Fashioning Spain

Fashioning Spain

From *Mantillas* to Rosalía

Edited by
Francisco Fernández de Alba and
Marcela T. Garcés

BLOOMSBURY VISUAL ARTS
LONDON • NEW YORK • OXFORD • NEW DELHI • SYDNEY

BLOOMSBURY VISUAL ARTS
Bloomsbury Publishing Plc
50 Bedford Square, London, WC1B 3DP, UK
1385 Broadway, New York, NY 10018, USA
29 Earlsfort Terrace, Dublin 2, Ireland

BLOOMSBURY, BLOOMSBURY VISUAL ARTS and the Diana logo are trademarks of
Bloomsbury Publishing Plc

First published in Great Britain 2021
Paperback edition first published 2022

A catalogue record for this book is available from the British Library.

A catalog record for this book is available from the Library of Congress.

ISBN: HB: 978-1-3501-6926-5
PB: 978-1-3502-4458-0
ePDF: 978-1-3501-6927-2
eBook: 978-1-3501-6928-9

Typeset by Deanta Global Publishing Services, Chennai, India

To find out more about our authors and books visit www.bloomsbury.com
and sign up for our newsletters.

For Alizah Holstein, molecular elegance.
For Yuri Morejón, fount of inspiration and strength.

Contents

Illustrations

Foreword

It gives me great pleasure to write this brief preface to the excellent, groundbreaking volume edited by Francisco Fernández de Alba and Marcela T. Garcés, *Fashioning Spain: From Mantillas to Rosalía*.

Back in 2003, I wrote a book chapter on the subject of fashion. With pedagogic intent and moving from the general to the particular, I began with a survey of fashion theory, from Barthes to Bourdieu and continued with an overview of Spanish fashion based on industry sources; went on to describe the profile of a single label, Adolfo Domínguez, and his paradoxical crumpled elegance (famous slogan: *La arruga es bella* [The Crease is Beautiful]); before finally analyzing a single garment I had bought in Domínguez's hushed branch in central London's storied Regent Street: a grey-striped cotton long-sleeved T-shirt that was carefully poised, like the brand itself, between the formal and the casual.

One reviewer of my book wrote that this was the first time that a Hispanist had devoted so much space to laundry instructions (I noted that the expensive garment could only be hand-washed, thus requiring intensive labor from its owner or his domestic employee). The comment was typical of the frequent dismissal of fashion and fashion studies as vapid and trivial. Yet there has always been great interest in the topic. When I was much later invited to contribute to a panel on Almodóvar and fashion held at New York's Fashion Institute of Technology, a panel which included Spanish designer David Delfín who was to die tragically young, I was surprised to be greeted by one of the largest and most enthusiastic audiences in my career.

Moreover fashion shares with television (another medium whose serious study I have long sought to promote) a precious proximity to everyday life, which makes it both inseparable from the consumer and inescapable from the culture. Indeed, one could hardly imagine a closer connection between the aesthetic and the existential than in the fragile material that we wear next to our skin. Yet almost twenty years after my own essay, Spanish fashion remains relatively unstudied. And most visual culture specialists remain mesmerized by the art or auteur cinema which owes its hallowed distinction precisely to its seclusion from the messy reality of the everyday.

The successive sections of Francisco Fernández de Alba and Marcela T. Garcés's collection, whose essays are written by distinguished specialists, engage with questions and media that are vital for all students of Spanish culture: politics, history, gender, photography, film, music, and museums. They reveal the breadth and depth of a Spanish cultural studies that is now poised to expand its focus and deepen its analysis. The editors and contributors are to be congratulated for blazing a new trail through a field as complex and contradictory as it is sensual and pleasurable.

Paul Julian Smith
Distinguished Professor of Hispanic studies at the
Graduate Center of City University of New York

Acknowledgments

Chapter 3: "Women, Fashion, and the Spanish Civil War: From the Fashion Parade to the Victory Parade" by Kathleen Vernon is reprinted here courtesy of the University of Michigan Press. This book was edited thanks to the support of Siena College (NY) and Wheaton College (MA) scholarly funds.

Note on Translations

All translations are by the authors unless otherwise noted.

Introduction

Fashion in Spain: Catalyst for Affect and Identity

Francisco Fernández de Alba and Marcela T. Garcés

In the context of Spain, the word "fashion" conjures up countless images and associations. When we consider a material object such as Balenciaga's *Infanta* dress, and in the next thought imagine the latest lineup from Zara, our minds must make the sizable leap from appreciating a one-of-a-kind couture creation to evaluating the products emerging from complex commercial and industrial systems within a specific cultural context.[1]

Take, for instance, the front cover of this book. In this 1984 photograph taken by Nacho Pinedo, Lara Ubago models a design by Antonio Alvarado that mixes two distinct styles and consists of four key elements. The pillbox hat and gloves immediately recall a style popularized by Jackie Kennedy in the early 1960s. The high-waisted skirt and cropped jacket, meanwhile, remind us of later fashions such as the miniskirt and "hippy" styles. Our interest in this image, however, is not rooted only in Alvarado's ability to distill the key styles of the 1960s into a fresh look for the 1980s. Rather, the image is compelling, too, for its fascinating story: how this outfit came to be, and what it meant in the cultural context of 1980s Madrid. For one thing, the piece is an exercise in contradictions. It exemplifies some of the elements that define couture—a unique garment, tailored by hand—while at the same time, it expresses a mordant critique of the fashion industry.

To fabricate this ensemble, Alvarado used cotton hand-towel rolls stolen from bar restrooms and surplus linen tablecloths from the Palace Hotel. It was debuted in a 1981 fashion show entitled "Baja costura" ["Low Couture"] in Madrid's famous concert venue Rock-Ola.[2] Although it at first appears to be a provocative performance typical of Madrid's 1980s underground culture, the limitations imposed by the fabric make it a true tour de force. Classic white linen tablecloths and hand-towels, only forty centimeters wide with two red lines running along the selvage, had to be expertly patterned, cut, and sewn.

Alvarado's piece tells us about tailoring and the recycling of styles, but also about ingenuity and creativity.

We begin with Alvarado's suit constructed of simple, purloined linens executed using couture techniques because it represents a key point in contemporary Spanish history in which fashion played a pivotal role in the zeitgeist. During the long transition process after nearly four decades of military dictatorship (1939–75), fashion became a vehicle for expressing agency, creativity, and political leanings. As we will see in this collection, the work of successful designers and business models also consolidated in tandem with democratization and changes in patterns of consumption. The story of how fashion in Spain made it to this point, however, is just starting to be told. Despite being the origin of globally renowned designers and industrial models, Spain has not been deeply studied when it comes to fashion.[3] This is especially so for the twentieth century.

In contrast, the Spanish Golden Age (roughly the sixteenth and seventeenth centuries) and the centuries following it have received substantial scholarly attention.[4] Carmen Bernis's work on *Don Quijote* (2001) is foundational, and the two volumes edited by José Luis Colomer and Amalia Descalzo (2014) are comprehensive and indispensable for understanding fashion in this period. Amanda Wunder succinctly explains the challenges scholars face when studying fashions during a long-past historical period. For instance, the most widely available primary sources—polemics, laws, portraits, poems, and theatrical works—were produced by a small group of elite males from the court. Relying on evidence from the male-dominated court is limiting, however, because "such sources reveal very little about women's actual experiences" with clothing (2015: 141–2). By using a wider body of evidence that includes Inquisitorial depositions, letters, poems written by women, tailors' record books, and lesser-known portraits sitting in storage, women's voices and experiences have been reinserted into the historical narrative (2015: 142).[5] This expansive approach to archival research has deepened our understanding of Golden Age culture and fashion.

Interactions between society, fashion, and modernity during the eighteenth and nineteenth centuries have also been the focus of studies by Ana María Díaz Marcos (2006), Francisco de Sousa Congosto (2007), and Jesús Cruz (2011).[6] Among several works on these two centuries in Spain, we would like to highlight Rebecca Haidt's *Women, Work and Clothing in Eighteenth-Century Spain* (2011). This is an important interdisciplinary contribution to fashion studies in our discipline of Spanish cultural studies. Haidt's book is a cultural history of theatrical depictions of Madrid fashions such as the *maja* and the *petimetra*.[7]

It explores how garments offer a privileged location for thinking collectively about social changes in Madrid involving women, labor, immigration, and class. Clothes in eighteenth-century Spain were considered to be almost more valuable than money, since they immediately located the wearer within the social hierarchies of the moment. Haidt succeeds at mapping the multiple cultures of the city and the ways in which fashion was central for working-class women's agency and financial survival. Among scholars in Spain, the works of Mercedes Pasalodos Salgado (2007, 2012) and Pablo Pena González (2008) constitute essential reading for this period.

The twentieth and twenty-first centuries, meanwhile, have received less attention.[8] This is perplexing but not surprising, since some academics see contemporary fashion as a superfluous expenditure while others see it as a capitalist ploy to drive conformity and consumption. We, however, see fashion as a subject to be studied with attention and subtlety for what it conveys about social and cultural systems. Paul Julian Smith, for instance, wrote in 2003 about the interrelation of economic and aesthetic aspects of fashion in a case study of Adolfo Domínguez, a long-established Spanish designer. Smith detailed "the Galician localism of this global company" and the way in which brands like this helped incorporate Spain into the global fashion scene of the 1980s and 1990s (2003: 51). Elegantly connecting Roland Barthes's ideas about the instability of fashion as an object, Pierre Bourdieu's concept of *habitus*, Jennifer Craik's work on fashion systems, and the role of female museum curators as pioneers of the study of dress, Smith challenged scholars to connect the fashion object to theory in order to study the use of fashion in everyday life. He emphasized that "fashion is not to be minimized" and that its objects and artifacts are "witnesses to material culture" (2003: 34, 36). Smith's salient study ushered us into twenty-first-century thinking about the plurality of meanings that may be drawn from examining fashion in Spain. Inspired by Smith and others, we aim to show that fashion is much more than borrowed aesthetics and conspicuous consumption.

Those who give only a cursory glance to fashion's inherently exterior façade may fail to see the complexity it represents. This is not surprising since in Yuniya Kawamura's words, "fashion is not visual clothing but is the invisible elements included in clothing" (2006: 4). Fashion is certainly endowed with materiality, designed and produced within a specific social, technical, and economic context. If carefully studied in a structured way, art historian Jules Prown showed that any material object or artifact may reveal a wealth of information about a given society or community's beliefs, assumptions, values, or the organizing principles of its industrial systems (1982: 1). That his definition of material culture did not focus on fashion does not make it less useful.⁹ Prown, for instance, identified the importance of style: "If the cultural significance of a device is perceivable in its style rather than its function, then there is reason to conclude that, for purposes of material culture analysis, the aesthetic aspects of artifacts are more significant than the utilitarian" (1982: 15). Prown understood that style could eclipse function. We take this idea to heart as we explore the elusive and subtle elements in fashion.

Fashion is a sum of both material and intangible elements. From design to production, fashion is created by ghost labor, the "invisible hands" that make the garments we wear possible and that, in the case of couture, considerably raise its value. That phantasmagoric aspect of fashion also lends it important attributes, such as being a catalyst for affects and belonging. Wearing certain clothing can make us feel different, and act accordingly. Alternatively, the clothes we wear may cause others to see and treat us differently. Fashion is a vehicle for class distinction and upward mobility.¹⁰ It can be mobilized to change identities, mask origins, go incognito, or start anew.

Fashion also has its critics. Baudrillard, for instance, argued that fashion—and its ancillary, consumption—replace systemic change and social mobility. By channeling the need for transformation into cyclical changes of styles, fashion allows fundamental social structures to remain the same. Writing late in his career, he concluded that the impression of change embodied in fashion is also the illusion of democracy (1993: 78). From another perspective, Efrat Tseëlon described fashion as a form of "false consciousness" (1995: 79–91). Social conventions, fashion, and a male-pleasing standard of femininity lured women, according to this theory, into acquiescing to their exclusion from politics and the economy.¹¹ But fashion, as we will see, is neither a substitution for political citizenship nor mutually exclusive from it. In fact, they often go hand in hand—clothing may be a form of protest or resistance against social disciplinary practices. Baudrillard and Tseëlon thus offer suggestive but unavoidably limited interpretations of complex processes of collective changes in taste and agency.

Fashion, although understudied in Spanish cultural studies, has been a topic of discussion among artists and intellectuals. For some, fashion was something to be rejected, or, at the very least, disassociated from women. Already in the nineteenth century, Concepción Arenal rejected the gendered stereotype that attributed excessive interest in fashion and decoration to bourgeois women. She concluded that it was a lack of formal education and access to higher-minded jobs that limited women to those trifles over which they exercised control: "Women become slaves to the fashion illustration and the dressmaker, pinning their wellbeing to the elegance and ornamentation of their dress, and in the luxurious furnishing of their homes" (1916: 59–60).[12] In the late 1920s, Carmen de Burgos would similarly reject the organic pairing of fashion and women since "for a long time, women have had no other field than fashion to deploy their imagination" (1927: 252).[13] For Concepción Arenal and Carmen de Burgos, fashion was neither an instrument of social control nor a free-for-all. Instead, their work provides an early model of how to approach fashion studies, treading the fine line between agency and social conformity.

Approaching Fashion: A Question of Agency

In this collection, our approach to fashion will be the broadest possible, and always identity-focused as opposed to system-focused. While we try to "historicize" fashion in every chapter, to borrow Fredric Jameson's term, we do not attempt to take on the ambitious project of writing an encyclopedic history of fashion in Spain.[14] This volume is not about how fashion has been represented but rather about how fashion works as a cultural practice over time. In this sense, we rely on Jo Labanyi, who challenges us "[t]o treat cultural texts as forms of cultural practice [. . . in the sense that] cultural texts are 'things that do things': that is, things that have the capacity to affect us" (2010: 233). This collection sees clothes as cultural texts that, beyond their materiality, are produced and understood within a social context that both creates and alters affect and meaning.

Drawing on Teresa Brennan's *The Transmission of Affect* (2004), Labanyi notes: "affect means to be affected by and to affect; one person's affect affects others" (226). This suggests that affect is part of social relationships, and we see fashion as one of the affective linchpins in the complex social dynamics of identity and belonging. Labanyi's work relates to our idea of affect, in the sense that fashion objects can be a vehicle through which emotions are felt and experienced, conveying things other than social status and class. For instance, wearing certain fashion objects can make people feel empowered, or feel like they belong, or that they are a truer version of themselves.

In this vein, we explore questions such as: How did wearing items like *la mantilla* create different social and political meanings over time? How does couture communicate affects and meaning to film audiences? In what ways does commercial fashion photography become a political statement? How do fashion and comics help us to represent a historical moment and, at the same time, imagine alternative futures? How do people interact with clothing virtually, either shopping online or touring a virtual museum? In what manner do brick-and-mortar museums like El Museo del Traje in Madrid redefine what is worthy of collecting in an age of fast fashion? What do music and fashion tell us about the world as exemplified through a performer like Rosalía? And, fundamentally, how do we engage with reality through the clothes we wear?

Keeping these questions in mind, we turn to Margarita Rivière (1944–2015), a precursor of fashion studies in Spain, who argued that "fashion is communication" (1977). We cannot agree more. Fashion is an interface by which we relate to the world. In 1971, Rivière presented an expert analysis of fashion in the magazine *Triunfo*. For her, fashion was not simply a business, but a marker of group belonging.[15] Her essay, "Las monas vestidas de seda" ("Monkeys in Silk"), argued that fashion's main function is to simultaneously offer both the security of being accepted in a group, and the guarantee of originality and individual singularity. In other words, fashion represented the paradoxical affirmation of individuality within the illusion of differentiation (1971: 17–18). Fashion, not bad or frivolous per se, was after all an expression of the cultural structure of the West (1971: 18). Undoubtedly influenced by German sociologist Georg Simmel (1858–1918), Rivière identified the intersection of collective and individual identities as the site at which fashion becomes the mechanism for social articulation, integration, and differentiation.

As a language, fashion offers a deep semantic field. We explore some of these meanings in this collection, such as political expression and the communication of wealth and status. Like spoken languages, fashion does not exist without social interaction. Simmel emphasized this fundamental sociality of fashion. His sophisticated description of fashion at the intersection of space (in terms of which fashions are "in" or "out") and time (becoming fashionable or not) is essential for conceptualizing fashion as an evolving collective phenomenon (1923: 1–2).

Fashion is also a unique medium through which to think about the world. Marco Pecorari has argued that fashion is an epistemology. Inspired by Hans-Jörg Rheinberger's concept of "epistemic objects," Pecorari suggests that fashion objects generate concepts beyond the tenets of style (2016: n.p.). For example, consider the ripped fishnet stockings and safety-pinned black leather jackets common to 1980s punk culture in Spain and elsewhere. This fashion, which shaped and influenced social interaction, allows us to perceive the limits of propriety and acceptance of difference. Taken more broadly, certain fashion objects may signal societal change. Photographers such as Miguel Trillo, who captured images of the urban youth subculture fashions of the late 1970s and early 1980s, left little doubt that Spain had fundamentally changed since the end of the dictatorship.[16] Fashion objects, together with ideas and concepts, are therefore indispensable in the acquisition and formation of knowledge about the world and in the parallel construction and expression of identity.

The relationship between fashion and forms of identity, and how this relationship has changed over time, is one of the topics of this collection. At the end of the nineteenth century, the US American sociologist and economist Thorstein Veblen (1857–1929) was the first to theorize, in *The Theory of the Leisure Class*, that those who surround us influence our consumer choices ([1899] 2007). Others, also writing outside of Spain, such as American sociologist Herbert Blumer (1900–87), wondered to what extent fashion helps us to belong, and if class distinction and emulation are secondary to the desire to be modern and au courant in a constantly changing world (1969). As identity becomes plural, the meaning and expression of fashion becomes multiple too (Davis 1992: 17). We have arrived at a different understanding of fashion, where "the consumption of cultural goods, such as fashionable clothing, performs an increasingly important role in the construction of personal identity, while satisfaction of material needs and emulation of superior classes are secondary" (Crane 2000: 11). In other words, the construction of personal identity through clothing and the creation of affects and meaning is now more important than the fixed, class-bound reflections of status and distinction of the past.

Returning to the context of Spain, it is worth pausing to consider the ways in which people personalize fashion, whether out of necessity or through creative repurposing of clothing from flea markets like *el Rastro* in Madrid, *Mercat dels Encants* in Barcelona, *Open your Ganbara* in Bilbao, and vintage clothing stores everywhere. In postwar Spain, and especially during the 1940s and 1950s, secondhand clothing and shoes were the norm in cash-strapped Spanish households. These clothes, worn with dignity, were ideally clean and neatly repaired, signifying the virtuous identity markers of thrift and temperance born of necessity. In the 1970s and 1980s, parallel to the advent of prêt-à-porter and a wider sense of affluence, used clothes from flea markets became a cheaper avenue for expressing aesthetics, as well as personal, social, and political attitudes. Still, because clothing was expensive, mending and repairing clothes (a job taken on primarily by women) indicated a lack of purchasing power but also a sign of a good household economy. Today, in the era of easily accessible, mass-produced, and inexpensive fast fashion, new trends are emerging. Reusing or repairing clothing is considered a principled form of sustainable consumption, a trend endorsed and encouraged by a growing number of brands.[17] These shifting consumer practices reflect the historical changes of consumer capitalism, how people engage with the culture of the moment, and how they perceive and project themselves through clothes and fashion.

The do-it-yourself spirit of contemporary fashion confirms that "consumers are no longer perceived as 'cultural dopes' or 'fashion victims' who imitate fashion leaders but as people selecting styles on the basis of their perceptions of their own identities and lifestyles. The consumer is expected to 'construct' an individualized appearance for a variety of options" (Crane 2000: 15). Fashion is presented as a choice, rather than a mandate, and may not automatically recall class, political and environmental beliefs, or affiliations. In this spirit, we believe in agency and the creative impulse, while also recognizing that brands copy and co-opt people's aesthetic choices. Self-individualizing appearances have become the norm, thanks to social media. Kawamura describes it like this: "in postmodern cultures, consumption is conceptualized as a form of role playing, as consumers seek to project conceptions of identity that are continually evolving" (2006: 99). In this vein, those who broadcast their reconstruction and co-optation of looks via social media platforms instantly share their personal aesthetic choices with a wider community than ever before. Appropriating and broadcasting are no doubt fueled by the rapidity with which the latest fashions may be accessed, rather than waiting for fashion magazines to consecrate and publicize them, as was the practice in the past.

Conceptualizing Fashion in Twentieth-Century Spain

Over the course of the twentieth century, Spain's aristocracy reluctantly took a backseat to rapid industrialization driven by bourgeois, and later, middle-class values and interests, eventually pivoting toward democracy, mass culture, and a market economy. As regards fashion, the works of painters such as Raimundo Madrazo, Joaquín Sorolla, Santiago Rusiñol, and Ignacio Zuloaga provide numerous examples of turn-of-the-century dress. Fashion in early twentieth-century Spain can also be traced through popular magazines such as *El Correo de las Damas*, *La Ilustración Española y Americana*, and *Blanco y Negro*. What we see in these depictions are men and women sporting the latest fashionable European styles. It is worthy of note that Sorolla and Zuloaga were also very interested in regional dress, and were often commissioned to paint it.

Capitalizing on this growing Spanish bourgeoisie, French fashion designer Jeanne Marie Charlotte Beckers (also known as "Paquin"), a pioneer in the business of modern fashion, opened an atelier in Madrid in 1914, bringing the city into an international circuit of fashion.[18] A few years later, a modern multistory department store, Almacenes Madrid-París, would be purposely built on Madrid's main thoroughfare, Gran Vía, 32.[19] Taken together, magazines, paintings, and these new forms of consumption illustrate the way people came into contact with fashion and how it was at the center of their experience of modernity.

Industrialization meant the serialized and large-scale manufacture of products for a growing consumer base—something that did not escape the critical eye of intellectuals and artists. Among the many writing about fashion in the early twentieth century, Salvador Dalí (1904–89) offers a remarkable example of a cutting-edge artist theorizing on the spirit of his time and the mechanisms that made it move. For Dalí, the mass market represented the meaning of modernity and perhaps the destiny of art. Reaching that market was the goal of his collaborations with avant-garde artist and designer Elsa Schiaparelli (1890–1973).[20] In the 1930s, Schiaparelli transformed Dalí's art into wearable garments, so that his famous lobster migrated from the telephone to become a print on a dinner dress. Reflecting on the intersection of everyday life, modernity, and art, Dalí published a number of articles in favor of a popular and cosmopolitan "anti-art" based on technology and expressed in industrial buildings, cars, and planes—what today we would call industrial design.

Dalí captured the essence of the modern world as he envisioned it when he wrote in *L'Amic de las Arts* in 1928: "Modernity is not signified by Sónia Delaunay's hand-painted fabrics, nor Fritz Lang's *Metropolis*. It means: a hockey sweater made by an unknown English factory, it means a funny movie, also anonymous, of racy reputation" (1928: 279).[21] Aside from rebuffing "high" avant-garde art such as the geometric designs of Delaunay or the dystopian sensibility of *Metropolis*, what is interesting about this quote is the interaction of the concepts of style, mass culture, and anonymity that conflate different layers of experience into one, that of modernity. Groundbreaking films or paintings are no more indicative of the modern condition than a mass-produced garment or a titillating movie. The anonymous masses who find and define their aesthetic identity in a brandless, mass-produced sports sweater remain doubly anonymous in a dark movie theater watching risqué comedies that have stilled the radical elements of avant-garde art in order to produce en masse and distribute imaginary happiness.

Anonymity and standardization were not negative in Dalí's view. Similar to what Margarita Rivière would say decades later, Dalí identified the potential of technology as a social equalizer, both in the cheap mass production of textiles and in film. Inexpensive clothes and comedy films—fashion and entertainment—made possible by technology and the advent of a mass-market economy were, in Dalí's estimation, the gateway to the democratic experience of modernity. In the case of Spain, this would not begin to materialize until the long transition to democracy from the 1960s on into the 1980s.

At the end of the 1920s, however, Dalí's ideas clashed with those of philosopher José Ortega y Gasset (1883–1955), who doubled down on the concept of fashion as an expression of class distinction and privilege: "Elegant clothing always communicates latent social power, which is expressed in the soberest way possible. Elegance is the simplest modulation of a given fashion that seeks to express, in turn, the well-being of the upper social circles" (1928: 228).[22] Unwittingly perhaps, Dalí represents one side of the enduring rift between those who see the potential for creativity, equality, and enjoyment in the fashion industry and those who, like Ortega y Gasset, understand fashion as simply reflecting social status and conformity.

From Balenciaga to Prêt-à-Porter

In thinking about Spanish fashion design in the early twentieth century, two names immediately come to mind: Mariano Fortuny y Madrazo (1871–1949) and Cristóbal Balenciaga (1895–1972). Fortuny was a creator in the widest sense. He envisioned innovations in textiles, clothing, wallpaper, and lighting, and his inventions left their mark on fashion, opera, architecture, and photography. His best-known design is the Delphos gown, a form-fitting, pleated silk dress. A resident of Venice for most of his life, Fortuny found inspiration in the Mediterranean cultures of the past. His Knossos scarf and the fabric prints he designed are good examples of how Muslim and ancient Greek material cultures came together in modern fashion.

Balenciaga, too, developed a successful career outside of Spain. The Basque couturier, already well established in San Sebastián, Madrid, and Barcelona, moved abroad to avoid the Spanish Civil War (1936–39), settling in Paris, where in 1937 he opened an atelier. In the 1950s and 1960s, Balenciaga produced his best-known works, becoming Europe's most sought-after couturier and the teacher of several generations of fashion designers. For photographer Cecil Beaton, reflecting on the designer's relationship to Cubism via his use of geometric shapes and his turn to abstraction, "Balenciaga was fashion's

Picasso" (Beaton 1954: 259 in Bowles 2010: 5). His designs, at once austere and fanciful, were sometimes inspired by Spanish culture (especially the fine arts, referencing El Greco, Goya, Velázquez, Zurbarán, Tàpies, and others) as well as Catholic ritual garments, liturgical vestments, clerical dress, and other Catholic accoutrements as Balenciaga was a deeply religious man, monastically devoted to his work (Bowles 2010: 6). His designs are fundamentally structural, reinterpreting chasubles and robes and even the nun's wimple. Volumes and forms are purposely enhanced and, at the same time, protect the body's true form. For instance, he adopted "the colorful *mantón de Manila*, the embroidered shawl worn by flamenco dancers, which in his hands became a sinuous evening gown that wraps the body as the dancer's shawl envelops her" (Bowles 2010: 5). The advent of prêt-à-porter convinced Balenciaga that the era of couture as he understood it was over, leading him to close his atelier in 1971, shortly before his death.[23] His work, nevertheless, remains the benchmark of top craft.[24]

Putting aside these two remarkable examples, Spanish couture began to reorganize in Barcelona soon after the Spanish Civil War despite the destruction of the industry, massive poverty, rationing, ideological repression, and extreme Catholicism. Top couturiers, taking inspiration from the French *Chambre Syndicale de la Couture Parisienne*, launched the *Cooperativa de alta costura* in 1940.[25] Those involved included Pedro Rodríguez, Manuel Pertegaz, Asunción Bastida, Santa Eulalia, and Dique Flotante. They would later be joined by, among others, Pedro Rovira and Carmen Mir, and eventually Elio Berhanyer. Surviving records of the *Cooperativa's* earliest work are few, since to protect their designs they did not allow press coverage of their shows until well into the 1950s. One early record of such an event, however, is a 1949 No-Do that depicts one of the first public fashion shows by Spanish *alta costura*.[26] On the patio of a bar in Barcelona's *Poble Espanyol*, smiling young women saunter down a catwalk while a formally dressed jazz band plays to a small, indifferent audience composed mostly of men (No-Do: 339).

As reflected in this No-Do, *alta costura* served the "leisure classes": the aristocracy, old bourgeoisie, and the new rich emerging from the postwar black market and the economic reorganization that benefited the winners of the Spanish Civil War. Rafael Abellá has documented the existence of luxury shops in Spanish cities during the 1940s and 1950s, postwar years known in popular parlance as *los años del hambre* "the hunger years" (1939–49) (1990: 30–43).[27] These high-end shops sold products such as shirts, jewelry, suits, dresses, fur coats, and hats and were at the service of the powerful who were newly enriched by the autarchic and isolationist policies of the Franco regime.[28]

Not everything was couture, and many ways to acquire clothes at different market levels developed over the years. For the poor and the working class, there were *tiendas de confección*—bazaars that sold cheap, mass-produced clothes that fulfilled the functional needs of workers or farmers. *Tiendas de confección* sold mostly knits, including socks, underwear, working clothes, and wool garments. For special occasions, tailors and dressmakers made what was for most of their clients a single piece of formal attire, one that often lasted a lifetime. By 1954, rationing had been curtailed but low incomes, limited availability of commodities, and a do-it-yourself tradition, driven by need, meant that well into the 1960s many clothes worn in Spain were still made mostly by women at home, or, for the more fortunate, by tailors and dressmakers.

After the economic and social disaster of the autarky years of Franco's regime, the 1959 *Plan de Estabilización* freed the fashion industry from the strict controls that the Francoist government had hitherto imposed upon every sector of the economy.[29] To attract tourism and foreign capital that would help save the Spanish economy—and, by extension, the regime—Franco's government invested in changing its international image. One way of promoting Spain and its textile and garment manufacturing industries abroad was to send Spanish *alta costura* designers to trade shows with the intention of breaking into international markets. Pasalodos has noted the massive promotion of Spanish *alta costura* at the 1958 World's Fair in Brussels, where Asunción Bastida, Marbel, Pertegaz, Dique Flotante, Pedro Rodríguez, Vargas Ochagabia, and Santa Eulalia presented their designs (Pasalodos 2008: 30). Simultaneously hijacked and supported by Franco's regime, the Spanish fashion industry and *alta costura* designers became reliant on government support and favorable tax deals.[30]

Alta costura became a mainstay of the fascist government's broader economic plan that, by heavily promoting Spain abroad, helped to soften the dictatorship's image. At the New York World's Fair in 1964, the Spanish pavilion prominently featured its fashion sector.[31] Audiences were treated to fashion shows by leading designers such as Pedro Rodríguez, Manuel Pertegaz, and Asunción Bastida.[32] Although traditional Spanish trades and customs were also highlighted, the pavilion flaunted an aesthetically au courant Spain, a country where world-class architecture, art, and design were produced and actively fostered (Rosendorf 2014: 81). Finally, the pavilion projected the impression, through *alta costura*, that Spain was a glamorous gathering place for celebrities and VIPs (2014: 81). Pieces like Richard Avedon's "In the Blaze of Spain" (1965) in *Harper's Bazaar* reinforced this image of Spain on an international scale. Wealthy tourists and

Hollywood celebrities could tour Spain's historical sites and acquire the latest bespoke fashion made by *alta costura* masters.[33]

The reign of *alta costura*, however, was not destined to last. During the long transition to democracy, changes in the collective sensibility, the emergence of prêt-à-porter and a new generation of fashion designers eventually rendered *alta costura* unsustainable. Even during the military dictatorship, trends signaling its demise were clear. Rebellious youth culture, a modestly affluent and growing middle class, and a desire for democracy, together with the sexual revolution and women's liberation movements, made couture's ethos of exclusivity suddenly seem passé, even for those who could afford it.

Margarita Rivière developed these arguments in her book *La moda: ¿comunicación o incomunicación?* (1977). Her central argument was that the production and consumption of mass fashion was, in fact, a step toward a more egalitarian society. For Rivière, prêt-à-porter paradoxically became a tool of liberation from clothes that automatically associated the wearer with a particular class.[34] The emergence of prêt-à-porter fashion constituted a puzzling success for capitalism in that it made the "irrational" act of buying unnecessary garments into an act of freedom from the visual markers of the class struggle that this economic system produced (1977: 25).[35] Rivière was not denying uneven social and economic relations but, rather, indicating how fashion could protect people from class bias and hierarchies driven by exclusion. In Spain, ready-to-wear had more than just stylistic significance. For the aspirational Spanish middle class, ready-to-wear design was one way of reducing the gap between social classes inherited from Franco's regime. Integrating modern design and the production of ready-to-wear garments was another step toward the general condition of equality needed for a democratic society.

Concomitant with the new collective sensibility of democratic equality was the spirit of embracing fun and joy through lifestyles and consumption. These outlooks contrasted with the Franco regime's philosophy of compliance, submission to authority, sobriety, and saintly stoicism in the face of adversity and pain. After being buttoned-up for so long, many were ready for styles that embraced freedom and expansion. For many, this meant a form of biopolitical rupture and an effort to openly live new lives (Labrador 2017: 309). Unable to transform themselves in the shadow of the ready-to-wear tsunami and the modern democratic sensibilities of consumers, by 1978 most *alta costura* houses had closed.[36]

While Franco's government was investing in *alta costura*, a youth market driven by subcultures and their styles of dress emerged, forcing the fashion industry into new ways of designing, producing, distributing, and selling clothes. It soon became clear to international couture brands that the rapidly changing mores of youth fashion could be a handsomely profitable industry. In Spain, youth confronted limited incomes, strict dress codes associated with class respectability, and a paucity of fashionable retail outlets. "Ye-yés," early adopters of international fashion in the 1960s, found it hard to come by clothing that identified them as part of this group, notwithstanding social pressure and condemnation from both the political right and left.[37] Employing tailors and dressmakers was their only way to be à la mode. By the mid- to late 1970s, youth subcultures such as Mods, Rockers, Heavies, and Punks emerged, contributing to the aesthetic renewal that was consolidated during the 1980s with *la Movida*'s popularization of fashion design.[38] Some purchased clothes in London or Amsterdam, others crafted their own by altering clothing found at flea markets like *el Rastro* in Madrid, or down market department stores such as SEPU or SIMAGO.[39] In the midst of these aesthetic, political, and social changes, the emerging fashion designers of the 1970s prepared new designs for a decade that promised freedom and experimentation for everyone.

Designers Adolfo Domínguez and Francis Montesinos opened stores in 1972 in Orense and Valencia, respectively. Jesús del Pozo inaugurated his Madrid atelier on Almirante Street in 1974, the same year that Manuel Piña bought his knit factory in Carabanchel for producing and selling his designs. Zara opened its first store in 1975, launching the behemoth of fast fashion that today is the Inditex group.[40] Many more designers followed, including Antonio Alvarado, Andrés Andrea, Paco Casado, Alfredo Carral, Domingo Córdoba, Gaspar Esteve, Luciano Pineda, Pepe Rubio, Juan Rufete, Nacho Ruiz, Ágatha Ruiz de la Prada, and Ignacio Sierra.[41] Later in the 1980s, Devota y Lomba, Victorio y Lucchino, Purificación García, and Sybilla, among others, emerged. Some, as we will see, built sizable brands with international recognition and sales. Others became fashion victims, falling prey to the ruthless economics of the industry or to *la Movida*'s lifestyle of excess.

The main challenge for these designers was to produce clothes that responded to the new zeitgeist of the Transition. To design clothes that were "democratic," it was essential that the garments did not automatically recall class hierarchy or couture. In this way, Manuel Piña summarily stated his intention "to generate affects through design" (Figueras 2007: n.p.).[42] Avoiding class conflict or reference to the dictatorial regime, fashion became a vehicle for new affects, like a sense of cosmopolitan modernity, as well as for new ways of engaging with Spanish cultural traditions. While it cannot be denied that distinction, in Baudrillard's terms, continued to drive the new styles emerging during the 1970s, this emerging fashion was not rooted in the prescribed mores of the old bourgeoisie, but in a search for novel structures of taste and meaning.

In this search, designers saw the world and everything in it as inspiration, including traditional Spanish cultural forms formerly appropriated by Franco's regime. These designers' cutting-edge clientele dismissed anything considered passé, boring, or bourgeois. And so, fashion designers, as with their fellow travelers of *la Movida*, moved away from any connection to either the Franco regime or its political opposition, choosing instead to craft a completely distinctive image for the nascent democratic state. The new socialist government and the elites adopted the sleek aesthetic proposed by these designers. Once again, the state and the mass media relied on fashion to redraw the country's international image. As Hamilton Stapell has commented, "the promotion of the colorful, and at times chaotic, cultural movement proved to be an essential piece in the development of a new regional sense of place based on inclusion and greater cultural participation" (2007: 178). What began as a peripheral and scrappy fashion experiment (as exemplified in some early films of Pedro Almodóvar) had become culturally central. This image was also important to consumers. A 1989 study by the Ministry of Industry and Energy's Center for the Promotion of Design and Fashion studied the buying habits of Spaniards from 1985 to 1989. It found that for modern Spanish consumers, "fashion epitomizes the new face of the country, and is bought for reasons of national pride—it is recognized as fully able to compete with that of other European countries" (Dent Coad 1990: 76). Echoing Rivière's point, fashion in the 1980s was communication, the medium to project Spain's new identity into the world. For Spanish citizens, fashion was an international language they could now speak.

Fashion Acumen, Business Models, and International Success

The 1990s saw the consolidation (and the collapse) of designer labels and a shift in the industry model. Emma Dent Coad's *Spanish Design and Architecture* (1990) narrates how, on the cusp of the new decade, things were already beginning to change:

> The tidal wave of media attention given to the fashion designers of La Movida has now been transferred to the more serious and established designers. The Spanish strengths in tailoring, colour and the production of high-quality, interesting and

wearable clothes have been encouraged by the government, and fashion clothing
has become a flourishing and virile industry. (Dent Coad 1990: 18–19)[43]

She mentions designers such as Pedro del Hierro, Manuel Piña, Jesús del Pozo,
and Ágatha Ruiz de la Prada. They symbolize a fresh type of successful fashion
figure that is part designer, and part entrepreneur seeking access to international
markets.

Designer Ágatha Ruiz de la Prada exemplifies this trend. During the 1980s,
she had become known for her eccentric, creative, and colorful designs for a
niche clientele. But by the 1990s, she was selling her designs for the masses at El
Corte Inglés, Spain's largest department store. Thus, from her roots as a designer
whose main concerns were quirkiness and pushing limits, she evolved into an
entrepreneur focused on commercial potential (Plaza 2000: 153). A survivor of
the creative ebullience of early 1980s Spain, Ágatha Ruiz de la Prada exemplifies
the 1990s turn toward commerce. Taking this one step further, many fashion
design firms expanded in the mid-1990s into adjacent market sectors such
as perfumes and housewares. In this manner, Ágatha Ruiz de la Prada began
selling dinnerware and children's clothing at El Corte Inglés, and her product
line now ranges from jewelry to notebooks to curtains to towels. With a retail
presence in 150 countries, Ruiz de la Prada personifies a fashion business model
that used couture and design as a launching pad for a much wider vision of
success. By embracing a diversified concept of fashion that includes affordable
but whimsical clothing design as well as household objects and jewelry, Ruiz de
la Prada has achieved international success.[44]

That the horizons for Spanish fashion were shifting from domestic to
international from the 1990s into the 2000s is reflected in other ways as well.
Since the mid-1980s, for example, promotional efforts such as the *Pasarela
Cibeles* and *Salón Gaudí* (sponsored by the Ministry of Industry) sought to put
Madrid and Barcelona on the exclusive map of fashion capitals.[45] Large fashion
shows brought the cities into the circuit of fashion weeks, where local design was
displayed to international buyers and media.[46] The impetus for the contemporary
international fashion show grew out of the need to create mass media hype and
spectacle to enhance brand recognition that, in turn, would sell lower-priced but
more profitable accessories.

In parallel to the advent of the international fashion show, Spanish ready-to-
wear brands were developing business models that relied not on groundbreaking
styles debuted on the catwalks but rather, on their ability to mass-produce top
designers' concepts at better price points. These brands include Zara (Galician

Inditex group 1975–present); Barcelona-based Mango (1984–present); Pronovias (whose claim to fame is being the first company to create ready-to-wear wedding dresses from the 1960s onward); and Cortefiel and Loewe (brands that emerged in the late nineteenth century).[47] Though it might be tempting to dismiss some of these brands as being machines for plagiarism or bargain prices, the truth is more complex. Stealing or replicating styles, after all, is a centuries-old practice in the fashion business as well as on the street. It is, furthermore, only one of many elements contributing to the success of these labels, whose sophisticated operations have, at their core: an acute sense of the market; an agile command of the supply chain; technical mastery of the production process, which includes designing, pattern-making, cutting, and sewing; and finally, robust distribution networks and a flexible but reliable system of logistics. To respond quickly to changes on the street, all of these elements are necessary. Not unlike IKEA, these companies have developed a unique product delivery system that hits the sweet spot of design and price point so valued by contemporary consumers.

Despite their success, we do not find the global presence of these brands to be automatically positive. That Spanish firms have conquered large segments of the market both locally and globally generates multiple concerns. For example, there is a legitimate debate over ethical and sustainable practices in the manufacture of massive quantities of clothing that are not designed to last. Others, meanwhile, are more concerned with the fashion industry itself. Sociologist and fashion critic Pedro Mansilla, for instance, has lamented that large chains like Zara and Mango have hindered smaller designers in Spain who cannot compete (Pareja 2012: n.p.). We would like to add two other issues that dampen the prospects of smaller ateliers: the ubiquitous presence of large retailer storefronts, and consumers' need to wear recognizable new trends, which, as Margarita Rivière proposed, offer both a sense of differentiation and conformity. Finally, like Mansilla, we worry that the dominant business model of the day is stifling a generation of local creative agents and designers, suffocated by the incredible speed, and low cost, at which large retailers are able to reinterpret designs for a mass market.

Más Tela Que Cortar (More Cloth to Cut)

If Dalí's sense of modernity was mass-produced sport clothing and risqué films in a movie theater, ours is fast fashion and on-demand television series that may be streamed on multiple platforms through portable devices while broadcasting on social media about them. Fashion and mass media have experienced momentous changes since the 1990s, some of which we have briefly explored in this introduction. However, there remains much research to be done on fashion in Spain. For this reason, in the following section, we offer some preliminary ideas on possible areas of investigation for future scholars. Consider these next paragraphs as invitations to study fashion as a privileged site for understanding contemporary culture.

Fashion-focused television, for one, is increasingly popular in the early twenty-first century.[48] Television programs such as *Maestros de la costura* demonstrate that stories about producing fashion attract sizable audiences.[49] With judges like designers Alejandro Gómez Palomo, creative director of Palomo Spain, María Escoté, and Lorenzo Caprile, the show connects accomplished designers with aspiring ones, affirming the dream that anyone can become a famous designer if given the chance. The virtual interaction between mass media and fashion has reached a point in which spectators are encouraged to judge fashion made for their visual consumption without experiencing its physical characteristics. On the one hand, these shows reveal and celebrate the labor that was once largely invisible. Made-for-TV clothing becomes Pecorari's epistemological fashion object, teaching us about artisanal processes and practices. On the other hand, the program encourages spectators to imagine themselves as part of the team—whether judging the clothing or showing appreciation for the creativity, craftsmanship, and execution of the designer's work. The program also encourages audiences to participate through social media outlets like Twitter by commenting, voting, and even sharing their own designs with their community of users. Echoing Labanyi's idea that cultural texts are "'things that do things': that is, things that have the capacity to affect us" (2010: 233), these media products show how clothing shapes identity, both by wearing it and by participating virtually as it is made, discussed, and judged.

To further illustrate Labanyi's point, mass media has reported on the popularity of do-it-yourself initiatives such as the increase in sewing machine purchases. Perhaps due to the 2008 financial crisis, rediscovered practices were echoed by highly stylized television adaptations of novels like *The Time in Between* (*El tiempo entre costuras*) by María Dueñas (2009); (Antena 3, 2013–14) that inspired viewers to innovate and still be fashionable in times of tighter budgets.[50] The repercussions of such series on many internet platforms shows once again that "fashion [television] programming is increasingly reliant on fashion to attract viewers and as such, magazine articles, internet blogs and websites contribute to promoting onscreen fashion outside of the text"

(Warner 2014: 13–14). The same is true of television series such as *Velvet/Velvet Colección* (Antena 3, 2014–19), which has also become successful on Netflix. Sanz and Alekseeva have noted that both series evoke nostalgia for a bygone era while simultaneously providing space for audiences to "safely articulate their urban identity among the city's masses, which have grown more indistinct in the context of fashion's relative democratization through the model of prêt-à-porter," noting that the fictitious Velvet galleries are located at Gran Vía, 34, the address of a Zara store today (2006: 178).

We would be remiss if we did not emphasize the relevance of social media to the fashion industry. The advent of social media has not only furthered the internationalization of fashion by providing global access to personal or local looks. It has also forced fashion designers to market styles on multiple platforms and appeal to "influencers" who wield significant branding power and who are able to direct young consumers' purchasing power. New research is emerging on this topic. For instance, Mañas-Viniegra, Veloso, and Cuesta (2019) track and analyze the interactions of users in Spain and Portugal with fashion brands on the social network Instagram, looking particularly at body positivity and self-esteem. Their work reveals the power of social media to shape identities and to foster discussion of important social issues. Other forms of serialized digital spoken-word programs, such as podcasts, are increasingly popular. For instance, *Un podcast de moda* (housed at *S Moda* in the newspaper *El País* since 2018) addresses fashion in Spain and worldwide. This podcast has 4,071 followers on Instagram (June 2020), thereby creating a community of people who learn about and discuss fashion online.

Thinking about fashion in recent years vis-à-vis community and culture, we wonder about the impact of the 2008 financial crisis on fashion. More specifically, what did the anti-austerity 15-M *Indignados* movement in 2011 teach us about street fashion in Spain? Seen from the early 2020s, the fact that leaders of Podemos, the party that emerged from those protests, are part of a coalition government is nothing short of astonishing. One of its leaders, Vice President Pablo Iglesias, is notorious for his ponytail, his disheveled look, and his refusal to wear a suit and tie. Is Iglesias's sartorial choice a populist move rejecting the uniform of sleek professional politicians and bureaucrats, or rather the hopeless style of the political science university professor that he is?

Finally, we cannot avoid wondering what changes the 2020 coronavirus pandemic will bring to markets and fashion.[51] Are face masks destined to become just another profitable accessory? Will remote work spell the end of business attire or encourage people to dress up more when they have the chance? Will we spend more on a few key pieces now that some of us don't have to go to the office every day or will we make do with what we have? Will home confinement encourage nesting and the concomitant comfy clothes or will it push us to retake the streets with panache? Will lockdowns and limits in stores and factories mean the end of the fashion industry as we know it? Are digital fashion weeks here to stay? How will Computer-Generated Imagery affect the modeling profession? In a time of upheaval as 2020 seems to be, what will the new fashions say about our aspirations, values, identities, or sense of belonging? These are all questions that scholars will have to answer in the future. For the moment, fashion and its designers are quickly adapting, as they have always done. In the Spanish context, Basque designer Eder Aurre, for instance, has pivoted to designing face masks and also wedding outfits with matching face coverings, and just as with the nature of fashion, time will tell what styles remain and what other adaptations and alterations might be made in the Spanish fashion context.

Book Organization

This volume is not organized in chronological order, but instead, its framework mirrors the cyclical nature of fashion. Fashion's ideas and material objects go in and out of style with each new season, and are revived, appropriated, adapted, and redeployed at different moments. Our approach highlights themes that allow us to see these recurrent threads. We write with the knowledge that to detail the recent history of fashion in Spain is a momentous task, as many aspects of this contemporary period have yet to be studied and understood.[52]

The first section, *Identity: Politics and Futures*, deals with material objects as diverse as the *mantilla* and comic books. In "Accessorizing the Nation: *Mantillas*, Cultural Identity, and Modern Spain," Inés Corujo-Martín analyzes how the *mantilla*, the garment most closely associated in the collective imaginary with traditional Spanish femininity, has become a contradictory signifier of both Catholic womanhood and seduction. Corujo-Martín's cultural history demonstrates how the *mantilla* has been employed for political purposes. Alberto Villamandos's chapter contribution, "Bodies of the Future: Comics, Fashion, and 1980s *Movida*," shows how at the end of Franco's regime, comics, music (punk, rock, pop), and, of course, the latest fashions intersect to create a narrative of social change. Villamandos argues that comics chronicle the fashion choices and social changes during this transitional period by presenting the cacophony of styles competing to make the scene.

The second section is titled *Picturing Femininity: Film and Photography*. In "Women, Fashion, and the Spanish Civil War: From the Fashion Parade to the Victory Parade," Kathleen M. Vernon explains the importance of fashion on the front lines of different political affiliations. In particular, she details the ambiguous relationship that the Falangist women's organization known as *Sección Femenina* had with fashion. While one role assigned to this organization was recovering and preserving local cultures, including traditional dress, its focus on fashion paradoxically mirrored the advances in consumer culture that the Franco regime desperately needed to survive. Olga Sendra Ferrer's chapter, "From Market to Feminism: Fashion Photography during the Franco Dictatorship," explores how a group of avant-garde photographers inserted their artistic and political views into their commercial fashion photoshoots by calling attention to the contradictions of class, high fashion, and the authoritarian regime. She highlights women photographers who represented the female body differently from their male counterparts.

The third section, *Designing Fashion Stars: Film and Music*, begins with "Fashioning Spanish Film Stars: Balenciaga and Conchita Montenegro," which unveils the personal and professional relations between Cristóbal Balenciaga and 1940s film star Conchita Montenegro. Jorge Pérez argues that Montenegro occupies a special place in Balenciaga's professional career, because Montenegro allowed Balenciaga to experiment with the Spanish touches that would make his designs famous. In "Rosalía and the Rise of *Poligonera* Chic," Mary Kate Donovan presents an early reflection of the musical phenomenon of Rosalía by critically examining the role of urban fashion, class, and cultural appropriation in this artist's ascent to global stardom. In this contribution, Donovan evaluates how trends take on varying meanings depending on context.

The fourth section, *Museums: From Closets to the Cloud*, brings this collection to a close to reflect on the process of collecting and curating fashion. "The Museo del Traje's Research on Spanish Prêt-à-Porter" explains the methodological evolution of what is now a museum devoted exclusively to fashion, but grew out of ethnographic collecting. Juan Gutiérrez, a museum curator at the Museo del Traje, details what it means to collect, conserve, and research fashion when we see it both as a social and cultural phenomenon. Nicholas Wolters discusses a different type of museum in "Curating Catalan Cultural Identity through Dress in the Virtual Fashion Museum of Catalonia," which explores the digital environment for preserving and protecting cultural and material heritage. Wolters reveals the ways in which one museum uses twenty-first-century digital tools to fulfill its mission of both preservation and dissemination to the widest possible audience.

To conclude this introduction, we return to Margarita Rivière, who offered an explanation for the growing interest in fashion reflected in mass media, scholarship, and in institutions such as museums. She stated in 1971 that the key to truly grasping fashion is "to think of fashion as a language still in need of translation" (1971: 18).[53] Her words still ring true today, as the chapters in this volume continue to decode the ever-evolving language of fashion in the context of multifaceted communities and identities in Spain.

Notes

1 For the sake of clarity, we use the term "couture" to refer to any fashion that is original, hand finished, and bespoke. "Haute couture" will be reserved for work by members of the *Chambre Syndicale de la Couture Parisienne*. Similarly, "alta costura" will be used for designs by those who joined the *Cooperativa de alta costura*. As one may do with *Champagne*, *Cava*, *Crémant*, or *Prosecco* we do not imply any form of value judgment by the use of these terms.

2 Alvarado would also design the clothes for Alaska in *La bola de cristal*, as well as for many movies by Almodóvar. For a visual history of his work, see www.antonioalvarado.es/.

3 The use of "Spain" in this collection implies the political and cultural diversity of this state.

4 For a great overview see Amalia Descalzo (2017).

5 See also Bass and Wunder (2017).

6 For work from one of the first antiquarian historians of dress, see, for instance, Puiggarí (1886).

7 The *maja* and the *petimetra* are opposing figures. The *maja* is the eighteenth-century popular, urban, and plebeian female figure that progressively became the emblem of "authentic" feminine Spanishness (Zanardi 2016: 121; Haidt 2011: 45). The *petimetra* is an aspiring woman fascinated with novelties and luxuries from France. The origin of the term (and its male counterpart, the *petimetre*) derives from the French word *petit-maître*, meaning "little men" (Haidt 2011: 254).

8 This is not to say that there are no publications or research on fashion in the Spanish state. For example, *Datatextil* has been published consistently since 1998, by the Circuit de Museus Tèxtils i de Moda a Catalunya. *España de moda* (2003) is an example of interdisciplinary work that sums up biographies, interviews, and history to provide a general sense of the industry. The Museo del Traje has reinitiated the publication *Indumenta*. Published from 2004 to 2006, *Indumenta* was re-launched in 2020 to commemorate the Museum's fifteenth anniversary. In addition, the first Col·loqui d'Investigadores en Textil i Moda (Colloquium

for Textile and Fashion Researchers) took place in 2017, and the conference proceedings include work by close to seventy attendees on a variety of fashion "moments" in Spain. The work of Eduardo Villena Alarcón provides a quantified indicator of the increasing interest in studying fashion in Spain in recent years, with a study titled "Production of Knowledge in Doctoral Theses on Fashion in Spain" (2019), which examines eighty-two dissertations from 1994 to 2018 produced at twenty-nine Spanish universities. The study also details which Spanish universities offer studies in all aspects of the fashion industry, and demonstrates an increase in fashion studies from 2014–19 (219–20). This bodes well for the field.

9 Since then, other fashion-focused methodologies have emerged, such as *The Dress Detective* by Ingrid Mida and Alexandra Kim (2015).

10 For more on this, see Baudrillard (1993) or Bourdieu (1995).

11 For further discussion see Finkelstein (1996).

12 "La mujer se hace esclava del figurín y de la modista, cifrando su bienestar en la elegancia y en la riqueza del traje, y en que la casa esté lujosamente amueblada."

13 "Durante mucho tiempo no ha tenido la mujer más campo que la moda para emplear su fantasía."

14 In *The Political Unconscious* (1981), Jameson recommends that we always "historicize," that is, that we concern ourselves both with the object of analysis (in his case, literary texts) and the cultural framework that provides its meaning.

15 *Triunfo* was a cultural and political magazine published in Spain between 1946 and 1982. It published pieces by leading public intellectuals on both national and international topics, achieving a wide readership by the mid-1960s. *Triunfo* became one of the most influential sources for democratic ideals in opposition to Franco's regime.

16 Miguel Trillo (b. 1953) systematically recorded images from Madrid's urban tribes during the late 1970s and early 1980s in his fanzine *Rockocó*, a play on words which evokes the extravagance of the Baroque style "Rococo" and subverts the word by applying it to the rock and roll bands of *la Movida*, known for its excess as well. Even though the readership of this fanzine was naturally reduced and self-selective, Trillo's pictures have become important archival material frequently reproduced in print media and exhibited in museums to illustrate the period.

17 Whether this is a form of "greenwashing" or not is a discussion for another time.

18 Before Madrid, Paquin had opened stores in London (1896), Buenos Aires (1912), and New York (1912).

19 The Almacenes Madrid-París was funded by French capital in 1923. By 1930 this upscale store folded due to lack of demand. Four years later, SEPU (Sociedad Española de Precios Únicos) opened in the same building. Today, this building is the flagship Primark storefront in Madrid.

20 Iconoclast Elsa Schiaparelli collaborated with Dalí to come up with now legendary pieces such as the ribbed skeleton dress, the lobster dress, the trompe

l'oeil tear dress, and a hat resembling an upside-down shoe. Visible zippers on dresses, fur boots, a necklace encrusted with insects, and the wrap dress are some of her iconic designs. Schiaparelli and Dalí were collaborating in the context of Parisian couture.

21 "Modernitat no vol pas dir teles pintades de Sónia Delaunay, no vol pas dir *Metropolis* de Fritz Lang. Vol dir: jersey de hockey d'anònima manufactura anglesa, vol dir pel·lícula de riure, també anònima, de reputades poca solta."

22 "El traje elegante anuncia siempre un poderío social latente, el cual se expresa en la forma más sobria. Toda elegancia es modulación más simple de una moda dada, y la moda, a su vez, pretende expresar el bienestar de los círculos sociales superiores." Ortega's simplistic formulation of elegance and fashion is puzzling since in 1923 he had translated and published one of the earliest translations of Simmel's work on fashion in *la Revista de Occidente*.

23 See Emilas (2017) and Balda (2020) for new evidence that suggests that Balenciaga was actually involved with Esparza in a ready-to-wear venture after he retired.

24 The House of Balenciaga still exists, and exhibits such as *Balenciaga: Spanish Master* from 2010–2011 at the Queen Sofía Spanish Institute in New York pay homage to his skill and versatility. Since 2011, the stunning Cristobal Balenciaga Museoa in his birthplace of Getaria, a small coastal village not far from San Sebastián, is a testament to his life's work, and was the first museum dedicated exclusively to a couturier.

25 The history of the *Cooperativa de alta costura* is yet to be written.

26 Noticiarios y Documentales (No-Do) were newsreels used by Franco's regime as a propaganda tool. Their exhibition was mandatory before movie screenings until 1975. No-Do was produced between 1943 and 1981.

27 Author Carmen Martín Gaite provides a rich description of early practices of consumption and fashion in *Usos amorosos de la postguerra española* (1987).

28 For example, it was during the "hunger years" that the cultivation of flax in Galicia, which was used to weave linen for the whole of Spain, was halted when farmers had to turn their land over to food production due to Franco's isolationist policies, which meant that an autochthonous clothing tradition and local industry dating back hundreds of years came to an end (Dent Coad 1990: 74).

29 This liberalization would last only until 1965, when textile and garment production were subjected to new norms that basically protected the status quo of the industry by making it almost impossible to expand or open new factories given exaggerated government-mandated minimums on machinery, production, and reinvestment of profits. Five years of liberalization gave way to the stagnation of the sector. For more on this, see Buesa and Pires.

30 Until the 1970s, industries in Spain contributed a negotiated amount to finance the state. In order to join the European Economic Community and later the European Union, Spain had to reform its system to tax purchases and sales. See Comín (2012)

for a description of the tax system and *Boletín Oficial del Estado* (1962) for a sample
of the agreements between Franco's government and the fashion industry.

31 The pavilion cost seven million dollars and hosted a mini-museum with
masterpieces by Velázquez, El Greco, Picasso, and Miró, among other artists. It also
boasted three restaurants and an auditorium. Extensive archival content, including
images, of the Spanish Pavilion at the New York World's Fair collected by Bill Young
may be found at http://nywf64.com/spain01.shtml.

32 Pertegaz and Herrera y Ollero would eventually sell their lines in US department
stores such as Lord & Taylor (Pasalodos 2008: 30).

33 See the work of Neal Rosendorf for the many ways in which US media represented
Spain in uncritical ways that furthered the Franco government's objective of
whitewashing its history. *Seventeen* (1963); *Cosmopolitan* (1964), *Ladies' Home
Journal* (1965), and *National Geographic* (1965) are but a few examples of the
depiction of this "new" Spain in US media (96–98).

34 See Arnold for a discussion of the mix of high and mass fashion through the
prêt-à-porter revolution (2001: 83). Customers' freedom to mix vintage, designer
and street-market finds results in the collapse of categories. See Lipovetsky for
an explanation of how the middle-class market, and the desire to be fashionable,
brought fashion to the streets at an affordable price (1994: 90).

35 Rivière explains how the struggle against the exclusivity of elites has been waged
since the Middle Ages around access to clothing that would not reinforce social
class (1977: 16, 44). During the 1970s and 1980s, some fashions such as punk and
grunge erased adopters' class distinctions.

36 Asunción Bastida closed in 1970, the same year in which Dique Flotante moved to
producing only prêt-à-porter; Pertegaz closed his Madrid atelier in 1975 and his
Barcelona one in 1978, the same year that Pedro Rodríguez, Pedro Rovira and Santa
Eulalia also closed.

37 The term *ye-yé*, also used in France, Portugal, and Italy to refer to 1960s pop music
and fashion, comes from the Beatles chorus "She loves you, yeah, yeah, yeah." In
Spain, it often refers to the song "La chica Ye Yé" by Concha Velasco, 1965. For
more on early ye-yé fashion adopters see Dueñas (1965).

38 *La Movida* was an avant-garde, experimental, and underground cultural movement
that, originally known as *la nueva ola* [new wave] came to dominate the late 1970s
and 1980s and ushered Madrid into modernity.

39 La Sociedad Española de Precios Únicos (SEPU) was a popular department store
in Spain founded by Swiss immigrants in 1934. SIMAGO was a chain of popular
bazaars founded in 1960 by a group of Spanish and Cuban impresarios fleeing
the Cuban revolution. For more on the history of department stores in Spain see
Arribas and Toboso Sánchez.

40 Founded by Galician entrepreneur Amancio Ortega, Inditex is the world's largest
fashion group, consisting of eight brands: Zara, Zara Home, Massimo Dutti,

Bershka, Oysho, Pull and Bear, Stradivarius and Uterqüe. Operating 75,000 stores worldwide, the success of the Inditex brands has made Ortega one of the richest people in the world (Forbes).

41 These designers (in addition to already established Toni Miró, Francis Montesinos, Manuel Piña and Jesús del Pozo) presented lineups in "Vogue," a contemporary Spanish fashion show that took place at the Museo Español de Arte Contemporáneo in spring 1981. Today's Museo del Traje is at the site of the former MEAC, which became the Reina Sofía Museum.

42 "Crear emociones por medio del diseño."

43 Dent Coad's survey was the most comprehensive one available in 1990.

44 While there remain a few ateliers sustained by a small, faithful clientele, a strategy embracing growth and diversification seems now to be the most likely path to success. For more on Ruiz de la Prada's international success and her use of e-commerce see González Litman (2018).

45 This fashion show is now known as the Mercedes-Benz Fashion Week Madrid. The name change is an interesting twist. Switching the name from a local monument (Cibeles) recognizable to national audiences to an international upmarket car brand (Mercedes-Benz) signals both a change of audience and the acceptance of the hierarchy of fashion shows. Madrid's fashion week is a franchise in an international series of fashion weeks sponsored by the German car brand (Miami, Istanbul, Mexico, Russia, Australia, Berlin). The name change also calls attention to the fact that haute couture is often run at a financial loss by labels that only make profit on their affordable and down-market products such as perfumes or purses. In order to maintain their brand status, fashion labels have accepted sponsorship by larger transnational companies.

46 For more on Madrid and Barcelona catwalks see "Pasarelas" in *España de moda* (2003): 384–393. For a historical overview of state policies to improve the competitiveness of the Spanish fashion industry see Sojo Calvo (2012).

47 This sector represents 2.8 percent of the Spanish GDP and 9 percent of its exports ("Informe" 2020). Loewe has been owned since 1996 by the global luxury conglomerate LMVH, though it continues to manufacture in Spain.

48 See *Televising Restoration Spain. History and Fiction in Twenty-First Century Costume Dramas* by David R. George, Jr. and Wan Sonya Tang (2018) for an in-depth reading of recent television programs that look into and re-present the past through fashion.

49 The show has run 2018–present (2020) and has a season planned for 2021 produced by Televisión Española in collaboration with Shine Iberia. It is a spinoff of *The Great British Sewing Bee*, distributed by BBCW, and is similar to the US-based fashion design show *Project Runway*. The audience share for *Maestros de la costura* is consistently high: 11.5 percent in 2018, 11.5 percent in 2019, and 13.9 percent in 2020 (Formula TV 2018, 2019, 2020).

50 Within the airing of the first four episodes of the series, the website Amazon.es saw a 135 percent overall increase in the purchase of sewing machines; notably, the machines were sold during the hours in which people watched the series (Monday nights between 10:00 p.m. and midnight) proving that the show had a demonstrable effect on sewing machine sales: ("El tiempo [. . .]" El Mundo). For more on this series and the novel, by María Dueñas, which inspired it, see "Reading Between the Seams in *El tiempo entre costuras*," Garcés (2020).

51 For an early evaluation of the impact of the coronavirus pandemic on the fashion industry see the "Informe sector moda en España," a report by the auditing and consulting firm Ernst and Young (2020).

52 Since Margarita Rivière, many journalists and scholars have continued to write about fashion. For instance, María Isabel Menéndez has researched the failure of *Marie Claire* and *Cosmopolitan* in their 1970s debut in Spain. Pilar Toboso Sánchez's work on the history of department store El Corte Inglés is fundamental to understanding the evolution of department stores in Spain. Journalist Lola Gavarrón continues to explore fashion in her books, from its symbolic functions to women's lingerie and unheralded characters such as María Rosa Salvador. Pedro Mansilla's extensive work thinking about and promoting fashion should also be recognized. Pablo Pena's blog offers remarkable pieces of research by a professor of design history.

53 "Considerar la moda como un lenguaje todavía por descodificar."

References

"#6 Amancio Ortega" (2020), *Forbes*, March 26. Available online: www.forbes.com/profi le/amancio-ortega/#53effac2116c (accessed on June 7, 2020).

Abellá, Rafael (1990), *La vida cotidiana en la España de los años cuarenta*, Madrid: Editorial del Pardo.

Arenal, Concepción ([1889] 1916), *La mujer del porvenir. La mujer de su casa*, Madrid: Librería general de Victoriano Suárez.

Arnold, Rebecca (2001), *Fashion, Desire, and Angst: Image and Morality in the 20th Century*, London: I. B. Tauris.

Avedon, Richard (1965), "The Blaze of Spain," *Harper's Bazaar*, 107–28.

Balda Arana, Ana (2020), "Balenciaga and la vie d'un chien," *Fashion Theory*, DOI:10.10 80/1362704X.2019.1704523 (accessed on September 22, 2020).

Bass, Laura and Amanda Wunder (2017), "Innovation and Tradition at the Court of Philip IV of Spain (1621–1665): The Invention of the *Golilla* and the *Guardainfante*," in Evelyn Welch (ed.), *Fashioning the Early Modern: Dress, Textiles and Innovation in Europe, 1500–1800*, 111–33, Oxford: Oxford University Press.

Baudrillard, Jean (1993), *Symbolic Exchange and Death*, trans. E. Hamilton Grant, London: Sage.

Beaton, Cecil (1954), *The Glass of Fashion*, London: Weidenfeld and Nicolson.

Bernis, Carmen (2001), *El Traje y los tipos sociales en El Quijote*, Madrid: El Viso.

Blumer, Herbert (1969), "Fashion: From Class Differentiation to Collective Selection," *The Sociology Quarterly* 10 (3): 275–91.

Boletín Oficial del Estado (1962), 6, January 6: 253.

Boletín Oficial del Estado (1962), 148, June 2: 8659.

Bourdieu, Pierre (1995), "Haute Couture and Haute Culture," in *Sociology in Questions*, London: Sage.

Bowles, Hamish (2010), *Balenciaga: Spanish Master*, New York: Skira Rissoli.

Brennan, Teresa (2004), *The Transmission of Affect*, Ithaca: Cornell University Press.

Buesa Blanco, Mikel and Luis Eduardo Pires Jiménez (2001), "Intervencionismo estatal durante el franquismo tardío: un análisis del condicionamiento industrial," *Documentos de trabajo del Instituto de Análisis Industrial y Financiero* 22: n.p. Available online: http://eprints.ucm.es/6780/1/22-01.pdf (accessed on June 7, 2020).

Burgos, Carmen de (1927), *La mujer moderna y sus derechos*, Valencia: Sempere.

Colomer, José Luis and Amalia Descalzo (eds.) (2014), *Spanish Fashion at the Courts of Early Modern Europe*, 2 vols., Madrid: Centro de Estudios Europa Hispánica.

Comín Comín, Francisco and Rafael Vallejo Pousadab (2012), "La reforma tributaria de 1957 en las Cortes franquistas," *Investigaciones de Historia Económica* 8: 154–63.

Crane, Diana (2000), *Fashion and Its Social Agendas: Class, Gender, and Identity in Clothing*, Chicago: University of Chicago Press.

Cruz, Jesús (2011), *The Rise of Middle-Class Culture in Nineteenth-Century Spain*, Baton Rouge: Louisiana State University Press.

Dalí, Salvador ([1928] 1969), "Poesía de L'útil Standaritzat," in Paul Ilie (ed.), *Documents of the Spanish Vanguard*, 277–80, Chapel Hill: The University of North Carolina Press.

Davis, Fred (1992), *Fashion, Culture, and Identity*, Chicago: University of Chicago Press.

Dent Coad, Emma (1990), *Spanish Design and Architecture*, London: Studio Vista.

Dent Coad, Emma (1995), "Designer Culture in the 1980s: The Price of Success," in Helen Graham and Jo Labanyi (eds.), *Spanish Cultural Studies: An Introduction*, 376–80, Oxford: Oxford University Press.

Descalzo, Amalia (2017), "Vestirse a la moda en la España moderna," *Vínculos de Historia* 6: 105–34.

Díaz-Marcos, Ana María (2006), *La edad de seda. Representaciones de la moda en la literatura española (1728–1926)*, Cádiz: Servicio de publicaciones Universidad de Cádiz.

Dueñas, Jesús de (1965), "Madrid Yé-Yé," *Triunfo* 152: 30–37.

"'El tiempo entre costuras' dispara las ventas de máquinas de coser," *El Mundo*, 18 November 2013. Available online: www.elmundo.es/television/2013/11/18/528 a006e61fd3db33e8b4578.html (accessed on June 18, 2020).

Emilas, Mariu (2017), *Balenciaga: mi jefe*, Almería: Círculo Rojo.

España de moda (2003), Segovia: Artec Impresiones.

Ferrero, Clara and Carlos Megía [Podcast], *Un podcast de moda*. Available online: https://smoda.elpais.com/tag/un-podcast-de-moda/ (accessed on June 7, 2020).

Figueras, Josefina (2007), "Homenaje a Manuel Piña," *As Moda, Revista de Moda y Cultura* 15. Available online: www.asmoda.com/Articulos/Articulo?articuloID=137&num=18 (accessed on June 6, 2020).

Finkelstein, Joanne (1996), *After a Fashion*, Carlton: Melbourne University Press.

Fouce, Héctor (2006), *El futuro ya está aquí*, Madrid: Velecío Editores.

Formula TV (2018), "'La Voz Kids' lidera con un magnífico 23,3% y deja a 'Maestros de la costura' en un aceptable 11,5%." Available online: www.formulatv.com/noticias/77530/audiencias- 5-marzo-la-voz-kids-lidera-deja-mastros-de-la-costura/ (accessed on June 18, 2020).

Formula TV (2019), "'Maestros de la costura' termina con un 11,5%, 'La Voz' inicia directos con un 15,9% y 'GH Dúo' (22,3%) lidera." Available online: www.formulatv.com/noticias/audiencias-20-marzo-maestros-de-la-costura- termina-la-voz-inicia-directos-90527/ (accessed on June 18, 2020).

Formula TV (2020), "'Maestros de la costura' (13,9%) marca máximo y recorta distancias con 'Vivir sin permiso' (14,5%)." Available online: www.formulatv.com/noticias/audiencias-24-febrero- maestros-de-la-costura-maximo-vivir-sin-permiso-99894/ (accessed on June 18, 2020).

Garcés, Marcela T. (2020), "Reading Between the Seams in *El tiempo entre costuras*," *Revista de Estudios Hispánicos* 54 (2): 455–75.

Gavarrón, Lola (2010), *La gran dama de la moda*, Madrid: Esfera.

George Jr., David R. and Wan Sonya Tang (eds.) (2018), *Televising Restoration Spain. History and Fiction in Twenty-First Century Costume Dramas*, New York: Palgrave-MacMillan.

González Litman, Tamara (2018), "Ágatha Ruiz de la Prada se lanza al mercado virtual en Colombia," *Fashion Network*, August 31. Available online: https://pe.fashionnetwork.com/news/agatha-ruiz-de-la-prada-se-lanza-al-mercado-virtual- en-colombia,1009089.html (accessed on 7 June 2020).

Haidt, Rebecca (2011), *Women, Work, and Clothing in Eighteenth-Century Spain*, Liverpool: Liverpool University Press.

"Informe sector moda en España. Análisis del impacto de la crisis del Covid 19" (2020), Ernst and Young. Available online: https://www.ey.com/Publication/vwLUAssets/ey-informe-sector-moda-en-espana-covid-19/$FILE/ey-informe-sector-moda-en-espana-covid-19.pdf (accessed on June 16, 2020).

Jameson, Fredric (1981), *The Political Unconscious: Narrative as a Socially Symbolic Act*, Ithaca, NY: Cornell University Press.

Kawamura, Yuniya (2006), *Fashion-ology. An Introduction to Fashion Studies*, New York: Berg.

Labanyi, Jo (2010), "Doing Things: Emotion, Affect, and Materiality," *Journal of Spanish Cultural Studies* 11 (3–4): 223–33.

Labrador, Germán (2017), *Culpables por la literatura. Imaginación política y contracultura en la transición española (1968–1986)*, Madrid: Akal.

Mañas-Viniegra, Veloso and Cuesta (2019), "Fashion Promotion on Instagram with Eye Tracking: Curvy Girl Influencers Versus Fashion Brands in Spain and Portugal," *Sustainability* 11 (14): 3977. Available online: https://doi.org/10.3390/su11143977 (accessed on June 7, 2020).

Martín Gaite, Carmen (1987), *Usos amorosos de la posguerra española*, Barcelona: Anagrama.

Menéndez Menéndez, María Isabel (2013), "Prensa femenina internacional en la transición española, el fracaso de *Cosmopolitan* y *Marie Claire*," *Ambitos, Revista Internacional de Comunicación* 23: 1–16.

Mida, Ingrid and Alexandra Kim (2015), *The Dress Detective. A Practical Guide to Object-Based Research in Fashion*, London: Bloomsbury.

No-Do (1949), [Film] *Noticiarios y Documentales* nº 339A. Available online: http://www.rtve.es/ filmoteca/no-do/ (accessed on June 7, 2020).

Ortega y Gasset, José (1996), *Meditación de nuestro tiempo: las conferencias de Buenos Aires, 1916–1928*, México: Fondo de Cultura Económica.

Pareja, Custodio (2012), "Pedro Mansilla: 'En la moda española no hay más genios porque el país no los quiere'," *moda.es*, October 15. Available online: www.modaes.es/back-stage/pedro-mansilla-en-la-moda-espanola-no-hay-mas- genios-porque-el-pais-no-los-quiere.html (accessed on June 7, 2020).

Pasalodos Salgado, Mercedes (2007), "Algunas consideraciones sobre la moda durante la *Belle Époque*," *Indumenta Revista del Museo del Traje* 00: 107–12.

Pasalodos Salgado, Mercedes (2008), "Haute Couture. High Fashion in the 50's," *Indumenta Revista del Museo del Traje* 1: 23–48.

Pasalodos Salgado, Mercedes (2012), "Ir de compras por Madrid. Los grandes almacenes y sus catálogos ilustrados," *Datatèxtil* 27: 6–21.

Pecorari, Marco (2016), "Points of Touch: Towards a Fashion Epistemology," *The Fashion Studies Journal*, September 11. Available online: www.fashionstudiesjournal.org/essays/2016/9/11/points-of-touch-towards-a- fashion-epistemology?rq=Pecorari (accessed on June 7, 2020).

Pena González, Pablo (2008), *El traje en el Romanticismo y su proyección en España, 1828–1868*, Madrid: Ministerio de Cultura.

Plaza, José María (2000), *Corazón Ágatha. De la movida madrileña a la conquista de París*, Barcelona: Plaza & Janés Editores.

Prown, Jules David (1982), "Mind in Matter: An Introduction to Material Culture Theory and Method," *Winterthur Portfolio* 17 (1): 1–19.

Puiggarí, José (1886), *Monografía histórica e iconográfica del traje*, Barcelona: Juan y Antonio Bastinos.

Rheinberger, Hans-Jörg (2010), *An Epistemology of the Concrete. Twentieth-Century Histories of Life (Experimental Futures: Technological Lives, Scientific Arts, Anthropological Voices)*, Durham, NC: Duke University Press Books.

Rivière, Margarita (1971), "Las monas vestidas de seda," *Triunfo* 454: 16–21.

Rivière, Margarita (1977), *La moda ¿comunicación o incomunicación?*, Barcelona: Gustavo Gili.

Rosendorf, Neal (2014), *Franco Sells Spain to America: Hollywood, Tourism, and Public Relations as Postwar Spanish Soft Power*, New York: Palgrave.

Sanz, Esteve and Tatiana Alekseeva (2016), "Media Landscapes of a Well-Dressed Multitude: The City and the Individual in *Velvet* and *El tiempo entre costuras*," in A. Cordoba and D. García-Donoso (eds.), *The Sacred and Modernity in Urban Spain. Beyond the Secular City*, 177–92, New York: Palgrave Macmillan.

Simmel, Georg (1923), "Filosofía de la moda I," *Revista de Occidente* 1 (1): 43–66.

Simmel, Georg (1923), "Filosofía de la moda II," *Revista de Occidente* 1 (2): 211–30.

Smith, Paul Julian (2003), *Contemporary Spanish Culture. TV, Fashion, Art and Film*, London: Polity.

Sojo Calvo, Francisco José (2012), "Evolución y mejora en la competitividad de las empresas del sector textil-confección," *Economía industrial* 385: 39–46.

Sousa Congosto, Francisco de (2007), *Introducción a la historia de la indumentaria en España*, Madrid: Ediciones Istmo.

Stapell, Hamilton (2007), "Reconsidering Spanish Nationalism, Regionalism, and the Centre-Periphery Model in the Post-Francoist Period, 1975–1992," *International Journal of Iberian Studies* 20 (3): 171–85.

Tseëlon, Efrat (1995), *The Masque of Femininity: The Presentation of Women in Everyday Life*, London: Sage.

Veblen, Thorstein ([1899] 2007), *The Theory of the Leisure Class*, New York: Oxford University Press.

Villena Alarcón, Eduardo (2019), "Production of Knowledge in Doctoral Theses on Fashion in Spain," *Revista Prisma Social. La investigación en moda: nuevos formatos de comunicación y consumo*, 24 (January): 209–32.

Warner, Helen (2014). *Fashion on Television. Identity and Celebrity Culture*. London: Bloomsbury.

Wunder, Amanda (2015), "Women's Fashions and Politics in Seventeenth-Century Spain: The Rise and Fall of the Guardainfante," *Renaissance Quarterly* 68: 133–86.

Zanardi, Tara (2016), *Framing Majismo: Art and Royal Identity in Eighteenth-Century, Spain*, University Park: Penn State University Press.

Part I

Identity

Politics and Futures

1

Accessorizing the Nation

Mantillas, Cultural Identity, and Modern Spain

Inés Corujo-Martín

To an uncritical eye, accessories may be considered merely ornamental. Scholarship on the history of fashion often underappreciates the accessory, viewing it as an arbitrary and subordinate accouterment. However, accessories function far beyond their decorative qualities: they illustrate not only personal style but also, in some cases, help to shape and signify national identity. The question one must consider when interrogating the categorization of accessories as superfluous is: Why must anything that goes beyond the primary purpose of clothing the self be considered "extra"?

Jacques Derrida's theory of the supplement is of particular relevance here. According to Derrida, the logic of supplementarity consists of the relation of power that is established between the "original" (*ergon*) and the "supplement" (*parergon*), as well as the degree of dependence of the former with respect to the latter (1997: 144–5). For the French thinker, the supplement is not an optional complement to the original: it is the condition of the original. Derrida's analysis shows that the supplement, beyond its seemingly trivialized importance, is indispensable to and inextricably linked to the original because it fills an element the *ergon* lacks. The supplement operates as an optional appendix, while at the same time completing a necessary element.

In a likeness to the relationship between *ergon* and *parergon*, recent research has drawn attention to the crucial role that accessories have played throughout cultural history despite the lack of scholarly attention given to them. For instance, Susan Hiner comments that fashion accessories are fraught with complex meanings, and in nineteenth-century France they "became primary sites for the ideological work of modernity" (2010: 1–2). In a similar vein, Marni Reva Kessler looks to artistic depictions of the female veil in Paris during the late

1800s, arguing that veils served to shed light on debates surrounding the ways in which modern life was constructed, including those around public health, imperialism, and modernist art practices. As Kessler points out, accessories are "always politically, socially, and culturally determined" (2006: xxx).[1]

Drawing upon the methodological approaches employed by the aforementioned authors, the objective of this chapter is to demonstrate the multiplicity of values and associations—often conflicting—that women's fashion accessories convey over time. Specifically, this chapter focuses on the narratives and cultural functions of the most archetypal of all Spanish female accessories— the *mantilla*, a lace veil donned by women to cover their hair, shoulders, and upper torso. As I will analyze in the pages that follow, the *mantilla* functions as a privileged sartorial object upon which one can intellectually explore the social and political events in modern and contemporary Spain.

This chapter centers on three key chronological phases in which the *mantilla* played a decisive role in Spanish culture: its origins to the eighteenth-century phenomenon of *majismo*, the process of national redefinition in the nineteenth century, and the first two decades of the Francoist regime (1939–59) until now. Throughout time, this adornment raised countless controversies and bore powerful ideological messages to communicate a unified and traditionalist view of the Spanish State. Concurrently, it became synonymous with Spanish femininity and served to ambiguously forge an idealized notion of a "genuine" and exoticized Spanishness within and beyond national borders. Still today, the *mantilla* remains vividly alive in the Spanish imaginary with its complexities, its interrogations, and its politically charged understandings at the heart of cultural change.

The *Mantilla* in Context: From Its Origins to *Majismo*

Many historians connect the fashion for veiling to the Moorish influence produced in the Iberian Peninsula during the Middle Ages, although there is not a full academic consensus.[2] Whatever its actual origins, the *manto* (large cloak) became deeply ingrained in female dress—predominantly in the southern part of Spain—in the sixteenth century, presumably as a result of the long and fertile Hispano-Islamic cultural exchange. Various artistic and literary sources from the early modern period, such as *Velos antiguos y modernos en los rostros de las mujeres* (1641) by Madrid-based historian Antonio de León Pinelo, report on the use of a cloak or veil that, similar to the Moorish one, covered women's hair, face, and shoulders.[3] It was used by women of all ranks to *taparse de medio ojo* (one-eyed veiling), a rooted sartorial custom that protected women's identities in the public arena. As León Pinelo explains, the *tapado* or *manteo* fashion raised many controversies at the time and was forbidden by the *Cortes de Castilla* (Royal Council) in 1590 after numerous failed attempts, and again in 1594, 1600, and 1639 (Zanardi 2016a: 76).[4] On this subject, Elena Pezzi writes about how there were many decrees passed with regard to women veiling their faces, but they made little impact and women continued to freely cover themselves with *mantos* in public (1991: 14).[5] Despite the sumptuary laws enacted, it was popular for Spanish women of the sixteenth and seventeenth centuries to evade this restrictive legislation around *mantos* and *mantillas*, which explains why these outer garments were still being commonly used over a century later, in the midst of the Enlightenment.[6]

Although it is difficult to pin down the exact time when the *mantilla* became a fashion trend and extended to all social hierarchies in the Iberian Peninsula, according to art historian Carmen Bernis, it was first documented in 1483 as a luxurious object only accessible to noblewomen (1979: 102). As Ruth de la Puerta further illustrates, upper-class women first wore it as a sign of respect during Christian festivities, horseback riding, and social gatherings, representing the passage from early childhood to youth (1996: 201). By the mid-1700s, however, there was a visual proliferation of *mantillas* in portraits, costume albums, fashion plates, and prints, in which the accessory appears as a quintessential item of the *maja's* dress—the eighteenth-century popular, urban, and plebeian female figure that progressively became the emblem of "authentic" feminine Spanishness (Zanardi 2013: 155). The *maja's mantilla*, a lightweight and shorter version of the *manto*, was made of different materials, including fibers like silk, cotton, and wool, and fabrics such as tulle, felt, muslin, taffeta, and especially lace. The *mantilla* was either white or black, and it could be further embellished with decorative patterning. Other enhancements included printed designs, embroidery, and gold or silver thread, while braids, fringe, and velvet borders could be attached to the base fabric. Moreover, it was often sported with tall hair combs or *peinetas* to craft a striking cascading effect. In spite of the *mantilla's* "national" qualities, there were many regional differences, offering countless variations in style, size, color, and material, all of which carried distinctive meanings (Zanardi 2016b: 123).

In his *Colección de trajes de España tanto antiguos como modernos* (1777), Juan de la Cruz Cano y Olmedilla visualizes the *mantilla* as an essential component in the wardrobe of the *maja*, whose clothing was completed with a black *basquiña* (overskirt) that revealed her ankles, a striped fichu, a corseted top with tassels, a short and tight jacket with the flaps open, buckled shoes, white tights, and a fan (Figure 1.1). All these items of dress served to highlight her seductive female body and were evidence of her *castizo* (pure) persona. In particular, the *mantilla*, because of its ability to hide the wearer's face, contained a component of mystery and eroticism, and was linked to seductiveness and sassiness, both qualities that marked the *maja*'s popular conduct (Zanardi 2016b: 124). This enticing allure is already perceived in travel accounts from the end of the eighteenth century. In *A Journey through Spain* (1791), British traveler Joseph Townsend associates the *mantilla* with Iberian femininity, praising how graciously women sported it. As Townsend tells us: "No foreigner can ever attain their ease, or elegance, in putting on this simple dress" (quoted in Zanardi 2013: 146). For another traveler of the time, the Frenchman Jean-François Bourgoing, the *mantilla* is a flirty accessory with seductive and erotic potential. The author states in his *Travels in*

Figure 1.1 Juan de la Cruz Cano y Olmedilla, "Maja," *Colección de trajes de España, tanto antiguos como modernos que comprehende todos los de sus dominios,* vol. 1. Madrid: Casa de D. M. Copin Carrera de San Gerónimo, 1777. Credit: © Biblioteca Nacional de España, Madrid.

Spain (1789) that the garment is "one of its most seducing articles of dress, and, in favoring half-concealment, has indirectly encouraged the stolen glances of love" (quoted in Zanardi 2013: 146). Both travelers connect the accessory specifically to a distinct Spanish woman's identity, both in a practical and symbolic sense.

Additionally, as art historian Tara Zanardi has investigated in depth, *majas* not only wore *mantillas* but were also active agents in the *mantilla*'s production and manufacture, since their work was primarily confined to the textile factories of blonde—a type of silk lace with which the accessory was characteristically fabricated (Zanardi 2013: 142–6). In this sense, according to Zanardi, the donning and manufacture of *mantillas* by *majas*, being an item closely associated with popular feminine communities, contributed to laud female labor and native lace production, while signaling the alliance of women with national textile production.

In the last decades of the eighteenth century, the *mantilla*, intimately linked to the *maja* feminine figure and eminently popular, spread to women belonging to all social strata, coinciding with the cultural movement of *majismo*. *Majismo*, as an embodiment of the popular aesthetic, is a performative phenomenon, and is the fundamental component of images connecting types to traditional practices and dress (Zanardi 2016a: 68). The phenomenon is visible in lithographs from this period in which the *petimetra*—a fashionable upper-class lady influenced by French styles and symbol of feminine idleness—appears wearing the *maja*'s garment (Figure 1.2). In the last two decades of eighteenth-century Spain, the polarization produced in representations of these two models of women—the *maja* and the *petimetra*—was frequent.[7] While both female types shared a disproportionate fondness for clothing and accessories, unlike the *maja*—eminently popular and *castiza*—the *petimetra* was fascinated with the novelties and luxuries from France, an aspect often ridiculed in plays and popular poetry. Even the origin of the term (and its male counterpart, the *petimetre*) derives from the French word *petit-maître*, describing a character who excessively worries about his or her fashionable appearance. The alluring and sensuous qualities of the *mantilla* were vividly depicted in the images of *petimetras* at the end of the eighteenth century, producing a continual ascent of the popular accessory into the custom and style of the upper classes (Zanardi 2016a: 71).

As can be seen in Francisco de Goya's portrait paintings for the duchess of Alba and Queen María Luisa of Parma, spouse of Carlos IV—two of the most powerful aristocrats and fashion icons of their time—the *mantilla* had become a sartorial fetish for elite women (Zanardi 2013: 140) (Figures 1.3 and 1.4). Both paintings showcase the spread of the *mantilla* from the lower classes to the regal environment, as well as the fascination of the elite with folkloric elements.

Figure 1.2 Antonio Rodríguez, "Me espera mi amiga. Petimetra con basquiña de flecos de madroños y mantilla negra transparente con blondas," *Colección general de los trages que en la actualidad se usan en España: principiada en el año de 1801 en Madrid*, 19 x 12 cm, Inv. 24108. Credit: © Museo de Historia de Madrid.

Even though aristocratic women such as the duchess of Alba and Queen María Luisa wore *mantillas* of richer materials than women from lower classes, by wearing the popular style they asserted their identification with national types and elevated the *maja*'s attire to the realm of royal tailors and dressmakers (Zanardi 2013: 153). Queen María Luisa, specifically, incorporated the black lace *mantilla* as a compulsory garment in the *paseo* (walking) costumes for all the ladies in the Spanish court, which favored the spread of this garment in public

Figure 1.3 Francisco de Goya, *The Duchess of Alba as Maja*, 1797. (A102), Oil on canvas, H 210.2 x W 149.2 cm. Credit: © The Hispanic Society of America.

spaces, such as the Paseo del Prado, popular festivities, and bullfights (Noyes 1998: 202). Spanish bourgeois women quickly adopted María Luisa's *mantilla* as a fashionable trend.

Goya's paintings ultimately reflect the ways in which a popular sartorial tradition can ascend to the highest levels of society and fulfill the symbolic function of affiliating the Crown with the lower classes, while concurrently

Figure 1.4 Francisco de Goya. *Queen María Luisa in a Mantilla*, 1799, Oil on canvas, 210 x 130 cm. Credit: Photo © Patrimonio Nacional. Palacio Real de Madrid.

offering a distinct identifier of what is purely Spanish in opposition to the nation's European counterparts. The *mantilla* helped promote a sense of cultural unity across social classes at a time of political instability and uncertainty in the context of the French invasion and the following War of Independence against the Napoleonic forces (1808–14). Soon associated with the Spanish national dress, it served to counter French styles in vogue and came to embody quintessential Spanishness, reinforcing the awareness of belonging to a single political and cultural community (Zanardi 2013: 155).

Goya features the ambivalent use of the *mantilla* in other hybrid forms. In his portrait of famed Spanish actress Antonia Zárate Aguirre y Murguía, the

Figure 1.5 Francisco de Goya (1746–1828). *Portrait of Doña Antonia de Zárate*, c. 1805. Oil on canvas, 103.5 x 82 cm, Presented, Sir Alfred and Lady Beit, 1987 (Beit Collection). NGI.4539. Credit: © National Gallery of Ireland, Dublin.

black lace *mantilla* that elegantly falls over her shoulders plays a central role in the painting (Figure 1.5).[8] The contrast between the luminous yellow settee and the black lace veil that delicately frames her face creates a sophisticated and tantalizing style. As the image reveals, Antonia Zárate is a stylish woman who combines the fashionable empire-waist dress of French influence with the Spanish adornment.

The fusion of foreign fashions and national garments diversifies and updates the usual Spanish attire employed by the *maja*. Antonia de Zárate's *mantilla* serves to signal the alliance between tradition and modernity, between the local and the fashionable, configuring an aesthetic space where the identity of a Spanish modern woman is forged. The painting presents a feminine model who adapts her attire to the new pan-European styles while simultaneously maintaining her identity as definitively Spanish (Zanardi 2013: 140).

The case of the *mantilla* exemplifies the role that female accessories acquire in the construction of national and gendered identities during moments of political instability and national formation. Through its symbolic capacity, the item helped define and materialize a specific notion of "Spanishness," reinforcing a long-standing traditional custom among all social strata and expressing an idea of national unity and pride. At the same time, the accessory served as a marker of Spanish femininity, allowing the wearer to flaunt charm and seductiveness with its ability to cover and uncover parts of the face, neck, and shoulders. Far from interpreting it solely as a superfluous or excessive accouterment adorning the female body, the *mantilla*, as Zanardi points out, can be viewed as a "performative object" through which a Spanish woman was capable of expressing her femininity, personal style, and national allegiance (2016b: 124).

Mantillas and the Spanish Nation-Building Process

The spread of *mantillas* among women from all social spheres in the late eighteenth and early nineteenth century coincides with what scholar Susan Martin-Márquez has defined as "the second wave of nation building" in Spain (2008: 17). As Martin-Márquez explains, this period started with the War of Independence in 1808 and lasted until the loss of the last colonies in Latin America, resulting in the conclusive imperial dismemberment in 1898 (17). According to the author, this period was characterized by a deep national identity crisis and a complex process of national reorganization to reevaluate the concept of a unified Spanish identity.[9] Within the nation-building process, Spain embarked on a colonialist project in North Africa, which served, according to Martin-Márquez, as a "compensatory gesture" to balance the imperial decline in Spanish America (18). Northern Africa and its cultural legacy in Spain, represented by the southern region of Andalusia, appeared Orientalized and exoticized in the popular cultural imaginary (Fernández Cifuentes 2007: 133; Tofiño-Quesada 2003: 143).

Over time, Andalusia became a fundamental signifier in discourses on Spanish national identity, and a deep connection between a distinct idea of Spain and the south of the Iberian Peninsula developed. The associations between the Spanish "national" character, popular types, and Andalusia were significant. Although this bond between cultural, political, and geographical elements was already debated in the late 1700s, it took on greater meaning during the nineteenth century. Quoting Luis Fernández Cifuentes, in the nineteenth-century Spanish cultural imagination, the image of Andalusia represents "primitive but *authentic* national identity" (2007: 133; author's emphasis). As Fernández Cifuentes observes, any attempt to analyze the advent of modernity in Spain should pay attention to the decisive role played by the images of Andalusia produced in the construction of national identity (2007: 133).

The *mantilla's* popularity and dissemination in the nineteenth century, both in visual and textual accounts, can thus be understood in the light of imperialist and Orientalist discourses focused on Andalusia and northern Africa to reformulate and shape national values. It was an accessory that appeared within modern negotiations of nationhood, and it ultimately served to express and solidify an Orientalized and exotic vision of Spain. A sartorial item of seemingly Moorish origin rooted and developed in Andalusia, the *mantilla* visually and symbolically helped forge the idea of cultural hybridity that is at the base of nineteenth-century peninsular cultural discourses. Serving as a bellwether for larger political and sociocultural issues, the *mantilla* was frequently embroiled in contemporary tensions and controversies. As theoretical approaches associated with the "material turn" within the fields of literary and cultural studies have shown since the 1980s, objects can work as vital cultural symbols.[10] By putting objects into historical context and reading them in conjunction with other forms of culture, we can grasp a holistic understanding of the ideals and narratives that circulated in a given time and helped forge a distinct way of seeing the world. Because they are human-made artifacts, accessories reflect the anxieties of the individuals who wore and interacted with them, revealing by extension the concerns and beliefs of the culture at large.

As a distinctive female accessory, the *mantilla* moreover draws attention to the complex convergence of gendered and national identities. Floya Anthias and Nira Yuval-Davis in their collective volume *Women-Nation-State* illustrate how, during the nation-building processes around the globe, women are seen as either symbols of the nation, mothers of the nation, transmitters of cultural traditions, or border markers between nations.[11] Recent collective volumes, such as *Fashioning the Body Politic: Gender, Dress, Citizenship* (ed. Wendy Parkins) and *The Politics of Dress in Asia and the Americas* (eds. Mina Roces and Louise Edwards), have further studied the relationships between nationalism and gender by introducing the crucial role that dress has played in this dynamic.

Both works have contributed to challenging the simplistic perception of fashion as a frivolous topic, as well as viewing women as pawns manipulated by consumerism and the fashion industry.

Contrary to trivializing opinions of the intersections between fashion, womanhood, and nationalism, the previously cited studies provide a vital key to understanding fashion as a prominent site for political struggle that can help shape a special gendered construction of national identity. Fashion is a profoundly social process that compels individual and collective bodies to assume certain national identities through garments, and at times, transgresses normative limits. My exploration of the *mantilla* adds to the ongoing scholarship as it highlights the essential role that women's accessories play not just in adorning the female body or being an anecdote in the cultural history of dress, but also in shedding light on women's engagement in politics and their abilities to access public space during the nation-building process. As I show in the next section, the ideological values of the *mantilla* dramatically increased during the course of the nineteenth century as it transformed into a highly politicized object that attracted controversies and polemics, epitomizing the split between conservative and liberal political parties. The *mantilla* not only marked a significant moment of political transition and redefinition of national ideas but also granted women visibility and prominence in urban spaces.

Mantillas and Political Revolution in Nineteenth-Century Spain

Valerie Steele (1988) offers an account of how Paris became the indisputable center of fashion and modernity in the Western world throughout the nineteenth century. It is in the French capital where the first department stores emerged and designer Charles Frederick Worth—regarded as the father of haute couture—reinvented the female silhouette through his dressmaking at the second half of the century.[12] In the Iberian Peninsula, the influence of Parisian fashions and styles, which had already begun in the late 1700s as the aforementioned figures of the *petimetre* and *petimetra* reveal, intensified in the decade of 1830 during the *romanticismo costumbrista* (Pena González 2008: 34). Around this period the *mantilla* acquired strong political meanings in the press, embodying a type of Spanish "genuine" spirit and symbolizing national values against the French cultural invasion (Dendle 1982: 51–3; Díaz-Plaja 1952: 83–6).

Poet, playwright, and journalist Mariano José de Larra, director of *Correo de las damas* between 1833 and 1834, instigated one of the most famous and long-lasting controversies around the *mantilla*. The weekly fashion magazine subtitled "Periódico de modas" was primarily addressed to an upper-class and bourgeois female audience. It featured the latest sartorial novelties from Paris and included exquisite fashion plates and full-color illustrations. In some of his articles written for *Correo de las damas*, Larra praised the French female hats that were starting to replace the traditional *mantilla* in Madrilenian public spaces. For Larra, an intellectual of profound liberal ideas, the elegant and colorful Parisian hat was an indicator of the renewing spirit of modern times; it symbolized "a way to see and experience true freedom" in opposition to a traditionalist and old-fashioned Spain epitomized by the *mantilla* (*Correo de las damas*, July 10, 1833). When alluding to the return of Spanish political exiles after Ferdinand VII's Ominous Decade (1823–33), Larra writes that "where the effects of emigration are most felt is in the Parisian style costumes" that had taken over the Paseo del Prado—the center of nineteenth-century Madrilenian modern life (*Correo de las damas*, July 10, 1833). With the advent of European modernity, the *mantilla* symbolized a backward and outdated image of Spain, conveying "the appearance of a dark, distrustful people in mourning" (*Correo de las damas*, July 10, 1833). Larra asks: "Isn't there a certain relationship between the Inquisition and that monotony of the *basquiña* and the *mantilla*, that dark, black, oppressive, and poor garment of our mothers?" (*Correo de las damas*, July 10, 1833).[13] According to Larra, French hats symbolize the freedom of democracy and the penetration of enlightened values in opposition to the old-fashioned *mantilla*:

> See, on the contrary, those elegant Parisian hats that make their feathers flutter in the air with noble freedom and liberty: those wide and independent clothes, without hindrance or subjection, image of the ideas and march of a people in the possession of their rights: that infinite variety of shapes and colors, mirror of the tolerance of the uses and opinions. (*Correo de las damas*, July 10, 1833)[14]

As this excerpt illustrates, the *mantilla* functions as a privileged site to portray the reality of a nation divided into two opposing ideologies: the antiquated Spain of the *mantilla* and the *basquiña*, the *castiza* (pure) Spain of the Counter-Reformation defined by an austere, monotonous, and backward mentality; in contrast to a young, Europeanized, modern, tolerant, and free Spain that assimilates the fashions imported from Paris (Escobar 1983: 163).

The nationalist intelligentsia reacted to Larra's assertions and came out in defense of the *mantilla*, which they considered a national icon, disapproving of the female French hat. For instance, Antonio María de Segovia, writing under the pseudonym of "El Estudiante," editor of the *Correo de las damas* in 1835, declared that, although the newspaper would continue to report on Parisian fashions and styles, it would seek "to build a bronze wall in the Pyrenees" in order to protect the national spirit (*Correo de las damas*, January 7, 1835). Segovia, directly responding to Larra's statements, identifies the *mantilla* as the stronghold that will maintain true Spanish culture.

Segovia launched a patriotic campaign in defense of the *mantilla* for several months, urging Spanish women to not disdain its traditional and genuine use. Other intellectuals of the time joined the journalistic debate around the *mantilla* that had started between Larra and Segovia. For example, the journalist of conservative ideology Eugenio de Ochoa declared in an extensive article the "bitter humiliation and deep pain" to see a foreign accessory (French hats) triumph over a Spanish garment "so authentic and pure" as the traditional *mantilla* (*Correo de las damas*, February 14, 1835). Ramón de Mesonero Romanos confronted Larra's progressive cosmopolitanism in "El sombrero y la mantilla." In this short story, Mesonero acknowledges the political dimension that women's fashion had attained and its ability to reflect ongoing ideological tensions, reaffirming the view of *mantillas* as the bulwark of Spanish culture ([1835] 1965: 101). Finally, it is important to note the Orientalized description of the "true" Spanish lady he makes; in addition to proudly wearing a *mantilla*, she has a "a body worthy of the banks of the river Betis" and big, black eyes "that would not have looked bad in the paradise of Muhammad" (104).

The discussion over women's accessories in the press actively continued until the 1850s. Even in 1851, an anonymous writer under the initials T. Z. lamented in *La Ilustración* the battle between *mantillas* and French hats: "How much more attractive, how much more elegant have our *mantillas* always been, than those French hats that are introduced to us?" (April 7, 1851). *Fin-de-siècle* literary texts similarly expressed the need to bring back the old use of *mantillas*. This desire was the case of "Mantillas y paveros," a short story written by conservative author Eusebio Blasco (1895). In the text, once again the *chapeau* (hat in French) is confronted with the *mantilla*, which acts as a national hallmark that links the "true" Spanish people with their "authentic" past and identity.

The journalistic excerpts discussed here, all written by male authors, served to reinforce the *mantilla* as a powerful and influential political tool.[15] The symbolic power ascribed to this accessory escalated during the turbulent Restoration years with the so-called "*Mantillas* Rebellion"—a succession of sartorial protests led by Spanish noblewomen in March 1871 to express their rejection to Amadeo I (reigned 1870–73), the Spanish king of Italian origin.[16] Along with the fleur-de-lis (heraldic emblem of the Bourbon dynasty), women defiantly wore *mantillas* across the Paseo del Prado, arousing ardent debates and discussion in the press, all of which intensified the ongoing negative sentiments toward Amadeo I and his government. Donned to openly communicate nationalist stances and political adherence to the House of Bourbon, the *mantilla* offered women a vehicle to intervene in the public sphere, transcending their conventional, domestic roles. The *Mantillas* Rebellion was a sartorial protest organized and led by female aristocrats, albeit women from other social classes, emulating the higher ranks, also joined the processions.[17] *Mantillas* literally took over the Madrilenian streets, and the protesters' political dissent contributed to the abdication of the king.

The female rebellion inspired countless literary texts in *fin-de-siècle* Spain. For instance, in Jesuit Luis Coloma's *Pequeñeces* (1890), the protagonist, countess Currita de Albornoz, appears as the organizer of the sartorial protests, in which women wore the *castizo* accessory to protect purist national values.[18] Coloma's contemporary, writer Benito Pérez Galdós, also fictionalized the *Mantillas* Rebellion in *La desheredada* (1881). In this instance, once more, the strong political values invested in the *mantilla* become clear.[19] The *Mantillas* Rebellion ultimately exemplifies the ways in which a material object takes a central role in the nation-building process. Transcending its alleged accessorizing role and surpassing its mere decorative function, the *mantilla* traces the various national narratives that intersected and competed over time. As an object that became the embodiment of a specific notion of Spanishness and traditional conservatism, it helped express rejection of foreign customs and divided contending political factions. At the same time, as a trope of national femininity, it served as a visual and material tool with which Spanish women could express agency both in political and sexual terms.

Tracing the *Mantilla*: Then and Now

Even though the *mantilla* remained a ubiquitous Spanish accessory over the course of the nineteenth century, its presence progressively diminished at the turn of the twentieth century. With the spread of new ideas about the Modern Woman in the 1920s and 1930s in Western societies, one who dressed in comfortable clothes and wore short hair, the use of the *mantilla* gradually declined.[20] It was increasingly worn solely at religious and national festivities, such as bullfights, weddings, or during Holy Week celebrations. In the first two decades of the Francoist dictatorship (1939–59), however, the accessory experienced a revival in women's wardrobes. Over this period, traditional garments like the *mantilla* were incorporated into the iconography of National Catholicism and served as an instrument for Falangist propaganda (Vincent 2002: 15). In various media, such as advertisements, film, television, and the press, visual representations of *mantillas* helped recover traditionalist ideologies from the nineteenth century.[21] In the years following the Spanish Civil War (1936–9), the *mantilla* and the high *peineta* (hair comb) were employed together to create the patriotic hairstyle known as "Arriba España" (Upwards, Spain), which consisted of leaving the neck completely uncovered and the hair collected in curls at the top of the head. "Arriba España" was not only the most fashionable and widespread hairstyle during the end of the 1930s and 1940s among women of all social strata but also the official fascist salute employed in the Spanish State to show support of Franco's regime (Pelka 2014: 37). This instance is another example in which fashion trends and politics wildly collide through the *mantilla*. What better than a garment that had already been signified as truly and deeply Spanish to represent an emblem of National Catholicism, purism, and patriotism.

Both Franco's wife Carmen Polo and the founder of the *Sección Femenina* (Female Section of the Spanish Fascist Party), Pilar Primo de Rivera, publicly encouraged the austere and demure use of the *mantilla* in their public appearances. In contrast to the somewhat liberated female image from the Second Republic (1931–9)—when sporty clothing and shorter skirts became a major fashion influence—the visual model of the postwar period became attached to notions of modesty, virtuosity, and sobriety. Women's magazines addressed to the middle and lower classes that reached great popularity in the 1940s, such as *La Moda* and *El Hogar*, show the relative stagnancy of female fashions during this decade (Blanco Díaz 2015: 35; Muñoz Ruiz 2003: 15). Female dress aimed to mirror the nineteenth-century figure of the "angel of the home," whose functions were to be a mother and housewife, all tasks exteriorized in her modest clothing (Gracia and Ruiz Carnicer 2001: 93; Muñoz Ruiz 2003: 16). As costume historian Anna Pelka observes, in the 1940s a sartorial phenomenon named the "españolización de la moda" ("Spanishization of fashion") took place, which consisted in the articulation of a national fashion and the attempt to erase foreign influences (2012: 229–31). Particularly, French styles were overtly criticized in fashion magazines and advertisements addressed to the lower and middle classes, as they represented the corruption of moral and religious tenets (Pelka 2014: 39).[22]

In addition, in postwar Spain the control over the female dress was a frequent subject of concern for the Catholic Church (Vincent 2002: 167; Pelka 2012: 224). Dress, particularly for middle- and lower-class women, was determined by the religious code that forbade giving too much emphasis to the body and imposed a rigid clothing code. For instance, for going to church, women and girls needed to cover their heads with a *mantilla*, or lace veil, in addition to concealing their legs with black stockings (Muñoz Ruiz 2003: 528). Moreover, in every province, priests and bishops were responsible for determining the appropriate length of female sleeves and skirts (Muñoz Ruiz 2003: 528). Black was the color for *mantillas*, epitomizing the climate of repression and Catholic fundamentalism (Vaquero Argüelles 2007: 129). Deliberately promoted during the early decades of Francoism, the *mantilla* helped to identify the nation with the folklore of southern Spain, a component at the base of National Catholicism.[23] The accessory bore a great symbolic weight in Francoist Spain, propagating a sense of disciplined and purist national body, while at the same time providing visual uniformity. Overall, the *mantilla* highlighted the image of a picturesque and exotic Spain in tune with the notorious official slogan "Spain is different," formulated during Franco's regime by Manuel Fraga, Minister of Information and Tourism (1962–9), to promote the tourist industry.

In the late 1950s and 1960s, mainly triggered by foreign investments and the tourism boom, Francoist Spain underwent a phase of economic growth and profound social change after decades of cultural isolation. Those crucial transformations were reflected in women's fashion, and rapidly generated new styles of female dress influenced by European and North American trends. As a result, the *mantilla* became gradually relegated to official ceremonies and religious events, languishing especially from the 1980s onward. It is noteworthy, however, to mention the complex ways in which the *mantilla* continues to be associated with ancestral national and traditional values even today, particularly as it is still connected to southern Spain. As an example of this, there have been recent *mantilla* protests in Seville that, echoing the nineteenth-century *Mantillas* Rebellion, are organized and led by women to advocate for a specific "Andalusian femininity" (*ABC Sevilla*, March 23, 2018). In this context, female Andalusian designers grouped under the name "Sí, mantilla" employ the traditional accessory as a vehicle to praise Andalusian people's idiosyncrasies and their sociocultural and regional uniqueness (*Diario de España*, March 30, 2018).

In this same vein, activist Mar Gallego, founder of the Andalusian feminist group "Como vaya yo y lo encuentre," further explains: "The *mantilla* carries a lot of spirituality and many memories of a precarious people who use Holy Week as an excuse to remember their *female ancestors*, overturn their stolen and Spanished culture and also claim their own against other foreign discourses" (*El País*, March 30, 2018; author's emphasis).[24] Gallego, a strong female voice well known for her advocacy of the rights of working-class women, claims Andalusia's political and cultural independence from Spain through the *mantilla*. For Gallego and her counterparts, the *mantilla* serves as a powerful tool to express and display *andalucismo* (Andalusian nationalism)—a cultural and political current that calls for Andalusian autonomy, celebrating Andalusia's Muslim past and its geographic and cultural proximity to Morocco; all aspects that define Andalusia's difference and cultural uniqueness in contrast to the rest of the areas in the Iberian Peninsula.[25]

To further mystify the various notions and narratives currently enmeshed in the *mantilla*, European fashion designers from the last century—Yves Saint Laurent, John Galliano, and Jean Paul Gaultier, among many others—have persistently utilized this accessory as a sartorial vehicle to convey, appropriate, and perform an exoticized and erotized notion of Spain. In these modern interpretations of *mantillas*, the garment, notably voided of political meanings, is displayed on runways and in fashion magazines alongside castanets, *toreros*, colorful ruffles, and vibrant fans as a synecdoche of Spain. Images of women suggestively accessorized with exuberant *mantillas* communicate passion, erotic pleasure, and romantic travel to the viewer. The *mantilla* populates visual accounts of Europe's romantic, old fascination with Oriental Spain.[26] The twentieth-century sartorial representations of *mantillas* have ultimately contributed to ambiguously locate the essence of Spanishness in Andalusia and collaborate in the construction of an exotic and Orientalized conception of Spain.[27]

After this historical and cultural overview, one may ask, what does the *mantilla* truly represent? A sartorial instrument arbitrated by men to control the female body and link it to a specific national propaganda? A fashion choice employed by Spanish women to exert their own identity and actively assert their participation in the nation-building project? How can one single object within its materiality articulate a distinct idea of a Spanish national identity, symbolize an entire Andalusian feminist group, and be regarded as one of the highest forms of couture by European designers? Be that as it may, the *mantilla* does much more than simply fall across women's heads. In connection with Derrida's logic of supplementarity mentioned at the beginning of this chapter, the supplement (*parergon*), albeit detachable and marginal, completes the whole meaning of the work (*ergon*) it frames. The *parergon* is thus an indispensable and intrinsic element of the *ergon*. Taking into account the example of the *mantilla*, it is an accessory whose function goes beyond solely adorning or covering the female body. It allows us to explore the sociocultural and sociopolitical dynamics of a distinct period of time from a material perspective, bringing forward their subjacent and competing narratives and ideas. As a multifaceted item at the intersection of diverse realities and categories, the *mantilla* ultimately evidences the centrality of accessories within cultural history.

Notes

1 For further information on this subject, see *Accessorizing the Body*, edited by Cristina Giorcelli and Paula Rabinowitz. Some examples of recent works devoted to the study of garments are by Ariel Beaujout and Celia Marshik.

2 León Pinelo, the earliest historian on veiling, believes that this female fashion evolved out of Moorish practice. In contrast, Carmen Bernis argues that the *manteo* has no Moorish roots (2001: 257), while Ruth de la Puerta (1996: 198), Marco Antonio León León (1993: 274–6), Camilla Catarulla (2015: 199–200), and María Elena de Arizmendi Amiel (1988: 54), among others, suggest that it is the product of Arab-Christian contact.

3 Moriscas (converted Muslim women) wore a white veil called *almalafa* to cover their faces until the second half of the sixteenth century when King Philip II banned its use. As Bernis points out, Moriscas, in comparison to Christian women, revealed both eyes beneath their *almalafa* (2001: 257).

4 León Pinelo's book is the oldest testimony on the history of veiling in the Iberian Peninsula. The *tapada* that he describes is an emblematic element in the cultural imaginary of the Spanish Golden Age and constantly appears in *comedias* and popular poetry from the period. For more on the *manteo* tradition in Spain and Latin America, see Catarulla; Laura R. Bass and Amanda Wunder; Arizmendi Amiel; and León León.

5 All translations from Spanish into English are mine unless otherwise indicated.

6 In 1770, Carlos III (reigned 1759–88) issued a royal decree to prohibit the public use of any *manto* that was not made of either silk or wool to stop women from disguising their identities when mingling with others in public, which consequently blurred social lines and increased the potential for female misconduct. For an overview on the history and development of sumptuary legislation in Spain from the mid-thirteenth to eighteenth centuries, see Wunder (2019).

7 On *majas*, *petimetres*, and eighteenth-century cultural practices, Carmen Martín Gaite's *Usos amorosos del dieciocho en España* is essential reading.

8 Artist Francisco de Goya is undoubtedly the master painter of *mantillas*, giving this accessory a visibility without precedent. According to Aileen Ribeiro, Goya mastered the "most subtle and beautiful *mantilla* of all" in Zárate's portrait (2002: 84).

9 For an in-depth evolution of nationalism in nineteenth-century Spain, see José Álvarez Junco.

10 Among the large list of authors related to the "material turn" in the humanities and social sciences, see Arjun Appadurai (*The Social Life of Things*); Bruno Latour (*Matter, Materiality and Culture*); Bill Brown (*The Sense of Things*); and Barbara Johnson (*Persons and Things*). All of the scholars mentioned discuss the role of the material and the nonhuman in creating and shaping human subjectivity; more specifically, they seek to bring forward the vital role that objects, artifacts, and things—often disregarded as trivial—play in everyday life and social history.

11 For more on the intersection of gender and national construction, see Blom et al.; Sharp; Heng; and Yuval-Davis.

12 Worth, born in England and relocated to Paris in 1845, transformed women's couture into a big business and high art during the second half of the nineteenth century. On this subject, see Steele (117–37).

13 "¿No hay cierta relación entre la Inquisición y aquella monotonía de la basquiña y la mantilla, prenda oscura, negra, opresora y pobre de nuestras madres?"

14 "Véanse, por el contrario, esos elegantes sombreros parisinos que hacen ondear sus plumas al aire con noble desembarazo y libertad: esas ropas amplias e independientes, sin traba ni sujeción, imagen de las ideas y marcha de un pueblo en la posesión de sus derechos: esa variedad infinita de hechuras y colores, espejo de la tolerancia de los usos y opiniones."

15 Finding texts on *mantillas* written from the viewpoint of women at this time is a difficult task. Female journalism did not flourish until the middle of the nineteenth century and many female authors did not sign their articles or used pseudonyms. The fashion correspondent for *El Semanario pintoresco español*, Clementina, expressed a divergent opinion on *mantillas* in the late 1830s. In contrast to her male counterparts, Clementina praised the Spanish women's way of wearing this accessory, emphasizing its erotic and seductive dimensions. Decades later, we find a similar approach to the *mantilla* in Emilia Pardo Bazán's novel *Insolación* (1889).

16 The Spanish Restoration encompasses the period from 1874 to 1931. The term refers to the recovery of the throne by Alfonso XII, member of the House of Bourbon, after the Revolutionary Sexeny (1868–1874) .

17 Articles published in *El Imparcial* and *Revista de España* between March 20 and 30, 1871, report that women from all social hierarchies participated in the protests.

18 Curra Albornoz from *Pequeñeces* is based on the historical figure of Sofia Troubetzkoy, marchioness of Alcañices and duchess of Sesto, one of the most powerful aristocrats of the Madrilenian Court. As historical records evidence, Sofia Troubetzkoy was the instigator of the sartorial protests. For additional information, see Ana de Sagrera.

19 For further reading on the literary and journalistic representations of *mantillas* in nineteenth-century Spain, see Corujo-Martín.

20 The look of the modern, urban woman took central stage in the Western world after the First World War (1914–18). It promoted a more liberating and dynamic ideal of womanhood, coinciding with the rise of feminist movements and the entrance of middle-class women onto the public stage of work. Modern women's fashions borrowed menswear garments like trousers and suits (popularized by Coco Chanel, among others), and, in contrast to rigid corsets and full-length skirts, encouraged simple and practical clothing. On this subject, see Steele (215–27).

21 For more information on the influence of nineteenth-century nationalist values during Francoist regime, see Stanley P. Payne.

22 This did not apply to the upper class. Spanish couture in the 1940s paradoxically reached high artistic levels. Costly fashion magazines showcased exquisite outfits, and elite women often bought luxury garments at establishments from renowned designers, such as Cristóbal Balenciaga. On this topic, see Pelka (2012, 2014) and Vaquero Argüelles.

23 For more on this, see Josep Martí and Alexandre Cirici.

24 "La *mantilla* tiene mucho de espiritualidad y de memoria de un pueblo precario que usa la Semana Santa como excusa para recordar a sus *ancestras*, volcar su cultura robada y españolizada y reivindicar también lo propio frente a otros discursos extranjeros."

25 For a thoughtful and thorough overview of *andalucismo*, see José Acosta Sánchez.

26 Carmen, the myth immortalized by Prosper Mérimée (1845), is a prime example of this phenomenon, in which European authors from the Romantic period widely Orientalized the idea of Spain (Andalusia in particular). Other authors who contributed to the romantic construction of Spain are Byron, Hugo, Irving, and Chateaubriand, among many others.

27 For more on this subject, see "Visiones de España en la moda" by Lydia Kamitsis (21–7), and "Lo español en la moda" by Amalia Descalzo (29–39).

References

Acosta, Sánchez José (1978), *Andalucía: Reconstrucción de una identidad y la lucha contra el centralismo*, Barcelona: Anagrama.

Álvarez Junco, José (2010), *Mater Dolorosa. La idea de España en el siglo XIX*, Madrid: Taurus.

Anthias, Floya and Nira Yuval-Davis (1989), *Woman-Nation-State*, Basingstoke: Macmillan.

Arizmendi Amiel, María Elena de (1988), "Las tapadas," *Revista de Dialectología y Tradiciones Populares* 43: 53–8.

Bass, Laura R. and Amanda Wunder (2009), "The Veiled Ladies of the Early Modern Spanish World: Seduction and Scandal in Seville, Madrid, and Lima," *Hispanic Review* 77 (1): 97–144.

Beaujout, Ariel (2011), *Victorian Fashion Accessories*, Oxford: Berg Publishers.

Bernis, Carmen (1979), *Trajes y modas en la España de los Reyes Católicos,* vol. 2, *Los Hombres*, Madrid: Instituto Diego Velázquez, del Consejo Superior de Investigaciones Científicas.

Bernis, Carmen (2001), *El traje y los tipos sociales en El Quijote*, Madrid: El Viso.

Blanco Díaz, Violeta (2015), *Análisis de la moda española durante la dictadura franquista*, MA diss., Universidad de Sevilla, Sevilla.

Blasco, Eusebio ([1895] 1905), "Mantillas y paveros," *Obras completas*, vol. 16, 129–34, ed. Antonio Zozaya, Madrid: Librería Editorial de Leopoldo Martínez.

Blom, Ida, Karen Hagemann, and Catherine Hall, eds. (2000), *Gendered Nations: Nationalisms and Gender Order in the Long Nineteenth Century*, Oxford: Berg.

Catarulla, Camilla (2015), "The Erotic Play of the Veil. *Tapadas* in Lima," in Cristina Giorcelli and Paula Rabinowitz (eds.), *Extravagances. Habits of Being*, vol. 4, 198–218, Minneapolis: University of Minnesota Press.

Cirici, Alexandre (1977), *La estética del franquismo*, Barcelona: Gustavo Gili.

Correo de las damas. Periódico de modas (1833–35), Madrid.

Corujo-Martín, Inés (2017), "La mantilla entre tradición y modernidad: moda, género y cultura material en la España de los siglos XVIII y XIX," *Letras Femeninas* 43 (1): 28–45.

Dendle, Brian J. (1982), "Isidora, the *Mantillas Blancas*, and Attempted Assassination of Alfonso XII," *Anales Galdosianos*, 17: 51–4.

Derrida, Jacques (1977), *Of Grammatology*, trans. Gayatri Chakravorty Spivak, Baltimore: John Hopkins University Press.

Descalzo, Amalia (2007), "Lo español en la moda," in *Genio y figura. La influencia de la cultura española en la moda*, 29–39, Madrid: Museo del Traje.

Díaz-Plaja, Fernando (1952), *La vida española en el siglo XIX*, Madrid: Afrodisio Aguado.

Escobar, José (1983), "El sombrero y la mantilla: moda e ideología en el costumbrismo romántico español," in Jean-René Aymes (ed.), *Revisión de Larra, ¿protesta o revolución?*, 161–5, Paris: Les Belles Lettres.

Fernández Cifuentes, Luis (2007), "Southern Exposure: Early Tourism and Spanish National Identity," *Journal of Iberian and Latin American Studies* 13 (2–3): 133–48.

Giorcelli, Cristina and Paula Rabinowitz (2011), *Accessorizing the Body. Habits of Being*, vol. 1, Minneapolis: University of Minnesota Press.

Gracia, Jordi and Miguel Ángel Ruiz Carnicer (2001), *La España de Franco (1939–1975). Cultura y vida cotidiana*, Madrid: Síntesis.

Heng, Geraldine (1997), "'A Great Way to Fly': Nationalism, the State, and the Varieties of Third-World Feminism," in Chandra Talpade Mohanty and M. Jacqui Alexander (eds.), *Feminist Genealogies, Colonial Legacies, Democratic Futures*, New York: Routledge.

Hiner, Susan (2010), *Accessories to Modernity: Fashion and the Feminine in Nineteenth-Century France*, Philadelphia: University of Pennsylvania Press.

Kamitsis, Lydia (2007), "Visiones de España en la moda," in *Genio y figura. La influencia de la cultura española en la moda*, 21–7, Madrid: Museo del Traje.

Kessler, Marni Reva (2006), *Sheer Presence: The Veil in Manet's Paris*, Minneapolis: University of Minnesota Press.

León León, Marco Antonio (1993), "Entre lo público y lo privado: acercamiento a las *tapadas* y *cubiertas* en España, Hispanoamérica y Chile," *Boletín de la Academia Chilena de la Historia* 60: 273–311.

Marshik, Celia (2016), *At the Mercy of Their Clothes. Modernism, the Middlebrow, and British Garment Culture*, New York: Columbia University Press.

Martí, Josep (1996), *El folklorismo: uso y abuso de la tradición*, Barcelona: Ronsel.

Martín Gaite, Carmen (1981), *Usos amorosos del dieciocho en España*, Barcelona: Lumen.

Martin-Márquez, Susan (2008), *Disorientations: Spanish Colonialism in Africa and the Performance of Identity*, New Haven: Yale University Press.

Mesonero Romanos, Ramón ([1835] 1965), "El sombrerito y la mantilla," in María José Sáez Piñuela (ed.), *La moda femenina en la literatura*, Madrid: Taurus.

Muñoz Ruiz, María del Carmen (2003), "Amas de casa y trabajadoras: imágenes en la prensa femenina (1955–1970)," in Josefina Cuesta Bustillo (ed.), *Historia de las Mujeres en España. Siglo XX*, vol. 2, 331–70, Madrid: Instituto de la Mujer.

Noyes, Dorothy (1998), "La Maja Vestida: Dress as Resistance to Enlightenment in Late-18th Century Madrid," *Journal of American Folklore* 111 (440): 197–217.

Pardo Bazán, Emilia ([1889] 2005), *Insolación*, ed. Ermitas Penas Varela, Madrid: Cátedra.

Parkins, Wendy, ed. (2002), *Fashioning the Body Politic. Dress, Gender, Citizenship*, New York: Berg.

Payne, Stanley P. (1999), *Fascism in Spain 1923–1977*, Madison: University of Wisconsin Press.

Pelka, Anna (2012), "La imagen de la mujer. La moda femenina en la España de los años cuarenta," in Antoni Segura, Andreu Mayayo, and Teresa Abelló (eds.), *La dictadura franquista. La institucionalització d'un règim*, 223–34, Barcelona: Universitat de Barcelona.

Pelka, Anna (2014), "Mujer e ideología en la posguerra española: feminidad, cuerpo y vestido," *Historia social* 79: 23–42.

Pena González, Pablo (2008), *El traje en el Romanticismo y su proyección en España, 1828–1868*, Madrid: Ministerio de Cultura.

Pérez Galdós, Benito ([1881] 2011), *La desheredada*, ed. Germán Gullón, Madrid: Cátedra.

Pezzi, Elena (1991), *Los moriscos que no se fueron*, Almería: Editorial Cajal.

Puerta, Ruth de la (1996–97), "Moda, moral y regulación jurídica en época de Goya," *Ars Longa* 7–8: 205–17.

Ribeiro, Aileen (2002), "Fashioning the Feminine: Dress in Goya's Portraits of Women," in Janis Tomlinson (ed.), *Goya: Images of Women*, 71–87, Washington, DC: National Gallery of Art.

Roces, Mina and Louise Edwards, eds. (2010), *The Politics of Dress in Asia and the Americas*, Brighton: Sussex Academic Press.

Sagrera, Ana de (1990), *Una rusa en España. Sofía, duquesa de Sesto*, Madrid: Espasa-Calpe.

Sharp, Joanne P. (2006), "Gendering Nation. A Feminist Engagement with National Identity," in Nancy Hall-Duncan (ed.), *Bodyspace. Destabilizing Geographies of Gender and Sexuality*, 97–108, London: Routledge.

Steele, Valerie (1988), *Paris Fashion: A Cultural History*, Oxford: Oxford University Press.

Tofiño-Quesada, Ignacio (2003), "Spanish Orientalism: Uses of the Past in Spain's Colonization of Africa," *Comparative Studies of South Asia, Africa and the Middle East* 23 (1–2): 141–8.

Vaquero Argüelles, Isabel (2007), "El reinado de la Alta Costura: la moda de la primera mitad del siglo XX," *Indumenta. Revista del Museo del Traje* 0: 123–34.

Vincent, Mary (2002), "Camisas nuevas: Style and Uniformity in the Falange Española. 1933–1943," in Wendy Parkins (ed.), *Fashioning the Body Politic. Dress, Gender, Citizenship*, 167–88, New York: Berg.

Wunder, Amanda (2019), "Spanish Fashion and Sumptuary Legislation from the Thirteenth to the Eighteenth Century," in Giorgio Riello and Ulinka Rublack (eds.), *The Right to Dress. Sumptuary Laws in a Global Perspective, c. 1200–1800*, 243–72, Cambridge: Cambridge University Press.

Yuval-Davis, Nira (1997), *Gender and Nation*, London: Sage.

Zanardi, Tara (2013), "Crafting Spanish Female Identity: Silk Lace Mantillas at the Crossroads of Tradition and Fashion," *Revue de la culture matérielle* 77–78: 139–57.

Zanardi, Tara (2016a), "Majas, mantillas y marcialidad. Fashioning Identity in Late Eighteenth-Century Spain," in Jennifer Germann and Heidi Strobel (eds.), *Materializing Gender in Eighteenth-Century Europe*, 67–86, New York: Routledge.

Zanardi, Tara (2016b), *Framing Majismo: Art and Royal Identity in Eighteenth-Century Spain*, University Park: Penn State University Press.

2

Bodies of the Future

Comics, Fashion, and 1980s *Movida*

Alberto Villamandos

Comic creator Herikberto's *El Libertador* (1984)—*The Liberator*—offers a critical view of the new mainstream culture of 1980s Spain during the *Movida*. This comic "album," as this format is known in Europe, reflects on gender, sexual, and cultural identity in an increasingly consumerist society, while at the same time exploring how gender has been codified and constrained through garments and proposing a utopian liberation through punk ethics and aesthetics.[1] Herikberto's pictorial style encompasses a variety of textures and techniques, including acrylic, neon, metal, and fluorescent colors, and computer-generated effects. With references to artists like Bacon and Picasso, Herikberto's work distances itself from other 1980s underground comic trends and aims for ambitious readings of the times and the future to come. It takes the early *Movida* motto of "the future is already here" to the next level as it explores notions of the transhuman, the cyborg, gender fluidity, and new ways of coding and constructing the self through fashion.

Realistic comics tend to depict mainstream sartorial styles. In contrast, science fiction, graphic literature, and film have long been a source of inspiration for avant-garde fashion.[2] Dystopian comics invite the possibility of creating clothing styles that match an envisioned future world. It is within this visionary imagination that I place *El Libertador*, an aesthetically and thematically groundbreaking album that explores the idea of what it means to be modern in the spheres of fashion, art, and gender identity. The album introduced these themes just as Spain was transitioning from Francisco Franco's regime (1939–75) into democracy, embracing in the process the underground cultural movement known as *la Movida*. *El Libertador* presents punk aesthetics as a rebellion against traditional notions of identity and sexuality, while clothing serves as the technology underpinning the fluid gender of the future. The uniqueness of this album lies in its ability to both reflect upon a specific historical moment, and to connect with futuristic notions of identity such as the cyborg, a technologically enhanced human body. In this regard, *El Libertador* echoes Donna Haraway's "Cyborg manifesto" (1985), aiming to overcome traditional Western dual hierarchies such as self/other, mind/body, masculine/feminine, or civilized/primitive (1991: 164). Haraway imagined a world without gender—"which is perhaps a world without genesis, but maybe also a world without end" (1991: 151)—through the trope of the cyborg, "a cybernetic organism, a hybrid of machine and organism, a creature of social reality as well as a creature of fiction" (1991: 150).

"The Future Is Already Here": Enter the *Movida*

With these words, the pop-rock band Radio Futura summarized, in its 1980 anthem "Enamorado de la moda juvenil"—"In Love with Youth Fashion"—the optimistic and playful rebelliousness of the *Movida madrileña*. During the *Movida*, Madrid witnessed a cultural renewal with the influx of punk and New Wave styles, new music venues, and bands.[3] Visual artists such as movie director Pedro Almodóvar and comic artist Ceesepe also played a critical role in creating a sense of openness and freedom, and frequently collaborated with musicians.[4] Their collective works reflect the general optimism and hedonism of the time in spite of, or in contrast to, the dreary political narrative of rupture/reform, and the general disenchantment with the unrealized promises of the transition to democracy.[5]

The theme of "the future" was inherent to youth cultures of the late 1970s, especially British punk, which directly influenced the *Movida*.[6] Pedro Almodóvar has recalled on several occasions how a very young Olvido Gara—the singer and performer later known as Alaska—used to visit London in search of new music and the most shocking garments to bring back to Madrid. It was likewise in London that singer, music producer, and 1980s fashion icon Tino Casal found his glam, gender-fluid looks, which were adopted by others such as the painting collective Las Costus.[7] As Marcela T. Garcés has stated, changing urban styles provided "a window into the transformations" that were reshaping Spanish society and youth culture (2016: 156).

British punk, as performed and styled by *The Sex Pistols* and *The Clash*, expressed the prevailing political pessimism of the Margaret Thatcher years.

Their motto "no future" pointedly signaled the mood brought on by the economic crisis, Thatcher's privatizations and cuts to the welfare system, and the concurrent demise of the organized working class. On the other hand, the Spanish *Movida* demonstrated a surprising confidence about the present. Radio Futura's song "Enamorado de la moda juvenil" promoted a promiscuous notion of modernity. It equated sexual desire and commodity fetish: "I fell in love with the guys, with the girls/with the mannequins."[8] In Spain, new forms of mass consumption were developing, with the creation in 1975 of the chain store and brand Zara, known for its affordable fashion. While both countries were severely impacted by the international oil crisis (1973–4), Spain found itself in different historical circumstances after almost four decades of Franco's authoritarian regime. As bad as the economic situation was, there was no stopping Spanish citizens from embracing and expressing freedom and fun through social practices such as fashion, music, and the visual arts.

During the last decade of the regime and the transition to democracy, fashion was culturally central. It revealed "both the themes and the formal relationships which serve a culture as orienting ideas and the real or imagined basis according to which cultural categories are organized" (McCracken 1988: 59). A clothing metaphor, "cambiar de chaqueta" or "switching jackets," referred to the sudden acceptance of democracy by former Franco officials.[9] The clean-cut look of the conservative political elite found its opposition in the *Movida*'s loud, gender-bending punk-glam, which appealed to urban and working-class youth. This do-it-yourself notion of anti-fashion (Davis 2007: 98) could be found in *el Rastro*, the popular, centuries-old flea market in Madrid—a convenient venue for creating modern looks by combining old-fashioned or ill-fitting elements.[10] A meeting point for the young "misfits"—the singer Alaska and others first sold their fanzines there—*el Rastro* became a symbol of postmodern bricolage where queer performers like Fabio McNamara or Paco Clavel found pieces to combine for their *cutrelux* (trashy-luxe) outfits in the best punk spirit of shocking audiences.[11]

From the beginning of this cultural movement, personal style and collective statements became critical elements.[12] In its more upscale expression, some designers, who later would be part of the *Moda de España* branding campaign by the new Socialist—PSOE administration, opened ateliers on Almirante and Argensola streets.[13] Visual arts projected not only rebellious punk aesthetics but also the sophistication of those new designers. Almodóvar's film *Matador* (1986) included a fashion show by trailblazing designer Francis Montesinos, while another staple of the *Movida* and the *Moda de España* campaign,

Sybilla dressed the members of pop group *Peor Impossible* for their music video "Ortopedia" (1985).[14] In *Labyrinth of Passion* (directed by Almodóvar, 1982), the couture outfits of the protagonist Sexilia (played by Cecilia Roth) mingled with Fabio McNamara's punk-glam looks and ye-ye retro outfits.[15] Comic artist Ceesepe also represented the fashion-conscious youth of the early 1980s on the cover of magazines and fanzines like *Madriz* or *El Víbora* (*The Viper*), featuring stylish *modernos* in a bar in bright colors, skinny ties, shoulder-padded blazers, and even in a revisited Madrid traditional *chulapo*— late nineteenth-century working-class male of the country's capital—outfit (*El Víbora* 40: 1983). In contrast, Herikberto's album depicts his criticism of the snobbery, superficiality, and social- and gender-conformity of the new fashionable elite.

Herikberto: Sequential Art for the Future

Herikberto's work epitomizes the social and cultural changes of the time: bold aesthetics in the arts and the self.[16] He became a critical creator of *Movida* imagery through comic, a sequential art (McCloud 1994), reproduced mechanically, and therefore with political potential (Benjamin 1998). His illustrations appeared in fanzines such as *La Luna de Madrid* and comic magazines such as *Heavy Metal* (the English edition of the French *Métal Hurlant*), *Rambla*, and *Comix Internacional*.[17] Many of his science fiction illustrations portrayed a stylized futuristic dehumanization that was influenced by rock and punk culture—like the comic "¡Strok!" for *Rambla* in 1983—and became iconic when placed in other formats such as record covers and advertising. The album *El Libertador*, previously serialized in *Rambla* from December 1983 through the following year, combined the *Movida* cultural milieu with a futuristic fantasy. *El Libertador* was part of an unprecedented boom in Spanish comics (Pérez del Solar 2013).

At the time, two opposing styles were in competition. Fanzines such as 1973 *El Rrollo enmascarado* [*sic.*] (*The Masked Scene*), which published the work of Nazario and Miguel Gallardo, started a *línea chunga* ("bad" or "mean" style) similar to Robert Crumb's underground adult comics in the United States. This trend featured punk and grotesque aesthetics, combined with dark humor and sociopolitical commentary on countercultural subjects: music, drug use, and rebellion against power structures. Central to *línea chunga*'s rebellious character was its depiction of sexual and gender non-conformity, as if using Haraway's notion of the cyborg's post-gender world.

Another important trend was the revival of the 1940s–1950s adventure-filled *línea clara* ("clear line") initiated by French and Belgian authors such as Hergé, creator of *The Adventures of Tintin*. This style would turn increasingly towards adult content in the early 1980s with authors such as Joost Swarte. In Spain, magazines like *Cairo* (1981–91) adopted a similar style with bright, flat colors, detailed backgrounds, and defined lines. The differences between *línea chunga* and *línea clara* are reflected as well in the divergent fashion styles they depict, including leather jackets, mohawks, and piercings on the one hand, as against classic 1940s Hollywood raincoats and nightgowns on the other. According to Malcolm Compitello, illustrator Javier de Juan's well-dressed characters sporting fedoras, wide shoulder pads, skinny ties, and trench coats against the background of a busy metropolis show a "fixation on movement, internationalism and modernity" (2014: 216). The retro *noir*-inspired iconography of the *línea clara* was in sync with the 1940s American style revived by haute couture firms such as Yves Saint Laurent in the 1970s and what Fredric Jameson termed "nostalgia films" (1991) such as *Blade Runner* (1982). The counterpoint to these retro aesthetics was the *línea chunga*, depicting gritty urban tribes, in addition to transvestites and transgender characters like Nazario's *Anarcoma*.

Other publications, such as *Star*, *El Víbora*, *Cimoc*, or *Rambla* were more eclectic in their contents.[18] Herikberto's style drew elements from the *línea clara*, like the bright colors and the pictorial composition of the page as an artistic unit, but also from the *línea chunga*, with countercultural themes such as violence or sex. Unlike other comic artists in the 1980s like Ceesepe and El Hortelano, whose trajectory took them from fanzines to art galleries (Pérez del Solar 2013: 287), Herikberto started out as a classically trained artist and painter. His first exhibition was at the important Juana Mordó art gallery in Madrid, when he was only eighteen. In an interview for *Rambla* in 1984, Herikberto expressed his debt to twentieth-century painters: "Those who read my comics think me to be something that I am not, a guy from the *rollo* (scene), a *moderno*. When I create my comics, my influences are Tàpies, Millares, Van Gogh, American expressionism, Bacon" (36).

The album is divided into six chapters ("The Deserter," "The Liberator," "The Foreigner," "The Fighter," "The Destroyer," "The Creator") and features characters in different disguises.

From the young fashionable *moderno* to the hippie; from the conservative executive in a tailored suit to the futuristic subject, a crossover of human and machine, fashion is often presented as a spectacle. The different attire represent a variety of social types in 1980s Spain. However, by using graphic narrative as a "realm of possibility," this dystopian album becomes a projection of the future. Clothing, as a technology of gender (De Lauretis 1987), provides an axis for identity changes and the search for authenticity.

The setting for the album begins in a contemporary art museum, where a crowd of young people socializes. They are dressed in the iconic 1980s Italian Memphis Group style: bright solid colors, bold geometrical prints, big shoulder pads, skinny ties, and wide-brimmed picture hats (Figure 2.1). The museum and its public remind the readers of the connections between fashion and art, much as Gustav Klimt and Mariano Fortuny made textiles central to their paintings.[19] Ever since the Metropolitan Museum of Art's 1973 Balenciaga exhibition, as Chapter 7 of this volume explains, traditional art museums have increasingly embraced fashion brands in temporary collections with great accolades from the museum-going public (Mata Torrado 2003: 229).

The opening location symbolizes the newly relevant role of institutions of high culture as fashionable spaces in democratic Spain.[20] Private art galleries such as Buades, Moriarty, Estampa, and Vijande became meeting spaces for well-to-do *modernos* during the *Movida*.

Ultimately, galleries like these became a social and cultural legitimizing authority in a society increasingly dominated by mass media, consumption, and spectacle (Stapell 2010: 102).[21] Within this context, *El Libertador*'s opening scene represents this new urban elite obsessed with the latest trends. When rendering the snobbery and superficiality of this social group, Herikberto's album places them, as much as the art on the walls, as objects of the gaze.[22]

El Libertador displays a character's displeasure with what Herikberto considers superficial and commercialized art: "I'm sick of it! I cannot bear this expressionist Surrealism! Deep inside I feel conservative, a classicist!" (1984: 5). Rebelling against mainstream aesthetic trends, the character longs for Velázquez, Leonardo or Goya, but his friends remind him how "the left" promised great changes listed as— empty—commodities: "avant-garde fashion, fluorescent colors, sexual freedom" (1984: 6). The album criticizes the new democratic culture as shallow, conformist, and restrictive, to the point that a government official arrives unannounced to assess the required "anti-repressive sexual behavior" of all citizens. At that point, the character yearning for classicism attacks everyone with a "Cinetic" triangle (1984: 10), a weapon inspired by Victor Vasarely's Op Art style, triggering color

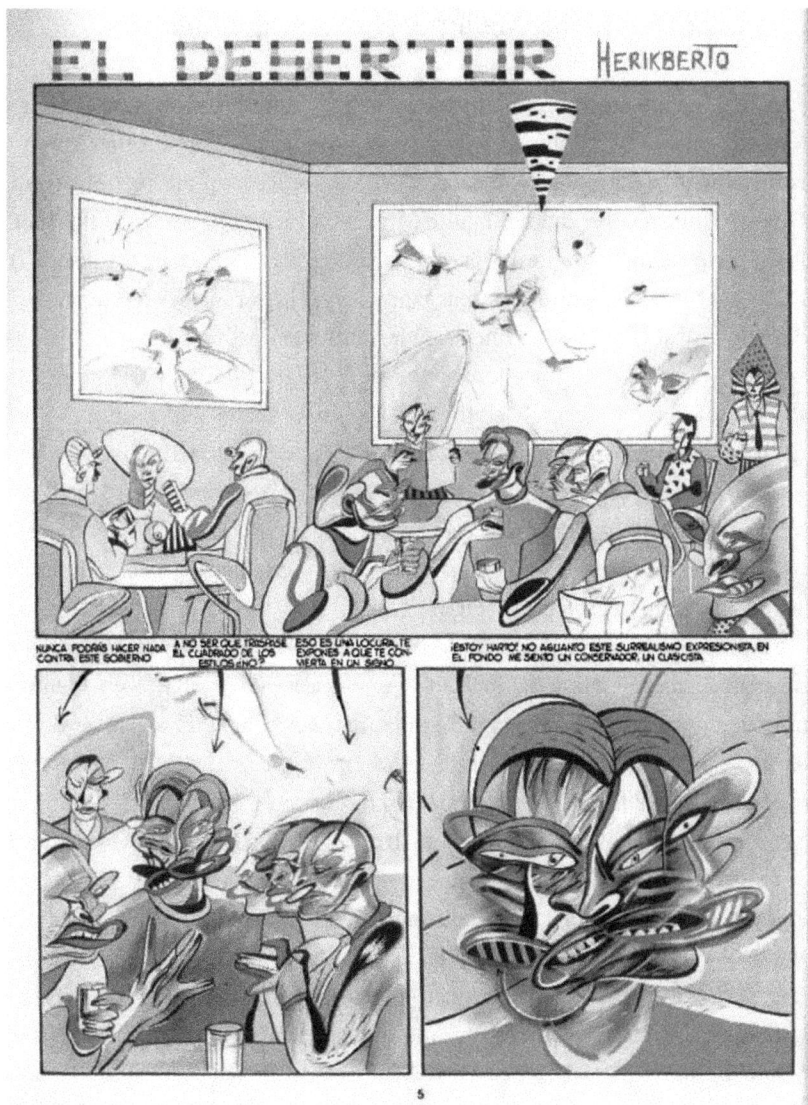

Figure 2.1 *El Libertador*, Bar. Credit: Herikberto MQ. *El Libertador* (1984).

gradations, and the change of people and space into geometrical forms. In this way, the album transports the reader to a futuristic modernity of dehumanized landscapes echoing art by De Chirico, graphic fiction by Moebius, or the film *Tron* (1982). The classicist character and his weapon provide an answer to the unformulated question that drives *El Libertador*: How do we stay authentic and connected to our roots in a (post)modern culture of spectacle and enforced pleasures? Art-driven metamorphosis seems to be the answer.

El Libertador: Metamorphosis at the Museum

In the next chapter, the protagonist known as "The Liberator" crosses over to a new dimension through a canvas-like monolith, entering another room of the museum. On the walls are displayed, side by side, art reproductions from a variety of centuries and styles: Manolo Miralles's abstract paintings of the 1960s, fashion advertising from the 1980s, and Bronzino's 1545 *Eleanor of Toledo*. The museum becomes a postmodern space: not only is linear history obliterated, but the distinction between high and popular culture—in this case, advertising—disappears. The commodification of the body (Baudrillard 1998) implies the codifying of gender through clothing. Next to centuries-old paintings, such as *Eleanor of Toledo*, depicting power, status, and gendered identity, images of modern advertising show traditional gender categories intertwined with capitalistic desire. In one scene, the protagonist merges with the image of a commercial poster selling men's suits and, in a chameleonic act, adopts the advertisement's look (1984: 15) (Figure 2.2).

The protagonist, now a smartly dressed businessman, is invested with the sign of male middle-class distinction, wearing a uniform that both identifies him with a group and erases his individuality (Crane 2000: 174). However, this unequivocal masculinity is destabilized when he merges with the advertising poster of a female figure. The character remains male on top, while the lower part of its body now wears a fluorescent green miniskirt, legwarmers, and dark-blue leggings (1984: 16). In a telling twist, these two conventionally gendered images from mainstream 1980s fashion, similar to those found in department stores like El Corte Inglés or Galerías Preciados, converge in one body. This two-gendered representation connects the protagonist with the Transition, a moment in which transvestites and transgender people symbolically represented the body politic.[23]

In this vein, Gema Pérez-Sánchez has stated that transvestism was "the true condition of Spanish democracy—la madre patria—subversively literalized as a gender bending figure for a new nation that is both male and female" (2007: 191). In her analysis of Eduardo Mendicutti's 1982 novella *Una mala noche la tiene cualquiera*, she notes that the main character, Madelón, a transgender woman, chronicles her life in a first-person monologue during the long night of the failed coup d'état of February 23, 1981. Although critics have offered differing interpretations, Madelón is generally seen as the embodiment of a country in the midst of change (Pérez-Sánchez, Garlinger, Fernández de Alba, and others). Fashion plays a central role in the novel, with Madelón pondering what to wear to each occasion: If the

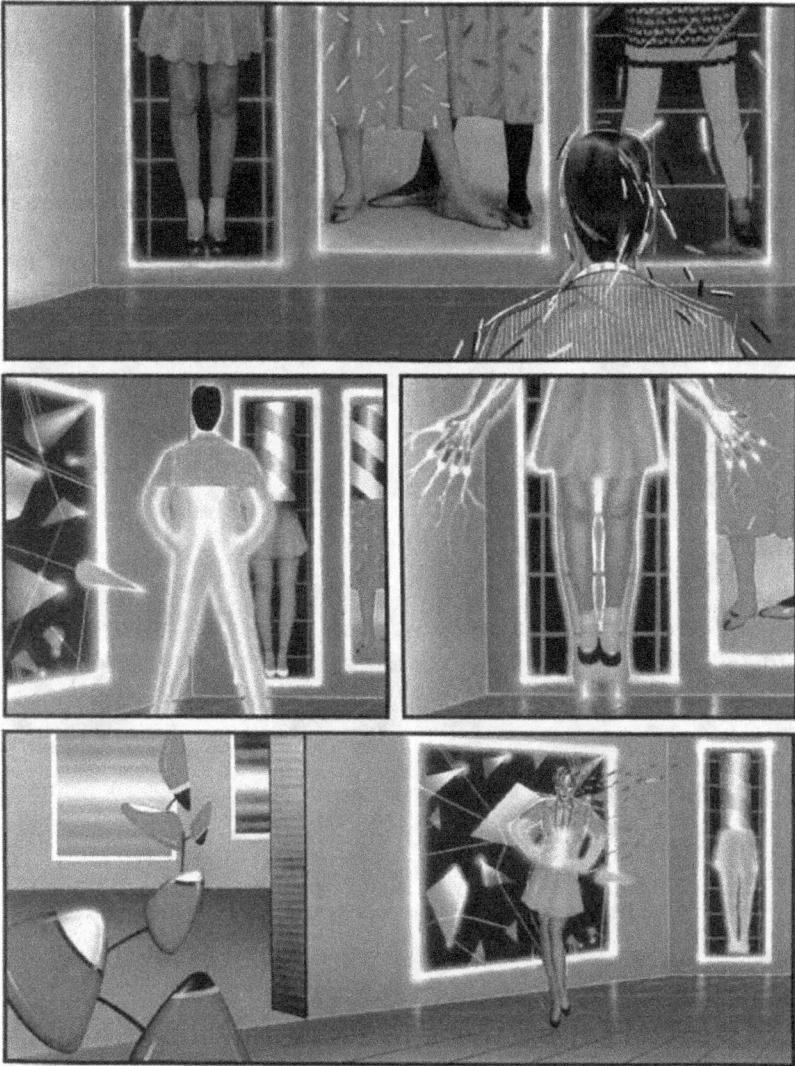

Figure 2.2 El Libertador, Cuadros Pop Museo (Pop Museum Paintings). Credit: Herikberto MQ. *El Libertador* (1984).

antidemocratic forces win, she fears she will be forced once again to wear her male military-service uniform.[24] *Una mala noche* offers an ambiguous reading of the political, due to its humor and camp value, and because Madelón maintains quite traditional binary gender politics. In contrast, *El Libertador* radically challenges gender structures, exuding an anti-status-quo energy, as demonstrated when the characters glimpse a new painting in the museum.

The new painting represents a red-skinned woman on all fours, wearing a tall black and rainbow-colored headpiece that resembles a pharaoh crown or an afro "box" hairstyle (Figure 2.3). The red woman, naked from the waist down, wears a black top with cutouts for her breasts.

Africanism, like that exhibited by music star Grace Jones in her videos "My Jamaican Guy" (1983) and "Slave to the Rhythm" (1985), was another sartorial

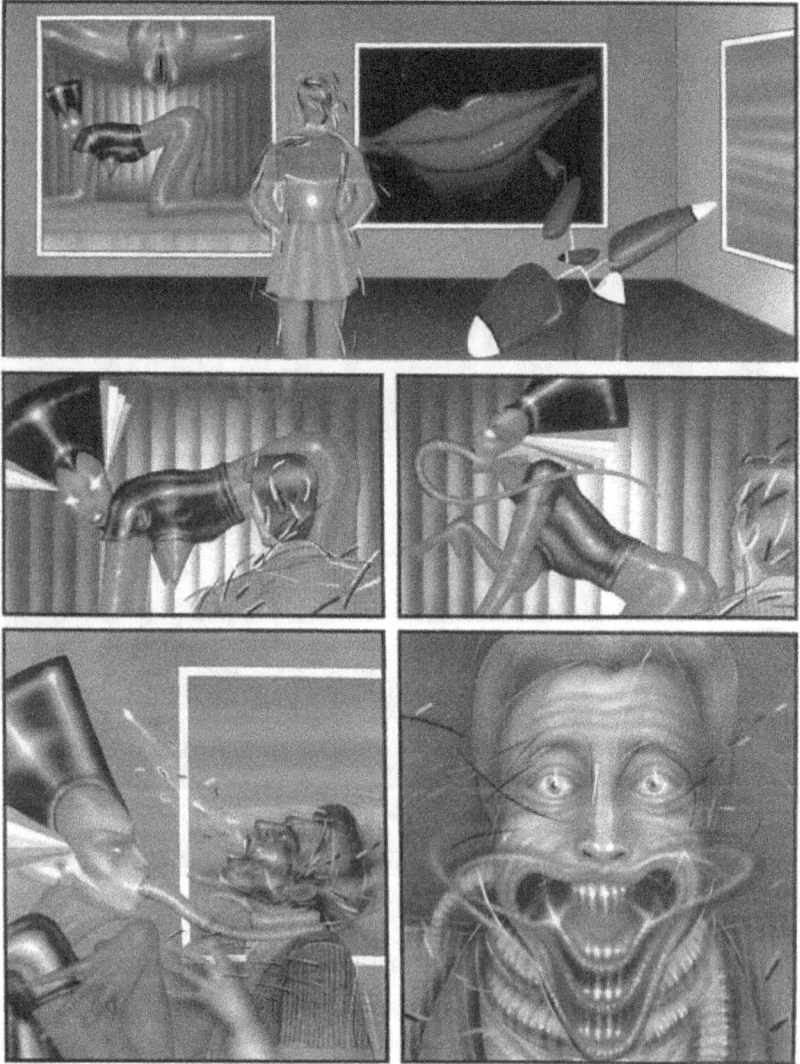

Figure 2.3 *El Libertador*, Mujer-Roja (Red Woman). Credit: Herikberto MQ. *El Libertador* (1984).

trend in Western countries in the 1980s. Whether or not cultural appropriation was considered, wearing African styles and colors was seen as another form of being modern. The African/punk red woman becomes a demiurge of ultramodern primitivism. This "image of the future," as Herikberto calls her in the brief introduction to the album, is shown to us as the epitome of the most creative and revolutionary modernity inspired by a futuristic monstrosity, Africa, and S&M sexuality. In Donna Haraway's "Cyborg Manifesto," the future to come was not Western politics—"the tradition of racist, and male-dominant capitalism" (1991: 150)—but rather a "creature in a post-gender world," the cyborg, "a condensed image of both imagination and material reality" (1991: 151). In *El Libertador*, before the cyborg becomes the high-tech character at the album's end, it adopts the appearance of revisited "primitive" cultures. Whereas the cyborg was "without origin" for Haraway, in *El Libertador* the subject of the future exists *before* history, while also comprising elements of those "urban tribes" (Hebdige 1979) such as punks.

For Valerie Steele, punk was "instrumental in bringing fetishism into fashion" (1996: 37). This was exemplified by Vivienne Westwood's London store, transformed into a fetish and bondage boutique called Sex (1974–6). However offensive and threatening S&M gear was to gender/social norms in the 1970s, by the early 1990s it finally made its way into the mainstream through prêt-à-porter designs by Gaultier, Versace, and *Vogue* magazine (Steele 1996: 33). *El Libertador* anticipates this turn in fashion, while adding a much more threatening layer. The red woman on the canvas comes alive and produces a long, green tongue that chokes the protagonist.

The whip-like tongue transforms the character into a green, gender-fluid being. The traditional dualism—masculine/active and feminine/submissive—which is "persistent in Western traditions" and "systemic to the logics and practices of domination" (Haraway 1991: 178) is upset once the red woman, wearing a strap-on, penetrates the other from behind (Figure 2.4).[25]

This scene, one of the most famous images from this album, combines the "forbidden content" (Hebdige 1979) of punk, while also adding what Amanda Feuerbach calls the "technoflesh aesthetic" that some fashion designers—Thierry Mugler, Jean Paul Gaultier—featured in the early 1990s, "when the body merges with its prosthetics" (2002: 11). These are "future bodies," half-human, half-machine, technologically enhanced, "a matter of fiction and lived experience," since the "boundary between science fiction and social reality is an optical illusion" (Haraway 1991: 155).[26]

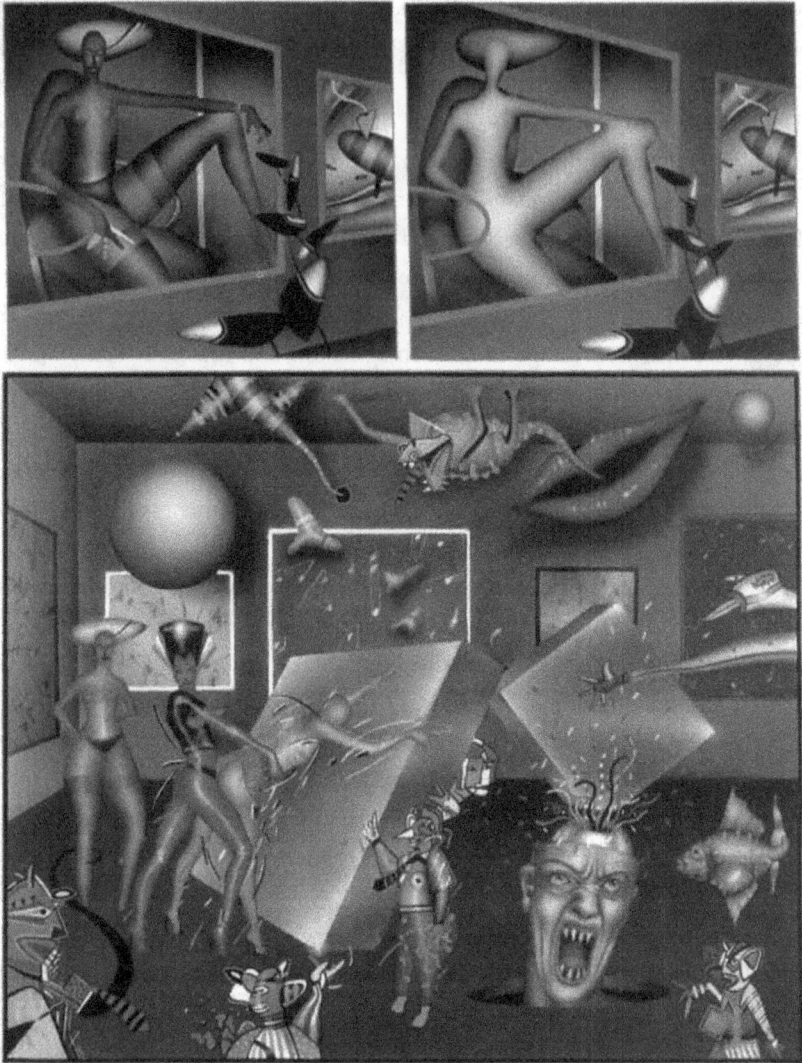

Figure 2.4 *El Libertador*, Explosión Surrealista (Surrealist Explosion). Credit: Herikberto MQ. *El Libertador* (1984).

In the context of groundbreaking science fiction films such as Ridley Scott's *Alien* (1979) and *Blade Runner* (1982), *El Libertador* revisits the trope of technologically altered and/or threatening female subjects. Like the unsettling imaginary of these movies, in *El Libertador* things are not as they seem, and the African punk rendering of a red-skinned woman in the museum transforms into a lethal, technologically enhanced body.[27]

Transhumanism, the "philosophy of human enhancement through technology" (Jeffery 2016: 11), is represented symbolically in the transition to the next chapter, "The Foreigner," when notions of future and primitivism merge. The suit-wearing protagonist from the first chapter enters another room of the museum, finding himself in an African savanna (1984: 22). Captured by warriors, he is taken to their village (Figure 2.5).

The depiction of the tribe's nudity, and of their makeup and jewels reminiscent of Maasai culture, reflects the imperial gaze (Pratt 1992) of the colonizer. This gaze, of course, has permeated documentaries and ethnographic museums, but also the Western aim for authenticity as it contemplates, and adopts from, "primitive" cultures.[28] Hebdige noted that in the 1970s, urban UK punk adopted aesthetic elements from traditional African cultures as, in part, "a white 'translation' of black 'ethnicity'" (1979: 64). In the album, the village members, with their body paint, shaved heads, tattoos, piercings, and other body modifications represent a time before History as well as the gender-bending, transhuman, punk cyborg of the future. In its exploration of the transformative effects of culture, *El Libertador* reflects an idealized, primitivistic notion of non-Western cultures as beacons of a perceived authenticity.

Traditional notions of class, gender, and sexuality have been lost in pursuit of utopian metamorphosis. One villager takes the protagonist's Western clothes in order to reenter the museum as a visitor. The subsequent chapter, "The Fighter," offers a poignant critique of the spectacularization of culture, visual arts, and fashion in the 1980s. Absorbed by another painting, the protagonist enters a dimension in which he becomes a blue futuristic warrior accompanied by an animal of shamanic power—a mandrill (Figure 2.6).

At this point, another humanoid figure emerges from a painting: a female warrior and her puma. After the animals fight to the death, it is the humans' turn. They, too, will die in the same horrid way. The episode concludes when an artist, Leo, acting as ringmaster, explains to a huge crowd that the battle was nothing but an art intervention: the blood spilled on the white floor has resulted in a painting. The critique of contemporary art and its evolution toward shock value is evident. Together with the theme of spectacularization of spaces for public culture at the beginning of the album, *El Libertador* points to the rising status of the designer as an artist, creator of spectacles and experiences, instead of material works.[29]

Indeed, *El Libertador*'s next chapter narrates how in late capitalist societies, where media reigns supreme, consumption of art or fashion becomes a subjective experience. In "The Destroyer," the artist Leo unveils his last spectacular work,

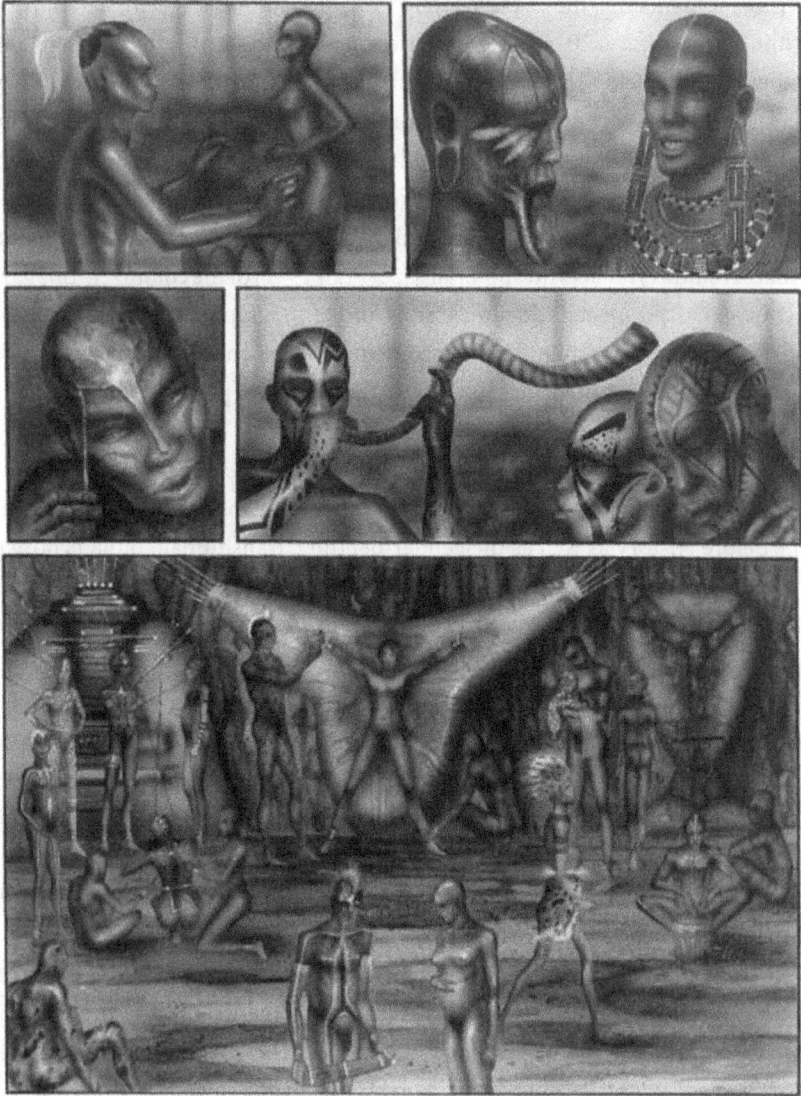

25

Figure 2.5 *El Libertador*, Arte Primitivo (Primitive Art). Credit: Herikberto MQ. *El Libertador* (1984).

a cube that can deconstruct and alter human bodies, sending them into new dimensions with transformed identities and looks, not unlike virtual reality or even fashion photography and advertising (Herikberto 1984: 39). *El Libertador* returns to the beginning of the story, the social milieu of the new *modernos* with the bright colors and outlandish fashion, who are mere followers of the

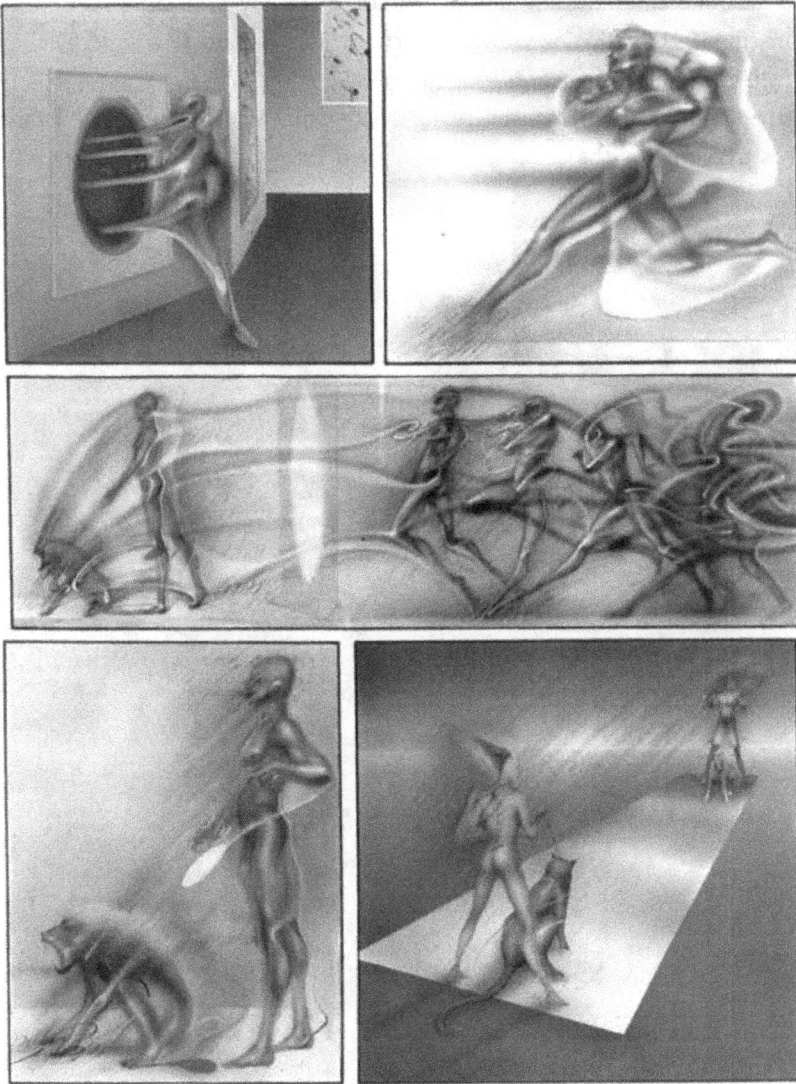

30

Figure 2.6 *El Libertador*, La bestia que llevamos dentro (The Beast We Carry Inside). Credit: Herikberto MQ. *El Libertador* (1984).

latest trends. The album's critique of their frivolity—the *Movida* in its more mainstream and commodified version—and their superficial embrace of newly acquired freedoms, gives way to an apocalyptic ending. The cube, a projector of future realities, turns out to be too powerful and mutates into a monster of many heads, "The Liberator," which devours all reality (Herikberto 1984: 42).

The machine embodies the power of mass media by producing only images (Jameson 1991), reducing contemporary art and fashion to a superficial and indistinguishable discourse lacking historical distinctiveness.

The album's end offers a surprising deus ex machina conclusion. When the chaos triggered by the cube becomes a fixed image of Picasso's *Guernica*, the

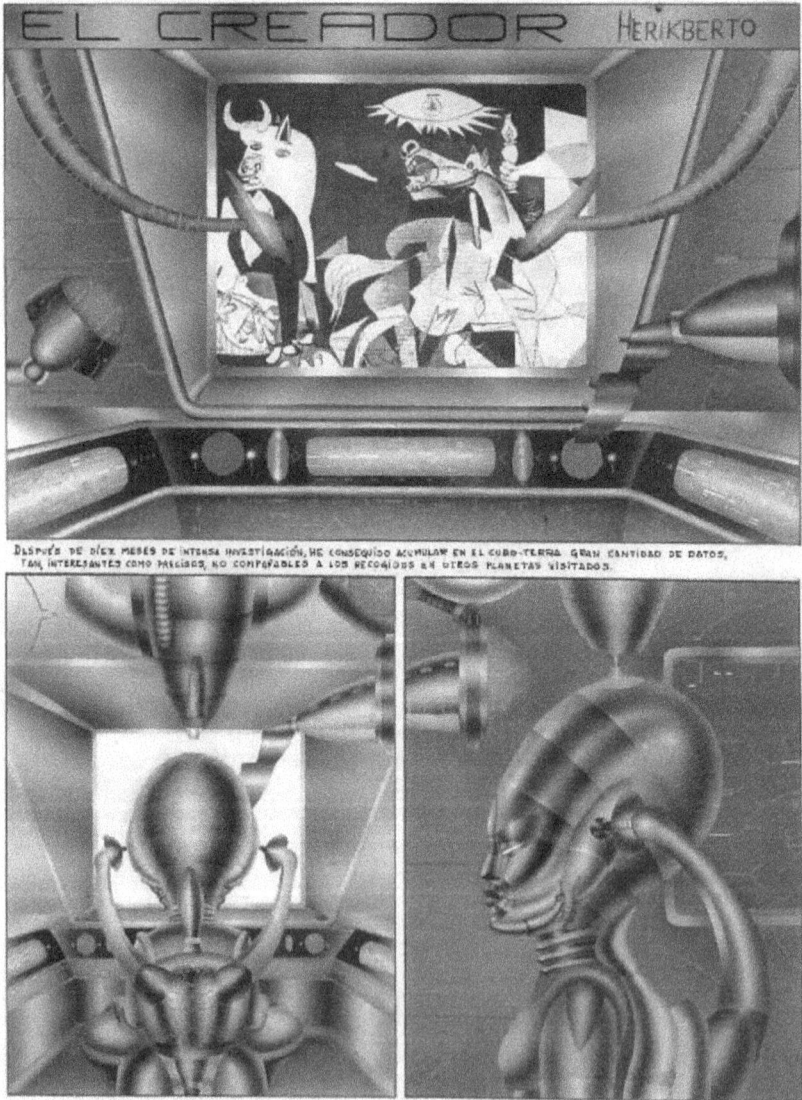

Figure 2.7 *El Libertador*, Androide. Credit: Herikberto MQ. *El Libertador* (1984).

epilogue, "The Creator," begins. Anticipating a similar theme in *Prometheus* (directed by Ridley Scott, 2012), the fifth installment of the *Alien* franchise, *El Libertador* presents an armor-clad humanoid figure. Whether the figure is an android, a cyborg, or an alien, readers cannot tell. A stylized and gender-ambiguous version of the "postmodern primitivism" previously seen, it has recorded all the dreamlike stories of the album in order to accumulate data about Earth (Figure 2.7). The epilogue poses more a question, a utopian hypothesis in the realm of science fiction, than a conclusion. The futuristic overseer, the "creator" of the chapter's title, is a character that returns readers to the notion of History—to the canon that Picasso now represents. Haraway ended her essay with a request for "regeneration, not rebirth": "the possibilities for our reconstitution include the utopian dream of the hope for a monstrous world without gender" (1991: 182). That seems to be the case in this artistically sophisticated album. During the story, the tensions between traditional and new punk notions of gender in early 1980s Spain are performed and revealed through fashion. However, the gender-fluid transhuman body that unites futuristic aesthetics and prosthetics fixates on the iconic representation of the Spanish Civil War by Picasso. This disquieting conclusion raises questions about both the origin of humanity and its regeneration—or its end.

Notes

1 Comic albums are print media, often large format and printed on high-quality paper, that may present a single narrative or several stories linked by a common theme. They fall somewhere between the graphic novel and the comic book.

2 Young French designers in the 1980s, like Thierry Mugler, were inspired by futuristic comic artists. Mugler's 1984–5 men's collection "Techniciens du ciel" featured large volumes, clear lines, and bright colors (Baudot) resembling the style of works like Moebius's *Arzach*.

3 Pentagrama, Vía Láctea, Marquee, El Sol, and Rock-Ola featured local bands like Kaka de Luxe, Aviador DRO, Derribos Arias, Vulpess, Gabinete Caligari or Nacha Pop. The Rock-Ola was "especially known for its mixture of different social classes, from lower-class *macarras* to upper-class *pijos*" (Stapell 2010: 106). Even though some early protagonists of the *Movida* were scions of the upper-middle urban class—for instance, Kaka de Luxe's members Alaska and Nacho Canut—the movement soon included working-class youth moving from rural areas or "provincias." An example is Pedro Almodóvar—see his text "Venir a Madrid."

4 Other active artists were photographers Ouka Leele and Alberto García-Alix, and painters Guillermo Pérez Villalta and las Costus. Another important comic artist was Nazario, author of the *Anarcoma* series, and member of the *Rrollo* comic trend in Barcelona. Teresa Vilarós analyzed his work in *El mono del desencanto* as part of Barcelona's *preMovida*.

5 For a timeline of the *Movida* and its actors, see Stapell (2010: 100–104).

6 See Gallero (1991) and Nichols and Song (2014).

7 For Alaska and her role in the *Movida*, see Cervera. The Museo del Traje in Madrid recently curated an exhibition on Tino Casal's wardrobe and his influence. See Gutiérrez (2017).

8 Another iconic 1980s song, Alaska & Los Pegamoides' single "Horror en el hipermercado" stated the new politics of desire and everyday life in urban Spain: "Horror at the supermarket/fear in the grocery section/My girl has disappeared/ and nobody knows how it happened." Texts originally in Spanish are my translation unless otherwise noted.

9 That political parties renounced some of their original principles during the Transition was exploited by humor literature, such as by notorious conservative author and bestseller Fernando Vizcaíno Casas in *De "camisa vieja" a chaqueta nueva* (1976)—*From Old Shirt to Brand New Jacket*. "Old shirt" is the sobriquet for the earlier members of the Spanish fascist movement.

10 For a cultural history of *el Rastro*, see Trapiello (2018).

11 Sociologist Dick Hebdige's classic book on punk, *Subculture* interprets the concept of style in "urban tribes" as "a form of refusal" (1979: 2), and as "transgressions of sartorial and behavioral codes" (1979: 91–2). Punk culture, which originated in a working-class environment in the UK, developed in Spain, where it adhered to the notion of style as bricolage (Hebdige 1979: 103) for its irony and masking effect (1979: 65–66). McNamara would buy 1930s-era music hall artist outfits at *el Rastro* and dress in tight pants, feathers, and patent-leather studded clothes while wearing makeup (Romo 2014). Even though *cutrelux* was the name Paco Clavel used for a 1990 LP, it can be considered another iteration of the subversive queer styles during the *Movida*, like "*chochonismo*" (Romo).

12 For Borja Casani, the *Movida* remained an underground movement, influenced by punk music and other urban cultures, until 1981; during its heyday (1981 to 1986), it was promoted by magazines like *La Luna de Madrid* (*Madrid's Moon*), art galleries and independent music companies; after that, local governments coopted the phenomenon, making it mainstream (Gallero 1991: 11–12). Stapell proposes the institutionalization of the *Movida* from 1984 to 1986, when public money financed publications like *Madriz* or *Madrid me mata* (*Madrid is killing me*) (2010: 104).

13 The Spanish administration of the late 1970s created a National Plan for Intangible Goods to activate the fashion industry and its exports (Mansilla), when the

liberalizing measures requested by the European Economic Community were threatening the national textile industry. The Plan was renewed by the Socialist government. Adolfo Domínguez, Sybilla, Ágatha Ruiz de la Prada, Jesús del Pozo, and Manuel Piña are some names associated with the *Moda de España* efforts to link democratic Spain with modern design (Stapell 102). For more information about the liberalization of the fashion industry, see Fernández de Alba (2020: 93–4; 139).

14 Montesinos, whose first shows took place in Madrid and Barcelona in 1979, became an inspiration to younger designers of the *Moda de España*. After working at the Yves Saint Laurent atelier, Sybilla became an overnight success with her first collection in Madrid at age twenty (Gallero 1991: 397–400). For other young designers of the time, such as Ruiz de la Prada, see Gallero (1991: 162–6). The band Peor Impossible [*sic.*]—Worse Off or Hopeless—which included among its members the later "Almodóvar girl" Rossy de Palma, started in 1983 for an event for the Sindicat de Dissenyadores in Palma de Majorca. The band recorded its only LP in 1985, *Passion*, and collaborated with photographer Ouka Leele (Peor Impossible).

15 The term ye-ye, also used in France, Portugal, and Italy, refers to the pop music and fashion styles of the moment. It comes from the Beatles' chorus "She loves you, yeah, yeah, yeah."

16 Born in Ourense in 1958, Heriberto Muela Quesada moved to Madrid with his family in 1966 and studied at the *Escuela de Artes y Oficios*. After publishing several comics, he focused on advertising and illustration, and movie design. He participated in the science fiction film *Solar Warriors* (dir. Alan Johnson, 1986), also known as *Solarbabies*. In the 1990s, Herikberto also wrote four young adult novels (www.herikbertomq.com).

17 *La Luna de Madrid* (1982–8) was one of the first publications to give voice to those young creators linked to the *Movida* and to articulate the latter as a postmodern movement. See Susan Larson (2003). *Rambla* (1982–5), founded by a group of comic artists, like Carlos Giménez and Alfonso Font, focused on adult comics by highly recognized Spanish and international authors like Guido Crepax and Alberto Breccia. *Comix Internacional* (1980–6) was published by Josep Toutain. Note that "comix" or "cómix" is used in Spanish when referring to countercultural, adult comics.

18 Pérez del Solar lists other titles, such as *Comix Internacional*, *Bésame Mucho*, *Hunter*, *Kirk*, *Metropol*, and *Mogambo* (2013: 31). By the mid-1980s, the adult comic boom came to a halt due to excess production and limited readership, which meant the closure of magazines like *Cairo* and *Rambla*. The market would not stabilize until the 1990s. For more information, see Pérez del Solar (2013).

19 Avant-garde movements like Dada and Surrealism incorporated their aesthetics into fashion. Salvador Dalí collaborated with designer Elsa Schiaparelli, and the

Bauhaus movement created striking stage costumes for the Triadic Ballet and a Mechanical Cabaret (Casablanca 2009: 163).

20 The PSOE (The Spanish Socialist Worker's Party) victory in 1982 ushered in a new approach to policy in educational and cultural institutions, especially art museums, with an increase of 511 percent in public investment (Quaggio 2014: 187). To educate general audiences on contemporary art and promote a modern view of the country abroad, several museums and art-centered initiatives, like the Spanish Program for Foreign Cultural Action (1983), the Reina Sofía Art Center (1986), and the international art fair ARCO (1982), were created (Quaggio 2014).

21 Situationist International leader Guy Debord defined the concept and its criticism in his book, *The Society of Spectacle* (1967).

22 Herikberto's critical view of the new fashionable elite was not an exception, and can be found in satirical comic magazines. Montesol's story "Vidas ejemplares" parodied the branding of a new music band *Memofobia* ("Dorkfobia") by a change of look: oversized checkered blazers and high-waisted 1940s zoot pants by designer "Alucinadas Müller." "You look great!" the manager says (*Cairo* 1984: 16).

23 After a unisex trend in the 1970s fostered by feminism and anti-Franco sentiment in Spain (Lara 2009: 328–329), fashion saw a return to binary forms. Some at the *Moda de España*, however, expressed interest in breaking apart from traditional notions of gendered fashion. For Pereda, men's clothes in particular were undergoing a revolutionary shift (1986: 23).

24 On other occasions, she wears her women's flamenco dress, or upscale prêt-à-porter. Transgender as a trope of political change and liberation is recovered in nostalgia films like Chus Gutiérrez's *El Calentito*, which also takes place during the coup on February 23, 1981. Antonia, the owner of the club, still open that night, would define herself as a "gender terrorist" (Garcés 2016: 162–3).

25 "Unlike the hopes of Frankenstein's monster, the cyborg does not expect its father to save it through a restoration of the garden; that is, through the fabrication of a heterosexual mate, through its completion in a finished whole, a city and cosmos." (Haraway 1991: 152).

26 "[I]n short, we are cyborgs. This cyborg is our ontology; it gives us our politics. The cyborg is a condensed image of both imagination and material reality, the two joined centers structuring any possibility of historical transformation." (Haraway 1991: 151).

27 Ridley Scott's *Alien* (1979) featured a female, prosthetic-tongued monster that, according to James Kavanagh, reunited the masculine and the feminine, death and life (1990: 76) as castrating mother, similar to the red demiurge in *El Libertador*. Ridley Scott's *Blade Runner* (1982) also explored the idea of cyborgs, or "replicants," with a "classically fetishized construction of female sexuality" of threatening eroticism (Feuerbach 2002: 137).

28 Margaret Maynard writes about the idea of "ethnic chic" (2004: 79) for Western
consumers as exotic, luxurious, or sensuous, or as evidence of a simpler way of life
(2004: 74).
29 Rebecca Arnold explains that in the 1980s, "catwalk shows" were "turning into
theatrical extravaganzas that combined music, lighting, effects and ever-more
famous models" (2001: 8). An example is Thierry Mugler's 1984 show, which
opened to a 6,000-member paying audience.

References

Alien (1979), [Film] Dir. Ridley Scott, US: Twentieth Century Fox.

Almodóvar, Pedro (1991), "Venir a Madrid," *Patty Diphusa y otros textos*, 106–110,
Barcelona: Anagrama.

Arnold, Rebecca (2001), *Fashion, Desire and Anxiety. Image and Morality in the 20th
Century*, New Brunswick, NJ: Rutgers University Press.

Baudot, François (1998), *Thierry Mugler*, New York: Universe/Vendome.

Baudrillard, Jean (1998), *The Consumer Society. Myths and Structures*, trans. C. T.,
London: Sage.

Benjamin, Walter (1998), "The Work of Art in the Age of Mechanical Reproduction,"
Illuminations, ed. Hannah Arendt, trans. Harry Zohn, New York: Schocken.

Blade Runner (1982), [Film] Dir. Ridley Scott, US: The Ladd Company.

Bourdieu, Pierre (1993), *The Field of Cultural Production*, ed. R. Johnson, New York:
Columbia University Press.

Casablanca Migueles, Luis (2009), "Diálogos entre la moda y el arte," in José F. Lorenzo
Rojas and María José Sánchez Rodríguez (eds.), *Lengua e historia social. La
importancia de la moda*, 142–192, Granada: Editorial Universidad de Granada.

Compitello, Malcolm A. (2014), "Sketching the Future Furiously. *La Movida*, Graphic
Design, and the Urban Process in Madrid," in William J. Nichols and H. Rosi
Song (eds.), *Toward a Cultural Archive of La Movida. Back to the Future*, 203–232,
Maryland: Fairleigh Dickinson University Press.

Crane, Diana (2000), *Fashion and Its Social Agendas. Class, Gender, and Identity in
Clothing*, Chicago: The University of Chicago Press.

Davis, Fred (2007), "Antifashion," in Malcolm Barnard (ed.), *Fashion Theory. A Reader*,
89–102, New York: Routledge.

Debord, Guy (1994), *The Society of the Spectacle*, trans. Donald Nicholson-Smith, New
York: Zone Books.

De Lauretis, Teresa (1987), *Technologies of Gender: Essays on Theory, Film, and Fiction*,
Bloomington: Indiana University Press.

El Calentito (2005), [Film] Dir. Chus Gutiérrez, Spain: Buena Vista Intl.

Fernández de Alba, Francisco (2020), *Sex, Drugs, and Fashion in 1970s Madrid*,
Toronto: University of Toronto Press.

Fernbach, Amanda (2002), *Fantasies of Fetishism. From Decadence to the Post-Human*, New Brunswick, NJ: Rutgers University Press.

Gallero, José Luis (1991), *Sólo se vive una vez. Esplendor y ruina de la movida madrileña*, Madrid: Árdora.

Garcés, Marcela T. (2016), "Fashioning Transitions and Designing Identities in *El Calentito*," in T. Gómez, P. Bolaños-Fabres, and C. Mougoyanni Hennessy (eds.), *Gender in Hispanic Literature and Visual Arts*, 155–170, Lanham, MD: Rowman & Littlefield.

Garlinger, Patrick Paul (2000), "Dragging Spain into the 'Post-Franco' Era: Transvestism and National Identity in *Una mala noche la tiene cualquiera*," *Revista Canadiense de Estudios Hispánicos* 24 (2): 363–382.

Gutiérrez, Juan (2017), *Tino Casal: El arte por exceso*, Madrid: Ministerio de Educación & Museo del Traje.

Haraway, Donna (1991), "A Cyborg Manifesto: Science, Technology, and Socialist-Feminism in the Late Twentieth Century," in Donna Haraway, *Simians, Cyborgs and Women: The Reinvention of Nature*, 149–181, New York: Routledge.

Hebdige, Dick (1979), *Subculture. The Meaning of Style*, New York: Routledge.

Herikberto (1984), *El libertador*, Colección Rambla Color 3, Barcelona: García & Bea.

Herikberto (1984), interview by Ana Salado, in *Rambla*, 13: 34–36.

Herikberto (1983), "¡Strok!," *Rambla*, 11: 35–42.

Jameson, Fredric (1991), *Postmodernism, or the Cultural Logic of Late Capitalism*, Durham: Duke University Press.

Jeffery, Scott (2016), *The Posthuman Body in Superhero Comics. Human, Superhuman, Transhuman, Post/Human*, New York: Palgrave Macmillan.

Kavanagh, James H. (1990), "Feminism, Humanism and Science in *Alien*," in A. Kuhn (ed.), *Alien Zone: Cultural Theory and Contemporary Science Fiction Cinema*, 73–81, New York: Verso.

Lara Gómez, Leonardo (2009), "Cambios sociales, cambios vestimentarios en la década de los 70," in J. F. Lorenzo Rojas and M. J. Sánchez Rodríguez (eds.), *Lengua e historia social. La importancia de la moda*, 327–347, Granada: Editorial Universidad de Granada.

Larson, Susan (2003), "La Luna de Madrid y la movida madrileña: un experimento valioso en la creación de la cultura urbana revolucionaria," in E. Baker and M. Alan Compitello (eds.), *Madrid de Fortunata a la M 40. Un siglo de creación urbana*, 309–325, Madrid: Alianza.

Mansilla, Pedro. Available online: www.madriz.com/pedro_mansilla_en_los_ochenta_la_moda_espanola_fue_un_sueno_notan_improbable/ (accessed September 21, 2018).

Mata Torrado, Francisco Manuel (2003), "Las exposiciones temporales de moda," *Museo. Revista de la Asociación Profesional de Museólogos de España* 8: 227–34.

Maynard, Margaret (2004), *Dress and Globalization*, Manchester and New York: Manchester University Press.

McCloud, Scott (1994), *Understanding Comics*, New York: Harper Collins.

McCracken, Grant (1988), *Culture and Consumption. New Approaches to the Symbolic Character of Consumer Goods and Activities*, Bloomington, IN: Indiana University Press.

Montesinos, Francis. Available online: http://francismontesinos.com/biography/ (accessed September 22, 2018).

Montesol (1984), "Vidas ejemplares," *Cairo*, June, 14–17.

Nichols, William J. and H. Rosi Song, eds. (2014), *Toward a Cultural Archive of La Movida. Back to the Future*, Lanham, MD: Fairleigh Dickinson University Press.

Peor Impossible. Available online: http://lascancionesperdidas.blogspot.com/2012/10/p eor-impossible.html (accessed October 21, 2019).

Pereda, Rosa María (1986), *Vestir en España*, Madrid: Ediciones del Dragón.

Pérez-Sánchez, Gema (2007), *Queer Transitions in Contemporary Spanish Culture. From Franco to la Movida*, Albany: State University of New York Press.

Pérez del Solar, Pedro (2013), *Imágenes del desencanto: Nueva historieta española 1980–1986*, Madrid: Iberoamericana.

Pratt, Mary Louise (1992), *Imperial Eyes: Travel Writing and Transculturation*, New York: Routledge.

Prometheus (2012), [Film] Dir. Ridley Scott, US: Scott Free Productions.

Quaggio, Giulia (2014), *La cultura en transición. Reconciliación y política cultural en España, 1976–1986*, Madrid: Alianza.

Romo, José Luis (2014), "Del 'chochonismo' a la pintura religiosa," *El Mundo*, March 30, 2014. Available online: www.elmundo.es/loc/2014/03/29/53357925e2704e37078b 4570.html (accessed October 10, 2018).

Stapell, Hamilton M. (2010), *Remaking Madrid. Culture, Politics, and Identity after Franco*, New York: Palgrave Macmillan.

Steele, Valerie (1996), *Fetish. Fashion, Sex, & Power*, New York: Oxford University Press.

"Sybilla." Available online: www.fashionencyclopedia.com/Sp-To/Sybilla.html (accessed September 22, 2018).

Trapiello, Andrés (2018), *El Rastro. Historia, Teoría y Práctica*, Barcelona: Destino.

Tron (1982), [Film] Dir. Steven Lisberger, US: Walt Disney Productions.

Vizcaíno Casas, Fernando (1976), *De "camisa vieja" a chaqueta nueva*, Barcelona: Planeta.

Part II

Picturing Femininity

Film and Photography

3

Women, Fashion, and the Spanish Civil War

From the Fashion Parade to the Victory Parade

Kathleen M. Vernon

Among the propaganda films produced by the Francoist side during and following the Spanish Civil War, a short eleven-minute documentary released in late 1939, *Ya viene el cortejo* (*Here Comes the Cortege*), directed by Carlos Arévalo and produced and narrated by actor and soon-to-be director Juan de Orduña, stands out for two very different reasons.[1] In the first instance, it represents the codification of a visual rhetoric that would provide the central model for subsequent documentary and fictional evocations of the civil war as a sacred crusade to recover and preserve the nation's timeless essence. Rejecting narrative or discursive argument for the poetic accumulation of iconic images of a supposed Spanish essence—medieval heralds and castles, panoramic natural landscapes, tolling bells, national flags, and crests—the film culminates in the ritual ceremony of the Victory Parade (Desfile de la Victoria), in a final sequence that anachronistically fuses imagery of the Reconquest against the Moorish invaders with the fascist pageantry of mass public spectacle: tightly choreographed displays of marching troops, modern weaponry, and political symbols (Figure 3.1).

Not surprisingly, the protagonists, individual and representative or massed and collective, of this mythmaking projection of the Spanish military's might and heroic deeds are exclusively male.

Yet a second matter overlooked in analyses of *Ya viene el cortejo* by Spanish film historians is a jarringly feminine interlude that occurs some four minutes into the film and lasts just over two minutes.[2] Set between shots of still more medieval heralds and ringing bells, the sequence is unmotivated and unintegrated thematically and formally into the rest of the film. The opening image shows an ornately carved wooden chest. Hands extend into the onscreen space to extract

Figure 3.1 Film still from Carlos Arévalo's *Ya viene el cortejo* (Here Comes the Cortege), 1939. Filmoteca Española. Credit: © Filmoteca Española.

Figure 3.2 Film still from Carlos Arévalo's *Ya viene el cortejo* (Here Comes the Cortege), 1939. Filmoteca Española. Credit: © Filmoteca Española.

embroidered fabrics and lace mantillas. Further shots offer women posing in traditional, regional garb juxtaposed against accessories, veils, and clothing animated as they rise, almost unaided, from chests and drawers. The camera work stresses a ritual quality of dresses and dressing while showing the models depicted posing for the camera and before a series of mirrors. Their practiced gestures and knowing smiles acknowledge the presence of other, admiring eyes on them (Figures 3.2 and 3.3).

All of these details prompt the question: what are these women doing in the film? The evocation of regional traditions and their sublimation into a unified national essence constituted a central topos of Francoist ideology. And the recovery and preservation of Spanish local cultures, including dress, was a charge taken up following the war by the Falangist women's organization, the Sección Femenina. Still, this scene is simply excessive, too long and loving to be easily explained or entirely subsumed into the film. When I consulted a colleague, a Spanish film historian, he pointed to the role of Orduña, a closeted gay man and "women's director" who would come to be known as the Spanish George Cukor. Coincidentally, Cukor's 1939 film classic *The Women*, based on the play by Clare Booth Luce, contains a similarly disruptive fashion show sequence, shot in color in an otherwise black-and-white film. However suggestive these hints of a shared cinematic cosmopolitan sensibility, I would argue that this case has a particularly emblematic value for our understanding of the struggle to incorporate women visually and symbolically into the image of the Francoist "New State."[3]

Victoria de Grazia and Eugenia Paulicelli have found evidence of a similar fusion of female fashion and fascist military spectacle in a staged public event that took place in Mussolini's Italy during the same year.[4] Working from contemporary newspaper reports and an Instituto Luce documentary, respectively, de Grazia and Paulicelli analyze the May 1939 "Great Parade of Female Forces" in Rome that assembled 70,000 women from diverse social strata, geographic origins, and professions. In the news report reproduced by de Grazia, the identification of the various groups, from rural housewives, women workers, and leisure-time troops to women professionals and artists, is threaded through with detailed references to articles of clothing and accessories: "scarves and shawls; wide skirts . . . jackets and corsets and belts . . . flowered aprons and lace . . . clogs, sandals and kerchiefs . . . azure jumpsuits" (1996: 352). The fragmented enumeration concludes with what de Grazia reads as an attempt to tie the heterogeneous collection of women and fashion paraphernalia to the fascist imperial project in its final evocation of the militarized advance of "the Red Cross nurses of the great wars for Africa

Figure 3.3 Film still from Carlos Arévalo's *Ya viene el cortejo* (Here Comes the Cortege), 1939. Filmoteca Española. Credit: © Filmoteca Española.

and Spain, on tanks and ambulances, severe in dress and demeanor, faces to the Duce, then straight ahead, their blue veils lifting off their white headbands" (de Grazia 1996: 352). Both de Grazia and Paulicelli are struck by a series of unresolved tensions and contradictions revealed in the scene, whether between the "local time-honored traditions" celebrated by the rural women in folkloric costume and the "modern woman wearing the military uniform" (Paulicelli 2004: 20) or more broadly in the clash between the subsuming and sublimation of individual identity into the massed collective and "the pursuit of exclusiveness and individuality typical of the workings of the modern fashion industry" (de Grazia 1996: 352).

Thus, the film *Ya viene el cortejo* and the Italian Great Parade reflect the difficulty of mobilizing women, or their representations, into a unitary force. The women depicted resist reduction to a singular essence, their heterogeneity on display in the juxtaposition of rural and urban, individual and collective, modernity, and timeless traditions. Furthermore, such binary distinctions themselves are blurred as the women incorporate seemingly contradictory traits and identities. In the Arévalo-Orduña film, despite their largely traditional dress, the women models strike a discordant note of modernity in their self-awareness and practiced exhibitionism. In the Italian parade, the variegated figures fail to coalesce into a single body of marchers, even at the level of visual spectacle, as Paulicelli points out in observing the contrast between the geometric precision of the women in uniform and the "more disorganized and scattered space" figured by the women in regional dress (2004: 20). That disparity is further emphasized in the description of the nurses' warrior-like pose, their purposeful theatricality set against the more random distribution of the "civilian" groups. De Grazia finds, in this persistent heterogeneity, a measure of women's troublesome resistance to efforts at visual symbolization that ultimately mark them as "too intractable, too volatile a subject for fascist rule" (1996: 353).

The issue of women's visibility as social and political actors, their move to the center of the frame, is closely tied in the Spanish and Italian documentaries and media accounts analyzed here to the role of fashion in framing and mediating debates over images and identities. Over the last decade, scholars have taught us to see fashion not as frivolous or inconsequential, the antithesis of wartime seriousness and scarcity, but rather as a source of crucial insights into ways of living, attitudes, and behaviors. As Dominique Veillon argues in her study of fashion in occupied France, the subject provides "an observation point from which to view the political, economic and cultural environment of an historical period" (2002: vii). This would seem to be particularly true at moments of political crisis and social and economic stress, and when more direct means of public expression are closed to certain population groups. Fashion, as a language or system, while susceptible to appropriation as an instrument for imposing conformity and social control, is also available as a vehicle for subverting such goals, whether part of a conscious program or as a result of fashion's very volatility, its function as a bearer of multiple messages. Wendy Parkins alludes to the inherent ambivalence of fashion's social meanings in noting the "multi-accentuality of dress in political contexts. . . [and] the semiotic capacity of practices of dress to either contest or reinforce existing arrangements of power and 'flesh out' the meanings of citizenship" (2002: 4).

Clothing styles and the choices they offered women became early recruits in the culture wars that preceded the military conflicts of the 1930s and 1940s in Europe. Fashion functioned, on the one hand, as the harbinger of modernity, the rapid turnover of styles and silhouettes linked to the influence of the media, radio, cinema, and advertising, all part of a burgeoning consumer culture that was key in circulating a cosmopolitan, transnational vision of the New Woman. Clothing could and did assume the role of standard-bearer of varying ideological messages. The cult of the healthy body, developed in fascist Germany and Italy, and adopted by the Sección Femenina in Spain, despite the disapproval of the Catholic Church, promoted streamlined styles of clothing that facilitated movement and quickness (de Grazia 1996: 343; Vincent 2002: 176). But such styles and attendant lifestyles also generated a backlash that spread across the continent (de Grazia 1996: 344). Helen Graham notes the conservative reaction among women themselves against the threat of social change embodied in the figure of the New Woman, more pronounced in Germany but evident in Spain as well, where middle-class women launched boycotts of "communist" and "Jewish" shopkeepers despite the fact there were no Jews in Spain (Graham 1995: 105–6). In this context, clothing also never lost its link with traditional femininity, or its role in situating women as pleasing ornaments and domestic decorations. This view of fashion effectively reinforced conventional divisions of labor. Clothing reigned at the core of women's work and women's play, a safe space of distraction and self-cultivation. It is little wonder, then, that these tensions played themselves out in the ritual staging of public patriotic and national spectacles, in the confrontation between traditional costume and modern everyday dress. Official rhetoric to the contrary, the need for special efforts and programs to preserve national and regional indigenous dress offers inadvertent confirmation of the dominance of international styles. Indeed, as Jesusa Vega documents in a study of Spanish regional dress, the battle may already have been lost in Spain by the early twentieth century. For when the organizers of a centenary celebration of Madrid's resistance against the 1808 Napoleonic invasion invited representatives from provincial capitals to attend in regional dress, the response from the Badajoz town hall in Extremadura was categorical: "[A]mong this population there is not one person who wears the typical dress of the old Extremeñans, nor is there a model that can serve to reconstruct said dress with accuracy" (Vega 2005: 214).

Fashioning the New Woman in Spain

Historians and cultural analysts continue to disagree about whether Francoism effectively endorsed or promoted a vision of the New Woman. As I have noted, the polarized political and social atmosphere under the Spanish Republic in the period before the 1936 outbreak of the Civil War was partially driven by anxieties over the changes associated with modernity, including perceived threats to the family and women's position therein. Yet, despite their calls for women to return to the home and traditional roles, the right moved in the early 1930s to mobilize women, initially through church organizations and later via the founding of the Falangist Sección Femenina in 1934 (Graham 1995: 104). This activity would continue, albeit "in an instinctive way and from the perception of their traditional roles" during the war itself (Graham 1995: 110). Mary Vincent reports on much more radical activities taken up by women who participated in Falangist street provocations, "girlfriends of Falangists who aided and abetted male violence, concealing guns in the lining of their coats or in the high boots that were coming into fashion," despite official opposition from the party (2002: 172). Nevertheless, she concludes in another article: "There was no 'new fascist woman' to complement the 'new fascist man,'" promoted by founders of the Falange (1999: 79). It is apparent, though, that for all its talk of exalting traditional Spanish womanhood, Francoist propaganda paid a certain contradictory lip service to the appeal of modernity. In her study of the treatment of gender roles in the regime-supported press in the immediate postwar period, Spanish novelist and essayist Carmen Martín Gaite finds vivid examples of the kind of "up-is-down and black-is-white" logic that opposed "fad-crazy girls, who adore outrageous things and are wild for anything foreign" with the "old yet always new" image of the modest and industrious Spanish woman (2004: 28). She emphasizes the pervasiveness of such campaigns, which were "devoted relentlessly to the task of turning the old fashioned yet ever-new woman into something fresh—that is, selling her as modern" (2004: 28).

Following the lead of Martín Gaite, but with a focus trained on the role of fashion coverage in attempts to redefine female identity, I turn to two magazines published by the Falange during the Civil War itself: *Vértice*, the organization's premier graphic and ideological showcase, which began publishing in April 1937; and the women's magazine, *Y* (named for Queen Isabela, using the archaic spelling of her name), sponsored by the Sección Femenina, whose first issue appeared in February 1938. As monthly publications, both *Vértice* and *Y* combined coverage of the arts—theater and cinema columns and reviews, short stories, features on photography, and graphic and plastic arts—and leisure activities, including fashion, with tendentious reporting on the progress of the war, admiring articles on Hitler (e.g., coverage of the Führer's birthday celebration in issue 10 of *Vértice* and a spread on Hitler's home in the Bavarian Alps in issue 3 of *Y*), and increasing contributions to the cult of personality building around General Francisco Franco and his immediate family (Sánchez 1938: n.p.; "La casa del Führer en los Alpes Bávaros" 1938: 18–19). Directed at a relatively elite and financially well-off readership in the Nationalist zone, far from the fighting or the aerial bombardments that targeted Republican-held territory, the two magazines promoted a sense of continuity and normalcy in the conduct of everyday life. Yet, their content inevitably betrayed a certain discomfort or anxiety about the appropriate occupation for women during wartime, on the one hand evincing a determination to maintain women in the frivolous and feminine activities proper to their sex and class standing and, on the other, seeking to enlist them in suitable acts of devotion to the cause of "nuestra España" (our—that is, Nationalist—Spain). The fashion coverage could not help but reflect this split agenda. Emblematic in this regard is an article from the inaugural issue of *Vértice* entitled "Moda: Crónica de abril" (Fashion: Chronicle of April), signed Márgara. In the opening lines, the author evokes the Paris spring in which she heard of plans for the new magazine to be published in "liberated" Nationalist territory. Prompted to act, she writes:

> I offered my name, my talent, my knowledge, my enthusiasm, my vision of life, a product of my many years removed from the hermeticism of Spanish life and my formation in a universal setting. I asked, imperiously, with all the force of my conviction, that I be allowed to speak to the women of Spain about something as trivial and as transcendent as Fashion.
>
> I thought about my country at war, I thought about the rarified state of all nations, turbulent and terrified, [which find themselves] at every dawn of every day at the edge of the precipice of war or social destruction. And I thought that Fashion is the symbol of the strong woman, the biblical woman, reserve of Humanity, [who is] pleasant and cordial even in the most adverse moments. (1937: n.p.)[5]

The passage is noteworthy for many reasons. The writer's Parisian and "universal" existence and vision gives her the authority to bring "the gospel of fashion" to an isolated, if not backward, Spain. And fashion is championed in all its contradictory glory as the attribute of strong, "biblical" women who are called to the heroic (but ultimately restricted) task of radiating feminine affability in a war-torn nation. Nevertheless, it is also clear that fashion and fashion journalism gave women like Márgara access to the public sphere—and to worlds beyond "hermetic" Spain—not just as models and specularized objects of the public gaze but as working professionals.

A case in point is the founding editor of *Y*, Marichu de la Mora, director of the Department of Press and Propaganda for the Sección Femenina, and sister of the Republican activist, Communist Party member, and director of international press relations for the Republic, Constancia de la Mora.[6] A collaborator in the subsequent Sección Femenina publications, *Medina* and *Ventanal*, and founder in 1940 of *La moda en España*, de la Mora shaped *Y* into perhaps the most visible representation of the values and concerns of Nationalist womanhood in all its contradictions. The magazine benefited from its geographic location, headquartered in San Sebastián on the northern Spanish coast not far from the French border and at a significant remove from the military capitals of Francoist Spain in Burgos and Salamanca, which allowed it to acquire "an apparently cosmopolitan touch" (Fuente 2006: 228). *Y* alternated sections charting the history of the Falangist Women's Section and its female leaders with pieces on more domestic topics such as menu planning and childcare. In contrast to the more aspirational fashion features in the decidedly upmarket *Vértice*, the April 1938 issue of *Y* offered its readers practical advice in an article titled, "Do You Know How to Take Advantage of a No Longer Stylish Dress?" (1938: 30). While *Y* sought to guide its audience concerning contemporary fashions, it also presented a series of pieces on fashion history. Thus, in the same April 1938 issue, an article explored the timely topic of "Military Influences on Female Fashion" (Lozoya 1938: 13). In June 1938, another considered the question of when brides first began to wear white wedding dresses (Torre Hermosa 1938: 7). And in May 1938, the magazine offered an account of governmental policies in the design and enforcement of sumptuary laws noting that "the freedom, today, to dress in green or blue, to cut one's hair short or let it grow long, is a very recent conquest" ("El gobierno y las modas" 1938: 17–19). This historical approach offered an implied critique of the essentializing and tautological vision of timeless womanhood espoused by Francoism. Not that such a view was absent from the pages of *Y*: an article by novelist Carmen Icaza in the March 1938 issue proclaimed the proper role of women in the work of reconstructing the nation. Up against alleged "Marxist" demands for women "mechanics, electricians or chemists," the Spain of Icaza "want[ed] its women to serve the nation exclusively as women" (1938: 52). In contrast, by recognizing fashion's imbrication in the contingencies of social, economic, and political life, the articles offered women readers a suggestive, if still restricted, sense of their stake in history. At the same time, the scholarly approach elevated fashion as a subject worthy of serious attention.

Perhaps in response to these varied and potentially disruptive implications of fashion, there also existed a clear push to instrumentalize its role. As in the film "Ya viene el cortejo," the magazines give evidence of an insistent if not always intentional linking of war and fashion. Both *Vértice* and *Y* enlisted fashion, along with so many other charged rhetorical practices during the Civil War, as a way to distinguish and separate Rebel identities, especially—though not exclusively—female identities, from those of the Loyalist side. In some cases, this meant explicitly claiming a sense of style or fashion as an index of taste and breeding and thus the proprietary attribute of the Nationalist side.

An article in the April 1938 issue of *Vértice* evokes the links between fashion and the (female) leisure class: "[W]ar has distanced us from the activities that previously filled our days. . . . Hospitals, the making of clothing for our troops, [and] social work now occupy the hours that before we devoted to films, bridge games and aperitifs. But the change of seasons necessarily brings our thoughts back to clothes for spring" (Blanco 1938: n.p.). These distinctions became more explicit still in the immediate postwar context as a famous advertisement published in 1939 proclaimed "Reds didn't wear hats" (Los rojos no usaban sombreros).[7] A page-one poem commemorating the Victory Parade in the inaugural issue of another Sección Femenina publication, *Ventanal*, presents a cautionary evocation of "Life as it is or as it might have been: I look out my window and see the troops of the Generalísimo instead of the horror of Stalin's legions" ("Así es" 1946: 3). The piece continues, contrasting the fashionably dressed women of Franco's Spain with the "muchachas desaliñadas," slovenly female supporters of the Republic (1946: 3). A particularly tendentious article by playwright Enrique Jardiel Poncela in the December 1939 issue of *Y* offers a depiction of Christmas in the Republican "Red zone" among a group of what he portrays as grotesquely unfeminine women soldiers, the portrayal highlighted by the photo of a grizzled militia woman dressed in overalls.[8]

The wartime continuity between fashion and political identity is strikingly on display in the work of artist and illustrator Carlos Sáenz de Tejada. A graduate of the Escuela de Bellas Artes de San Francisco, who lived in Paris from 1926 to 1935 and created cover art for *Vogue* and *Harper's Bazaar*, among other well-known fashion magazines, Sáenz de Tejada was also responsible for some of the most recognizable propaganda imagery on the Nationalist side.[9] That double identity is reflected in the first issue of *Vértice*, where his work appears on the cover and in a full-page color fashion illustration inside. The cover depicts a phalanx of billowing flags, the Spanish monarchist standard, the Falangist flag, and a red flag bearing a swastika, held aloft by uniformed men with muscular forearms. The fashion image shows three stylish blond women in coordinated black-and-white outfits—a black suit and frilly blouse, white blouse and long skirt combination, and a long dress with ruffled accents. Two women, both standing, wear hats and gloves, while the third sits before a low table bearing a silver tea service. Despite their very different themes, these two images share certain common tendencies in their depiction of the human body in the elongated and mannered figures that stretch to fill the available space. Sáenz de Tejada's signature traits become clearer still in two subsequent color illustrations, published in issue 4 of *Vértice*, that portray two groups of male marchers: Requetés, members of the Carlist militia, and Falangists, each in their distinctive uniforms, khaki with red berets in the case of the first and blue shirts with embroidered red Falangist emblems in the case of the second. In reference to these images, Mary Vincent has written of the artist's "highly stylized depictions of masculine strength and beauty . . . reminiscent of El Greco" (1999: 75). While the women models are not subject to the same reverent gaze, they are clearly idealized creatures, seemingly abstracted from everyday Spanish reality in their languorous, aristocratic bearing. A two-page color illustration signed "atc," in the first issue of *Y* brings a further synthesis of fashion and military imagery. There the blond models wearing the feminine version of the Falangist blue shirt project the slender and youthful insouciance and bodily self-awareness of the international "New Woman" as they pose first in a group of three against a minimalist white background, and then among male and female comrades in a more realistic three-dimensional space that suggests a social gathering or even a bar or other public, commercial setting. Vincent has emphasized the role of fashion as key to the essential "theatricality of the Falangist style or spirit," most evident in the provocative proletarian connotation deriving from the adoption of the blue shirt (2002: 167). In contrast to the traditional military uniform with its epaulets or gold braid, "the [blue] shirts were a new style for a new generation. Blue represented the *mono* or overall, which was the characteristic weekday dress of the Spanish working man" (2002: 169). Because of this message, she reports, wearing a blue shirt in public could be, and was, construed as an act of political defiance, and more so for women, who, during the Republic could be fined for appearing in blue shirts (2002: 170).

Clearly, the woman in uniform posed an especially suggestive and polyvalent image: on the one hand a means of potentially resolving tensions between the calls to selfless devotion to the cause and traditional notions of individualistic femininity, and, on the other, a means of managing anxieties over the potential blurring of male-female roles as women assumed more visible positions, as we have seen, even on the right. It is also likely that uniforms for women were the source of still more unease, as Vincent argues, as "self consciously modern" projections of control of the will (Vincent 2002: 176).

Fashion at the Front Lines, Left and Right

As much as clothing styles surely worked, as we have seen, to divide women along ideological and socioeconomic lines, the same fashion imagery could also serve to complicate the divisions between us and them. In his memoir,

El niño republicano, writer and journalist Eduardo Haro Tecglen evokes the cosmopolitan and womanly world of his childhood just before the war, recalling, "the lengthy afternoons of the only child . . . amid the machine-gun rhythms of the Singer sewing machine, looking and relooking at Mama's magazines, with [images of illustrators] Penagos, Baldrich, and Sáenz de Tejada [Sainz in the original]" (1998: 62). A photograph shot by Robert Capa in Barcelona in 1936 dramatically conveys a similar message. With the caption, "A Loyalist Militia Woman," it depicts a woman dressed in the characteristic *mono* worn by both male and female members of the volunteer Republican militia that carried out much of the fighting against the Francoists during the first months of the Civil War (Figure 3.4).

At rest on a city bench, her rifle at her side, she peruses the pages of a fashion magazine. Clearly, fashion had its place on the Republican side, in both the mental and material lives of women and men. And just as the image of the female Falangist *flecha* (arrow, the name given to blue-shirted women volunteers) or her more committed sister, the Falange-sponsored volunteer nurse in her white uniform, blue cape, and embroidered red crest, was subject to glamorization, the Republican *miliciana* herself could become a fashion icon. A photograph by Capa's companion in Spain, German-born photographer Gerda Taro, offers an obviously posed portrait of a woman dressed in militia garb. Shot at ground level against a nearly empty horizon, the image shows the woman tensed and seemingly poised for action in a kneeling crouch as her arm extends to the right, gun in hand. Just below and on the extreme left, the viewer notes her feet, clad in somewhat incongruous high-heeled shoes.

It is instructive to consider both the image and the aura attached to the *miliciana* in relation to a cover illustration to the February 1939 issue of Sección Femenina magazine *Y* (Figure 3.5). Two women in profile occupy the foreground: a blond nurse and a dark-haired *flecha.* They have adopted a warrior's pose, their arms raised in the Fascist salute. In the right rear of the frame, a third woman, wearing an apron with a large Falangist emblem, carries what appears to be a basket of laundry, her face in shadows. Not coincidentally, the first two women evoke the marching nurses in the Italian Great Parade of Female Forces, although here their "severe" dress and demeanor are tempered by the representations of cover-girl beauty. For her part, the *miliciana*, source of the "best-known female iconography of the war," also overshadowed her less visible and alluring sisters (Lannon 1991: 217) (Figure 3.6).

Denounced and demonized by the right, the *miliciana* never ceased to provoke strong reactions on both sides of the war. Nevertheless, the image ultimately bore

Figure 3.4 Robert Capa, "Barcelona, August 1936. A Loyalist Militia Woman," 1936.
Credit: © International Center of Photography and Magnum Photos.

little relation to the reality of women's roles. Just three months into the war, the
Republican prime minister was calling for the removal of women soldiers from
the front (Lannon 1991: 222). According to Helen Graham, the "real face of the
'new woman' in Spain" was the female factory or farm worker in the rearguard
(2005: 55).

> Most of the photographs of militia women we possess . . . [were] taken in the
> early days of the conflict and carry the unmistakable stamp of "war as fiesta."
> They are highly choreographed images, designed to maximize the decorative

Figure 3.5 Front Cover. *Y. Revista para la mujer.* February 1939. Collection of the author.

effects of their female subjects. Like the famous posters of the *milicianas* they are aimed primarily at a male audience . . . as a recruitment device to persuade the male audience to volunteer for military service. (Graham 2005: 55–6)

This phenomenon notably persists today. The image of the *miliciana* is still called upon to recruit readers and spectators, consumers of a potent conjunction

Figure 3.6 "Les milicies us necessiten," Cristóbal Arteche. Print Atlántida A.G., Barcelona (1936). Collection of the author.

of war and fashion, in ongoing efforts to make sense of the legacy of the Spanish Civil War.[10]

These continuities should not lead us to lose sight of the particular role of fashion and fashion imagery during the war years of the late 1930s in Spain, however. On both the left and the right, clothing styles and choices were mobilized at the front lines as marking a symbolic fault line between competing notions of gender identity, serving as a highly visible yet deeply embedded index of values, attitudes, and behaviors regarding women and modernity. The space for debate and dissent generated around the topic of fashion was soon to close, though, as wartime exceptionalism gave way to the imposition of ideological orthodoxy under the victorious Franco regime. In the context of this study, there is perhaps no better evidence of these changes than those seen in the redistribution of symbolic space in terms of gender as represented in the filmed depictions of the annual reenactments of the Victory Parade in the official Spanish newsreel founded in 1943, the Noticiarios y Documentales (NO-DO). In contrast to the setting of the parade in *Ya viene el cortejo*, with its disruptive two-minute, female-centered entr'acte, in the NO-DO women are kept safely consigned to the margins, visualized only in the inevitable cutaway shots of the audience, thus reaffirming women's proper place and role, on the sidelines lending support to the male protagonists.[11]

Notes

1 This essay stems from research conducted under the auspices of a grant funded by the British Academy, "Film Magazines, Fashion and Photography in 1940s and 1950s Spain." My thanks go to project director Jo Labanyi and fellow researcher Eva Woods Peiró for providing a collaborative context for this work. Special thanks also to Jordana Mendelson for sharing her expertise on Civil War magazines and graphic arts, and to Lou Charnon-Deutsch for technical and moral support.

2 See the coverage in Gubern (1986), 69–70; and Tranche and Biosca (2001), 296–8.

3 Historian Mike Richards studies the Francoist construction and implementation of a model of the "modern state" inspired by Germany and Italy with the goal of "reordering society in fundamental ways to face the challenges of the future" (1995: 176).

4 See Victoria de Grazia (1996: 337–58) and Eugenia Paulicelli (2004).

5 Ofrecí mi nombre, mis conocimientos, mi entusiasmo, mi visión de la vida, alejada tantos años de la vida hermética española y moldeada en escenarios universales … Solicité con toda la fuerza de mi convicción, imperiosamente, se me dejase hablar a las mujeres de España sobre algo tan trivial y tan trascendente como la Moda [upper case in original]. Pensé en mi país en guerra, pensé en el enrarecido ambiente de las naciones, todas, turbulentas y atemorizadas, al borde de precipicios sociales o bélicos a cada amanecer de cada nuevo día. Y pensé que la Moda era el símbolo de la mujer fuerte, bíblica, reserva de la Humanidad, placentera y cordial hasta en los momentos más adversos. (1937: n.p.)

6 Fuente (2006) is a fascinating dual biography of the two sisters, aristocratic granddaughters of conservative Spanish Prime Minister, Antonio Maura, whose

radically different paths offer insight into the political, social, cultural, and personal forces at stake in the civil war period.

7 In this regard see the catalog for the 2007 Bellas Artes exhibition in Madrid, Susana Sueiro (2007).

8 The author seems to have taken gladly to this cause of ideological gender warfare. In the July–August 1938 issue of *Y*, he provides a color-coded guide to the various inferior sub-species of Spanish women (green, red, lilac, and grey women) whom he contrasts unfavorably with the "mujer azul" (the blue Falangist or Nationalist woman). Enrique Jardiel Poncela, "Mujeres verdes, rojas, lilas, grises y azules," *Y*, July–August 1938, 36–7.

9 The family of Sáenz de Tejada has strongly contested his reputation as the prime artistic exponent of the Francoist cause. Professor Jordana Mendelson has shared with me her correspondence with Carlos Sáenz de Tejada y Benvenuti, a trained historian and the son of the artist, in which he details the chronology and nature of his father's commissions for the Falange and its organizations. He has also worked to document the alterations made to his father's illustrations and to identify falsely attributed images that continue to circulate.

10 The covers of two recent best-selling Spanish books that explore the role of women Republican activists during the war and immediate postwar, Fonseca (2007) and Chacón (2002), feature photographs of young, attractive *milicianas* whose frank, open gaze directly addresses the buyer–reader.

11 The DVD that accompanies Tranche and Biosca's *NO-DO* (2001), reproduces three examples from 1943, 1961, and 1973, that reveal the unvarying choreography of the ritual.

References

"Así es, así ha podido ser . . ." (1946), *Ventanal*, April.

Blanco, Lidia (1938), "Orientaciones," *Vértice*, April.

Chacón, Dulce (2002), *La voz dormida*, Madrid: Santillana.

de Grazia, Victoria (1996), "Nationalizing Women," in Victoria de Grazia and Ellen Furlough (eds.), *The Sex of Things*, 337–58, Berkeley: University of California Press.

"El gobierno y las modas" (1938), *Y*, May.

Fonseca, Carlos (2007), *Trece rosas rojas*, Madrid: Temas de Hoy.

Fuente, Inmaculada de la (2006), *La roja y la falangista*, Barcelona: Planeta.

Graham, Helen (2005), *The Spanish Civil War: A Very Short Introduction*, Oxford: Oxford University Press.

Graham, Helen (1995), "Women and Social Change," in Helen Graham and Jo Labanyi (eds.), *Spanish Cultural Studies*, 99–116, Oxford: Oxford University Press.

Gubern, Román (1986), *1936–1939: La guerra de España en la pantalla*, Madrid: Filmoteca Española.

Haro Tecglen, Eduardo (1998), *El niño republicano*, Madrid: Alfaguara.

Icaza, Carmen (1938), "Quehaceres de María y de Marta," *Y*, March.

Jardiel Poncela, Enrique (1938), "Mujeres verdes, rojas, lilas, grises y azules," *Y*, July–August.

Jardiel Poncela, Enrique (1939), "Navidades en la 'zona roja,'" *Y*, November.

"La casa del Führer en los Alpes Bávaros" (1938), *Y*, April.

Lannon, Frances (1991), "Women and Images of Women in the Spanish Civil War," *Transactions of the Royal Historical Society*, Sixth Series, 1: 213–28.

Lozoya, Marqués de (1938), "La influencia militar en la moda femenina," *Y*, April.

Márgara (1937), "Crónica de abril," *Vértice*, April.

Martín Gaite, Carmen (2004), *Courtship Customs in Postwar Spain*, trans. Margaret E. W. Jones, Lewisburg: Bucknell University Press.

Parkins, Wendy (2002), "Introduction: (Ad)dressing Citizens," in Wendy Parkins (ed.), *Fashioning the Body Politic*, 1–17, Oxford: Berg.

Paulicelli, Eugenia (2004), *Fashion under Fascism*, Oxford: Berg.

Richards, Mike (1995), "'Terror and Progress': Industrialization, Modernity and the Making of Francoism," in Helen Graham and Jo Labanyi (eds.), *Spanish Cultural Studies*, 173–82, Oxford: Oxford University Press.

"¿Sabes cómo aprovechar tu vestido pasado de moda?" (1938), *Y*, April.

Sánchez, E. Jorge (1938), "El cumpleaños de Hitler," *Vértice*, May.

Sueiro, Susana, ed. (2007), *Posguerra: Publicidad y propaganda (1939–1959)*, Madrid: Ministerio de Cultura.

Torre Hermosa, Marqués de (1938), "¿Cuándo empezaron las novias a vestirse de blanco?" *Y*, June.

Tranche, Rafael and Vicente Sánchez Biosca (2001), *NO-DO: El tiempo y la memoria*, Madrid: Cátedra/Filmoteca Española.

Vega, Jesusa (2005), "Spain's Image and Regional Dress: From Everyday Object to Museum Piece and Tourist Attraction," in Susan Larson and Eva Woods (eds.), *Visualizing Spanish Modernity*, 207–27, Oxford: Berg.

Veillon, Dominique (2002), *Fashion under the Occupation*, Oxford: Berg.

Vincent, Mary (1999), "The Martyrs and the Saints: Masculinity and the Construction of the Francoist Crusade," *History Workshop Journal* 47 (Spring): 68–98.

Vincent, Mary (2002), "Camisas Nuevas: Style and Uniformity in the Falange," in Wendy Parkins (ed.), *Fashioning the Body Politic*, 167–87, Oxford: Berg.

4

From Market to Feminism

Fashion Photography during the Franco Dictatorship

Olga Sendra Ferrer

In her reading of Plato's Allegory of the Cave, Susan Sontag finds a close bond between photography and the world, our cave. Photography, she says, shows us a new visual code that constructs narratives that "alter and enlarge our notions of what is worth looking at" (1977: 3), and in doing so can influence, guide, and condition our knowledge of the world. Historian Ian Jeffrey takes this connection a step further, using this characterization to define the field of the history of photography, which he claims should only concern itself with those moments when photography impacted the imagination of an era (2002: 24). In this context, according to Jeffrey, fashion photography does not have a say. Likewise, the general tenor of history books on Spanish photography is to ignore both the genre as a whole and any photographer whose work was exclusively dedicated to fashion, even though they do sometimes include photographers whose work had a fashion component.[1] However, such selection and exclusion erase social and cultural dynamics that are essential for the discursive makeup of an era. Consequently, by observing the practice of photography during the Franco dictatorship (1939–75), this chapter highlights the relevance of fashion photography as a way to stake out not just social and cultural norms but also, and especially, an aesthetic field through which those very same parameters can be questioned. In this quest, the work of the *Nova Avantguarda* and some of their successors will be of essence.[2]

On Fashion Photography

Since its beginnings at the dawn of the twentieth century, fashion photography has been closely connected to advertising, which situates it as a genre that bridges the commercial publishing industry and artistic photography (Martín Núñez and Marzal Felici 2016: 63). Consequently, although this type of photography is hemmed in by capitalist principles and clients' desires, it is nevertheless a field that offers the possibility of artistic experimentation and even social rebellion. In Francoist Spain (1939–75), this versatility fostered both the artistic development of photography, a field largely dominated since the Spanish Civil War (1936–9) by photographic associations' love of pictorialism, and a means of subsistence for photographers who might not otherwise find gainful professional employment. In due time, these photographers would put into practice the most innovative trends in photography imported from other parts of Europe. Once established as an artistic genre, fashion photography showcased the presence of women in public and enabled the critique and dismantling of certain limits imposed on them from the dictatorship's outset. Indeed, if the centrality of fashion allows for the negotiation of social and cultural status according to class, sexuality, gender, or ethnicity (Barnard 2017: 405), in Francoist Spain it was also a means to question the artistic parameters of photography and to expand the feminist struggle that would become so prominent in the final years of the dictatorship and the return to democracy in 1975.

Before continuing, it should be noted that fashion photography is characterized as "infraordinary" (Perec 2008: 22–3), that is, pertaining to objects that have not been conserved or archived, because they are seen as a part of everyday life as opposed to belonging to the artistic or aesthetic realm. Fashion photography has long appeared in magazines aimed at women, particularly housewives, and as such has tended to be considered ephemeral and unimportant. What material has been preserved is the fashion photography found in the archives of photographers whose oeuvre has been recognized for other artistic merits. This fact explains why the titles of the photographs referenced in this chapter tend to be descriptive, labeled so that they can be identified within the archive; only on rare occasions do they preserve information regarding the designer or place of publication. Again, fashion photography is extra-canonical, which does not imply that these images bear no weight in the construction of gender identity in dictatorship-era Spain, but quite the contrary.

Social and Historical Context

My analysis focuses on two decades under the dictatorship: the 1950s, when Francoism begins to open to the outside world in order to facilitate international economic aid; and the 1960s, known as the years of "developmentalism" (*desarrollismo*), a period when Spain underwent a modernization of all its economic sectors and opened up to mass tourism. Economic modernization led to a consumer society, which in turn ushered in the development of mass media and the rise of the middle class. In this context, visual culture, in particular photography, enables us to see fractures in the treatment and construction of womanhood during Francoism, specifically when the model of womanhood will evolve from the traditional woman confined to domesticity towards women as consumers.

Although the state promoted unidirectional cultural and social production from the top down, the opening of the country and the arrival of European and North American influences broadened the possibilities for the resignification of a chauvinist and conservative dictatorship that sought to make women responsible for embodying the virtues of the state and the survival of the family unit.[3] In this context, fashion photography, intimately connected to women's daily lived experience, enabled the development of a popular culture in which women began to show their sensuality, transgressions, and independence in the face of a puritanical society that would prefer them subject to inaction in the public sphere. Herein lies a contradiction: in the context of an international capitalist order that objectifies women, we find the possibility for change and aperture, moving from the market to feminism.

The *Nova Avantguarda* in Fashion Photography

In the context of Franco's regime, the *Nova Avantguarda* changed the panorama of photography and the role of photographers by opposing traditional formal elements of Spanish Francoist photography (composition, themes, exposure, lighting, etc.) and conceiving of theirs as a socially committed praxis, distanced from photographic associations, such as the Associació Fotogràfica de Catalunya (Photographers Association of Catalonia), and their *salonismo*.[4] Many of its members engaged in fashion photography, often to earn a living, but nonetheless always bringing to bear the techniques and topics that they were developing in their more social and artistic photographs.

The *Nova Avantguarda*'s images not only open a window into the world of fashion photography but, more importantly, they reflect the changing social and gender roles of the 1950s and 1960s. As the Catalan photographer and scholar Jorge Ribalta explains, the photographers that made up the bulk of the

Nova Avantguarda played a dual role: on one hand, they made contributions independently to artistic vanguardism with differing degrees of independence from the regime, but, on the other, they worked for the state (2007: 82), publishing their work in guides meant to promote tourism, for example. Simultaneously, the production of the *Nova Avantguarda* in Barcelona came about in the pivotal moment of neorealist and humanist photography, which sought to construct the image of a popular subject emerging in the wake of the Second World War.[5] The *Nova Avantguarda*'s representation of "the man of the street" in his urban context can be read as a dissenting view to the apparent perfection of the country presented by the Franco regime's propaganda, given how their images reveal the "dark" side of the alleged Francoist peace. At the same time, the local tradition of *costumbrismo* is entwined in these photos, producing a discourse that both connects with traditional literary culture and articulates a modern imaginary of the city. In this *costumbrista* tendency, the idyllic and monumentalized image of the city is substituted with a social architecture that focuses on the popular makeup of urban space. Concurrently, these images maintain a connection to civil society that can be read within the confines of the "normalizing" canons of the regime. That is, these photographs can be read as dissent, showing other realities that coexist with the official image put forth by the regime; or as part of the drive for legitimization and normalization of its practices, ultimately making up part of the façade of normality that the regime sought to impose upon a society in a state of exception. This ambivalent relationship situated photography, and mostly, fashion photography in a grey area that enabled a sort of social opposition that became enmeshed with everyday life without censorship.

This dialectic position is also found when it comes to the commercial fashion photography of the *Nova Avantguarda* (Figure 4.1).

In Oriol Maspons's photograph, we see the connection to the urban working class and, above all, the contrast between model and environment.[6] This dialectical relationship highlights the fragmentation between what is represented and its context, which could be interpreted as a question of class, that is, how the upper class exoticizes the environment of the working class, and how this exoticization happens through the dressed body, which is the nexus of this union but also the site of the clash it produces. In this way, the photograph can be read as a critique of the inequality between the model's clothing and her environment, between social classes and cultural practices, revealing in turn the fictionality and artificiality of fashion photography.

Moreover, the speed of street photography is substituted in this image by composition and a syntax and language that slow down the image and allow us

Figure 4.1 "El Born" by Oriol Maspons (Barcelona, 1956). Credit: © Artists Rights Society (ARS), New York/VEGAP, Madrid, 2020.

to carefully perceive the construction of a discourse and the positioning of the photographer. The speed of street photography establishes a direct relationship with an alleged objectivity that invites social commentary. In fashion photography, however, the construction, syntax of the image, and composition arrest the world's movement, and it is in this moment of pause that we can see not just the structure of the composition but also the "presence" of the photographer. The most interesting aspect here is how the act of stopping time portrays the nature of everyday life, in contrast, blurring the lines of an allegedly objective experience of perception, and in the process, revealing its fictionality.[7] In this sense, we are not dealing with, at least not exclusively, arresting time in a general sense, as photography does, especially when talking about street photography, which preserves fragments of the past "like flies in amber" (Wollen 2003: 77) by capturing those "fleeting moments" in an instant, in a past that is made relevant by its significance, as Jeffrey and Ribalta contend.[8] Rather, we are in the presence of the construction of a narrative, of a discourse that, although connected to everyday life, is ultimately a construction, crafted with a composition as carefully chosen as painters compose their work.

Oriol Maspons (1928–2013)

The photographic production of Oriol Maspons serves here to develop further the constructedness and the possibility of critique in fashion photography. He is one of the best representatives of the *Nova Avantguarda*,[9] publishing his most humanistic photography, portraits, fashion, and advertising work in *La Gaceta Ilustrada, L'Oeil, Paris Match, Boccaccio, Espression*, and *Elle*, among others. His work reveals the relationship that begins to develop between fashion and publicity in Francoist Spain. It shows the emergence of mass culture and a predominantly visual type of communication, independent of the object that is being sold. It reflects the influence and importance of everyday life. When it comes to fashion, his work inserts these images proscriptively into couture against a backdrop of daily life, which necessarily refers to a social context. Even though critic Roland Barthes stated that fashion photography has its own rules which have little to do with journalism, hobby, or other types of photography, the influence of different genres in Maspons's work contradicts this assertion. His work puts artistic and fashion photography on the same level and entwines their languages (Figure 4.2).

In the image, seduction, status, and the beauty of the dress are juxtaposed against a rough and grey setting accentuated by the graininess of the black and white, the latter an essential formal trait of the photography of the *Nova Avantguarda*. The urban theme that takes over both approaches makes manifest a latent sociohistorical dimension to the images, regardless of whether it is front and center or just in the background. In the move from humanistic photography to fashion, however, the image is hollowed out, stripped of social meaning as it becomes pure materiality, only objects without a direct reference to the present moment, items that would-be customers aspire to purchase.

This hollowing out of meaning does not affect the presence of the body in the same way. In these photographs, we essentially observe a mannequin whose most basic necessity is clothing her body, but through the fusion of art and advertising, she becomes pure meaning (Figure 4.3).

The pose punctuates the lack of any and all movement, the way the moment is frozen in time, and the exhibition of wares: body, pose, image. It is a state, not an action. The message written on this body, which seems initially inescapable, is connected to a social and cultural discourse that locks women in a masculine worldview—one that naturalizes their state of submission, an idea accentuated by the presence of both photographers in the mirror. The artistic nods to Goya's paintings (*The Naked Maja*, 1797–1800, and *The Clothed Maja*, 1800–5) and

Figure 4.2 "Two models in a bar" by Oriol Maspons (Barcelona, circa 1957). Credit: © Artists Rights Society (ARS), New York/VEGAP, Madrid, 2020.

E. J. Bellocq's photographs echo the repetition of a gesture that impregnates the female body.[10] These photographers create a series of signs that the very posture itself absorbs and which reinforces a number of important claims about the body. When subjected to the male gaze, the inactive posture points out the objectification and commodification, not just of the dress but also of the woman's body. Her passivity and rigidity stand out against the active gaze of the photographers, exposing asymmetry, difference, and the imposition of a male gaze and structure. They are like the social structures that we do not see because they have been naturalized.

The trope of the woman as muse in this composition reinforces the idea of art as the domain of men and the place of women as not outside of photography

Figure 4.3 "Oriol Maspons and Julio Ubiña photograph a model from Pertegaz" (1957). Credit: © Artists Rights Society (ARS), New York/VEGAP, Madrid, 2020.

but within it, as objects. As John Berger says, "men act and women appear. Men look at women. Women watch themselves being looked at" (1977: 47). Through this highly connotated positioning, the woman is inscribed into an artistic and historical discourse that is still being imposed upon the female body today. The "reclining nude," although in this case dressed, is a possession that belongs to the male spectator/owner. In the context of the dictatorship, where hiding bodies acquires a political dimension, the action of showing the clothed body in this particular context is politicized, as Jorge Marí explains, since the law is inscribed as if it were a text on the body, which is left demarcated, defined, and articulated by not just the law but also a social and cultural naturalization that legitimizes the male gaze (2003a: 130). Hence, although the body here is dressed, there is an unavoidable reference to the naked body, since Goya painted both a dressed and undressed version of the Maja. Considering the reference to Bellocq's photographs, this image highlights on the one hand the dress, of course, but also the woman's overt sexualization, passivity, and submission to the male gaze through an eroticization of the female body that could be read against the ideology of the regime. However, no matter in what direction the photograph is read—for or against the regime—the female body is always objectified: regardless of whether it is subject to the law that represents the regime's ideology, or how it is eroticized and used to subvert that law. Consequently, if as Barthes explains, fashion transforms clothing through the represented garment (which calls attention to the objects and other qualities that appear in the process of representation) what is being sold in this photo is not just the model's dress but also a social structure that keeps women subordinate to the male gaze. This structure is reinforced by law and by a patriarchal tradition that oppresses women, even when used as political or social dissent.

Even in the photographs where Maspons takes the models out to the street to stage them in the daily environs of city life that came to characterize the *Nova Avantguarda*, in the fixedness of the poses and discomfort of the models we can glimpse the imposition of that gaze and the structuring principles of fashion photography. On the one hand, this photographic style adheres to the rules of fashion photography at that time: the emphasis on the garments is achieved by eliminating the energy and personality of the models who wear them, by subjecting the body to the abstraction of the object. However, on the other hand, the uncomfortable posture of the women points toward their dehumanization, made manifest by their similarity to mannequins or dolls that, although capable of movement, can only flex to a certain extent, their extremities limited by an invisible force that refers back to the social and political control of female bodies. This lack of naturality underscores, therefore, the artificiality of the moment captured, which is in turn further underscored by the gazes of the people inside the establishment. They register the strangeness and awkwardness of the situation, as it breaks with the structure of everyday life, even as it is inserted in the very same structure. Out of this artificiality, a possible critique of the status quo arises from the contrast between the richness of the dress and the grimness of the space that envelops it.

We could say, then, together with so many images of prosperity, the work of the photographers of the *Nova Avantguarda* reconstructs and questions the myth of prosperity promulgated by Franco's regime. Nevertheless, when engaging in fashion photography, with its empire of the ephemeral and mass consumption, in which publicity and marketing are the principal discourses of capitalism (Sekula 2015: 155), the photographers of the *Nova Avantguarda* and their work embrace consumerism and utilize their humanist realism to transform that reality into a product to be bought and sold, especially insofar as the female body is concerned.

Xavier Miserachs (1937–98) and Leopoldo Pomés (1931–2019)

The approach to fashion photography began to change in the 1960s, when expanded policies for development take hold of the Spanish economy and capitalism floods Spanish consciousness. A new search for a modern, updated image emerges, that, thanks to new consumer products in the market, makes for a life that is more comfortable and pleasant, and also more beautiful and interesting. Marketing takes on a new, more casual and mobile tone, as may be observed in the works of Xavier Miserachs and Leopoldo Pomés, both members of the *Nova Avantguarda* at different times.[11] The work of both men in fashion photography is associated with the innovation that was being introduced to the country at that time: in the 1960s, a boom in synthetic fibers facilitated a change in the dynamics of thread production and the movement of women's bodies (Guillamón 2015: 90).[12] This change marks an important turn in the way both men approach their work in the fashion industry, now emphasizing movement, dynamism, and sensual sophistication (Figure 4.4).

Here, the body attains a flexibility that is missing from Maspons's photographs, but in both cases, the order of the day is still masculine structure and gaze, and the sexualized female body is subject to the sexual impulses of men. Xavier Miserachs has a similar photo, "Fashion Photography" (1960s),[13] where the photograph captures a group of women's legs, only from the waist down. As a product of manipulation and fetishization, the body is cut off, and its mutilation denies women the possibility to be whole beings that can speak and manifest subjectivity. There is no possibility for agency, only an objectification imposed by the emphasis on the object. In Pomés's photo, the adjective "Bellissimo" could be applied to both body and garment, simultaneously sexualized by the expression of the model.

In spite of this characterization and these limitations, the new approach to this type of photography enables movement and aperture, and leads to the creation of a new discourse of dissidence that might on the surface keep up the appearances of what is socially acceptable under the regime, but underneath opens the door to a feminist discourse and a critique of the male gaze. It is a matter not just of the physical movement in the image but rather of how this movement is extended and may be read, through the arrival of new ways of seeing and acting, as a notion of social movement, of culture in transition (Radner 2000: 128). As we see in these images, the women's level of control over this movement is ambiguous at best, which represents the paradoxes

Figure 4.4 Leopoldo Pomés, "Original photomontage of an advertisement for Piuma d'Oro raincoats" (1964). Credit: © Leopoldo Pomés, 2020.

being produced at this time. In one sense, we have the possibility of change, a new perspective of the body and, therefore, a new possibility for action; but in another sense, the definition of this change is still within the patriarchal parameters that define Spanish society. As visual studies scholar Hilary Radner explains, the evolution of fashion photography reflects a stylistic turn that will enable a new contextualization of the female body (2000: 129). If we apply Radner's statement to the photographic production of the 1960s in Spain, we see that fashion photography is evidence of the practices and ideals of a specific moment when women become active, in spite of the contradictions implied by being limited and objectified by a male gaze.

Colita (1940–) and Joana Biarnés (1935–2018)

At this point, the feminine gaze, specifically Colita's and Joana Biarnés's, becomes important.[14] As is the case with their male colleagues, the work of these two photographers does not primarily consist of fashion photography, but they did both carry out projects in this field. In so doing, they left their mark as they cracked an opening in the social structure as much for being female practitioners of photography as for the way they represented the female body. They engaged with notions of modernity, agency, and freedom comparable to the various feminist practices that were beginning to take shape toward the end of the 1960s (Figure 4.5).

Figure 4.5 "A Fashion Session in Barcelona." Credit: © Joana Biarnés, 1962.

They joined image, attitude, and association with the creation of a "look," which is as important as the content itself in their staging, and in the process, they visualized an identity that was at odds with socially prescribed limitations on women. Just like in the work of Miserachs or Pomés, we see women free to move, but here, this change is a result not of the application of techniques of the *Nova Avantguarda*, but rather from Biarnés's career as a photojournalist. She takes the model out to the street, but genuinely, not atavistically or as a muse; rather, her subject is made visible occupying plain public space as she is captured in the hustle and bustle of city life. She is not shielded from her surroundings, which in turn grants her an identity based on an agency and independence that is diametrically opposed to the physical passivity and overt sexualization seen previously. The dialectic with the regime's discourses and practices is self-evident within the image as the model's body dialogues with the other women present in the photograph. The supposed laxity of the woman that observes the model from behind is the first example: her lack of elegance is subordinated to the act of working, but her gaze questions what she sees, with a facial expression that is somewhere between surprise and incredulity at the existence of new possibilities. In the second example, the blurry female body captured to the model's left—a possible metaphor for what is disappearing and being lost—is also subordinate to the act of working, but here there is a certain degree of elegance expressed by the austerity of style and color. In the middle of this bleak panorama, the action and body of the model stand out all the more, like the first gasp for air after being underwater too long. She represents the independence of the body versus the submission seen in the work of Maspons: we are not in the presence of a silhouette that supports clothing but rather a flesh-and-blood woman reclaiming freedom of movement.

With Colita, the agency of the female body can be seen not just in the way in which she captures her subjects but also in how she sets up and then expands a critical stance from the get-go. In her series "Descuartizar un cuerpo" ("Carving Up a Body"), which started in 1965 and continued through 1977, Colita photographs sections of theater, film, and advertising posters in which the female body is objectified.[15] These photographs were later published in *Antifémina* (1977) together with writings by the prominent feminist and anti-Franco activist and writer Maria Aurèlia Capmany with the goal of kindling not just a female-specific culture but also the principle demands of their political struggle. In "Carving Up a Body," we can see how women's presence in public life was basically limited, despite their omnipresence in culture and society, or even what we could go so far as to characterize as their positioning at the center axis of the makeup of society. I also see a connection to Miserachs's image of several women's legs:

both photographers show how the act of looking is never neutral or objective, which feeds into one of feminist criticism's major themes—the active cultural component of power relations (Rosón 2017: 60). As scholar María Rosón Villena explains in reference to Colita's subsequent production in the 1970s (2017: 58), by portraying women outside of hetero-patriarchal norms, she makes possible new ways of existing and broadens the scope of what is visible and representable.

In the world of fashion, she gives us photographs like the one featuring an elegantly dressed woman in an empty study, eating a banana, while a man much older than her cleans one of her shoes.[16] In its emptiness, the setting puts the action right in the center of our focus, and recalls the ways in which a photograph can reconstruct the relationship between who sees whom (the woman directs her gaze at the man, who is lying on the floor) and from where. This image displays an eroticization that does not depend upon the objectification of the female body but rather an action, one that is the product of a female gaze and a role reversal that questions the origin of power, since it is the man who is working for her, cleaning her shoes, in an image of servitude that inverts traditional gender roles. Here, a critique emerges of the repertory of female bodies, and naked or semi-naked women, that was being produced during the last years of Franco's dictatorship as a response to the regime's censorship of film and magazines, not just on the level of popular culture but particularly in journals dedicated to social, political, and cultural analysis under the direction of writers and intellectuals such as Manuel Vázquez Montalbán or Francisco Umbral.[17] In these images, Colita differentiates between public presence and public exhibition, to borrow Rosón Villena's terminology (2017: 60), and does what years later Capmany will define as "visualizing the flip side of the dominant female image."[18] That is to say, Colita attempts not merely to represent a female image that distances itself from and criticizes the bodies that are objectified in their nudity and mutilation but also to show other possible realities in the social and cultural limitations imposed on those bodies. In the examples of both Biarnés and Colita, fashion implies the conceptualization of a "we," a collective that is conceived through two key elements that recall Barthes's distinction between a "real garment" and a "represented garment": the created object (the clothing) and the image that object exudes through its photographic composition.

Conclusion

The notion of women as objects captured and subordinated through the construction of images is a product of the inherent paternalism of society at that time. The fact that the body is the key element in this practice underscores to an even greater degree the operative control and crafting of an image. Maspons's photographs, as well as Pomés's and Miserachs's, are particularly enlightening in this regard, for the way they evince imposition and insertion in a tradition and a very specific structure that restricts the autonomy of the female body. Women here lose the possibility of being any other way that is not sanctioned by a male gaze, and go on to represent the social and moral values of the men who construct these images, which show "a deformed body with a view to achieving a certain formal generality, i.e., a structure" (Barthes 1983: 259). The body, per se, ceases to exist and becomes only what can be created through clothing and fashion: an image.

It is true that the same reading of fashion photography produced in Spain at this time could also apply to other countries, such as France or the United States. However, the censorship of the female body in Spanish society accentuates this act of rupture and, therefore, dissent, with the market providing a space for the development of feminism. In the context of the dictatorship, where uniformity is the norm, fashion can become a form of resistance by using photographic discourse and techniques as a critique of established and accepted systems. The ambiguity of the *Nova Avantguarda* and the photography of Colita and Biarnés create a reciprocity between fashion and society that allows opposition, dissidence, and rebellion, a direct reflection of the guiding principles that shaped their careers as photographers. These photographers create a crack in the regime's façade, where a new image that allows direct contact with the public eye can be created, enabling new possibilities and tendencies that facilitate the formation of more independent ways of being. In this case, we can affirm that the body is configured by a consumerism that forms part of the socioeconomic structure of the dictatorship and permits the gradual opening of a type of commerce that inserts Spain into international markets and brings with it the trends that were being developed in Europe and the United States in the 1970s. After all, fashion photography primarily operates in the market to sell clothing. Nevertheless, through fashion photography, a space for dialectical opposition in which women acquire agency and physical and social mobility is created.

Fashion photography represents, then, the clash happening at this moment in Spain: political and social aspirations based on the lived experiences of those at the bottom rungs of society versus the arrival of a cultural, social, and economic aperture that carried in its wake the adoption of a capitalist economic system. Photography is both an art and an industry. It is an instrument of contemplative materialism, and at the same time, it is a discourse and practice of identity formation that turns it into a social weapon. The combination of industry, art, and identity grant fashion photography its relevance. The transitory and transactional nature commonly attributed to fashion photography, which results from how it transforms the object it seeks to sell, fades away in these photographs that instead capture the imagination of an era. The products themselves are invaded by the moments they encapsulate, which does not remove their self-referentiality, that is, their constructedness as products, but it does highlight even more convincingly the dissidence that radiates from the work of photographers like Biarnés and Colita. Here at last appears the proof needed to convince Jeffrey of fashion photography's relevance and ability to impact the imagination of an era.

Notes

1   See Publio López Mondéjar (1996 and 1997), Joan Fontcuberta (2008), or Carmelo Vega (2017). For an alternative view, see the exhibits of the Museu de Disseny de Barcelona, "Distinción. Un siglo de fotografía de moda" (November 2015–April 2016), or the more recent "Antoni Bernard. Nord/Sud/Est/Oest" (May 2018–August 2018).

2   The periodization of the *Nova Avantguarda* was established by Josep Maria Casademont in the 1970s to denote the style that defines photographic production mainly in Barcelona between 1957 and 1964. It is characterized by a negation of the autonomy of art. Key photographers included Ricard Terré, Ramon Masats, Oriol Maspons, Julio Ubiña, and Xavier Miserachs, with precedents such as Francesc Català-Roca and Leopoldo Pomés, and culminating with the work of Joan Colom. The most salient feature of this group for my analysis is their connection to European humanist photography, developed by photographers like Otto Steinert in Germany, Henri Cartier-Bresson in France, and Edward Steichen in the United States, a connection also shared with the work of other Spanish groups of the moment including the Agrupación Fotográfica Almeriense (AFAL) or La Palangana in Madrid. The practice of the *Nova Avantguarda* does not differ from what their European counterparts were doing, but rather quite the contrary: they established a direct connection with them, which allowed for a modernization of photographic themes and techniques. For more on the *Nova Avantguarda* or the photography of this period, see Casademont (1972), Fontcuberta (2008), Terré (2006), or Ribalta (2009).

3   For more on the use of women's bodies in the development of the Francoist ideology, see Morcillo (2010).

4 Oriol Maspons, a member of the *Nova Avantguarda*, coined the term *salonismo* [exhibitionism] to define the institutionalized photography in photographic associations that continued to be pictorial and whose objective was to win awards. This type of photography prized technique, however superficial, above all else, perpetuating the vacuity of the subject matter (López Mondéjar 1996: 49). This approach put censors, the zealous guardians of a most fossilized orthodoxy, at ease.

5 For more on the relation between the *Nova Avantguarda* and Neorealism, see Terré (2006) or Ribalta (2009).

6 Other members of the *Nova Avantguarda* produced photographs with a similar theme. See Xavier Miserachs's photograph "El Born" in *Memòries* (2008) or Joan Colom's series "El Born, 1963" in Colom (2004).

7 I am not claiming that photography is objective; rather, echoing the belief that Street Photography, especially in the *Nova Avantguarda*'s work, seeks to capture a reality without the intervention of the photographer.

8 See Jorge Ribalta (2009) for an explanation of how the *Nova Avantguarda*'s work becomes the dominant image of Barcelona until the 1990s.

9 Maspons began his career as an amateur in the Associació Fotogràfica de Catalunya. In 1955, he moved to Paris where he rubbed elbows with important figures of European photography at that time, like Cartier-Bresson. Following his return to Barcelona, he became a professional photographer and began his collaboration with Julio Ubiña, with whom he would undertake many of his projects, whether in the world of art or in advertising.

10 E. J. Bellocq (1873–1949) was an American photographer known for the photos he took of prostitutes in the Storyville district of New Orleans. In several of these photos, women are stretched out on a sofa in the same position as Goya's Maja, with different degrees of mobility and agency. To consult these images, see the archive of the International Center of Photography. A selection of these photos may be found at the following site: www.storyvilledistrictnola.com/portraits.html

11 Xavier Miserachs is one of the most renowned members of the *Nova Avantguarda*, largely for his work *Barcelona en Blanc i negre* (1964). After abandoning his medical studies, he dedicated himself professionally to photography and advertising and collaborated with magazines that included *Actualidad Española*, *Triunfo*, *Magazin*, *Paris Match*, *Bazaar*, and the *Gaceta Ilustrada*. Leopoldo Pomés started taking photos in 1952 and in 1961 with Karin Leiz created Pomés Studios, where he developed his interests in film and commercial photography. In 1965, he won first prize in the Festival de Cinema Publicitaire in Cannes, which established him as one most important photographers of the time.

12 Pomés had to look for foreign models that would give him the natural poses he was looking for. For more, see Guillamón (2015).

13 This photo can be found in *Memòries de Barcelona. Xavier Miserachs i Colita* (104).

14 Colita (born Isabel Steva i Hernández in Barcelona, 1940) is one of the most important and famous photographers in Spain. Her work covers themes drawn from the social, cultural, and physical reality of Barcelona in the last four decades of the twentieth century. The work of Joana Biarnés (Terrassa, 1935–2018) was only recently recognized (*Joana Biarnés. Disparando con el corazón*, 2017, which followed the 2015 documentary *Joana Biarnés, una entre todos*), despite being the first graphic reporter of Spanish journalism. Realizing how financial concerns overtook the social function of journalism, she left photography to go into the restaurant business.

15 To view Colita's images, see: www.museoreinasofia.es/en/collection/artwork/descu artizar-cuerpo-carving-body-3.

16 This image may be found in *Memòries de Barcelona. Xavier Miserach i Colita* (103).

17 See, for example, Manuel Vázquez Montalbán (1985) or Francisco Umbral (1976). For more on this topic, see Jorge Marí (2003a and 2003b).

18 "Visibilizar el reverso de la imagen femenina al uso." My translation.

References

Barthes, Roland (1983), *The Fashion System*, trans. M. Ward and R. Howard, New York: Hill and Wang.

Barnard, Malcolm (2017), "Looking Sharp: Fashion Studies," in Ian Heywood and Barry Sandywell (eds.), *The Handbook of Visual Culture*, 405–25, London: Bloomsbury.

Berger, John (1977), *Ways of Seeing*, London: Penguin Books.

Biarnés, Joana (2017), *Joana Biarnés. Disparando con el corazón*, Barcelona: Blume y Fundación Photographic Social Vision.

Capmany, Maria Aurèlia and Isabel Steva (1977), *Antifémina*, Madrid: Editora Nacional.

Casademont, Josep María (1972), "La fotografía," in Enric Jardí (ed.), *L'art català contemporani*, 431–55, Barcelona: Edicions Proa.

Colom, Joan (2004), *Joan Colom. Fotografías de Barcelona, 1958–1964*, eds. David Balsells and Jorge Ribalta, Barcelona: Lunwerg Editores.

Fontcuberta, Joan (2008), "Barcelona: nuevo documentalismo," in Jorge Ribalta (ed.), *Historias de la fotografía española: escritos 1977–2004*, 77–85, Barcelona: Gustavo Gili.

Guillamón, Julià (2015), "Un caballo en París," in Sergi Plans (ed.), *Leopoldo Pomés. Flashback*, 89–91, Barcelona: RM.

Jeffrey, Ian (2002), "Entrevista," in Joan Fontcuberta (ed.), *Fotografía. Crisis de historia*, 18–29, Barcelona: Actar.

Joana Biarnés, una entre todos (2015), [Film] Dir. Óscar Moreno and Jordi Rovira, Spain: REC Producciones.

López Mondéjar, Publio (1996), *Photography in Franco's Spain*, Madrid: Lunwerg Editores.

López Mondéjar, Publio (1997), *Historia de la fotografía en España*, Madrid: Lunwerg Editores.

Marí, Jorge (2003a), "Desnudos, vivos y muertos: la transición erótico-política y/en la crítica cultural de Vázquez Montalbán," in José F. Colmeiro (ed.), *Manuel Vázquez Montalbán: el compromiso de la memoria*, 129–41, London: Thamesis.

Marí, Jorge (2003b), "El umbral del destape," in Carlos Ardavín (ed.), *Francisco Umbral*, 242–58, Gijón: Libros del Pexe.

Martín Núñez, Marta and Marzal Felici, Javier (2016), "Intervenciones digitales en la fotografía de moda: ficciones de la representación del cuerpo femenino," in Juan Carlos Alfeo and Luis Deltell (eds.), *La mirada mecánica. 17 ensayos sobre la imagen fotográfica*, 63–88, Madrid: Editorial Fragua.

Memòries de Barcelona. Xavier Miserachs i Colita (2008), Barcelona: Lupita Books.

Morcillo, Aurora G. (2010), *The Seduction of Modern Spain. The Female Body and the Francoist Body Politic*, Lewisburg: Bucknell University Press.

Perec, Georges (2008), *Lo infraordinario*, Palencia: Impedimenta.

Pomés, Leopoldo (2015), *Leopoldo Pomés, Flashback*, Barcelona: RM.

Radner, Hilary (2000), "On the Move. Fashion Photography and the Single Girl in the 1960's," in Stella Bruzzi and Pamela Church Gibson (eds.), *Fashion Cultures. Theories, Explorations and Analysis*, 128–42, New York: Routledge.

Ribalta, Jorge (2007), "AFAL como síntoma. La ambivalencia de la vanguardia fotográfica española," *El viejo topo. Crítica de la cultura* (228): 78–87.

Ribalta, Jorge (2009), *Paradigmas fotográficos en Barcelona, 1860–2004*, Barcelona: Quaderns del Seminari d'Història de Barcelona.

Rosón Villena, María (2017), "Colita en contexto. Fotografía y feminismo durante la transición española," *Arte y políticas de identidad* (16): 55–74.

Sekula, Allan (2015), "Desmantelar la modernidad, reinventar el documental. Notas sobre la política de la representación," in Jorge Ribalta (ed.), *Aún no: Sobre la reinvención del documental y la crítica de la modernidad. Ensayos y documentos (1972–1991)*, 153–68, Madrid: Museo Nacional Centro de Arte Reina Sofía.

Sontag, Susan (1977), "In Plato's Cave," in *On Photography*, 3–26, New York: Picador.

Terré, Laura (2006), *Historia del grupo fotográfico Afal (1956/1963)*, Sevilla: Photovision.

Umbral, Francisco (1976), *Crónicas post-franquistas*, Madrid: AQ Edicions.

Vázquez Montalbán, Manuel (1985), *Crónica sentimental de la Transición*, Barcelona: Planeta.

Vega, Carmelo (2017), *Fotografía en España (1839–2015). Historia, tendencias, estéticas*, Madrid: Cátedra.

Wollen, Peter (2003), "Fire and Ice," in Liz Wells (ed.), *The Photography Reader*, 76–80, New York: Routledge.

Part III

Designing Fashion Stars

Film and Music

5

Fashioning Spanish Film Stars

Balenciaga and Conchita Montenegro

Jorge Pérez

Conchita Montenegro (1911–2007) was by the 1940s a global film star at the peak of her career, making her persona the ideal platform from which to promote a couture brand in Spain, in this case, the House of Balenciaga. For the producers of the films in which she starred (all mainstream films seeking to attract massive audiences), the designer stamp helped increase her star appeal. In addition, the Balenciaga costumes contributed to "Hispanizing" Montenegro's image. This was crucial to incorporating her into the star system of Spanish cinema and, above all, to enabling the actress—whose star persona was quite sensual—to comply with the moral strictures of film censorship in Spain under Francisco Franco. My goal with this case study is to show that the relationship between fashion and film is multidimensional and contains layers of meaning—commercial, theoretical, aesthetic, and even patriotic and political—that merit our critical attention.

In the early 1910s, Parisian couturier Paul Poiret began to film his fashion shows to promote his collections (Leese 1976: 9), ushering in a period of fruitful collaboration between the fashion and film industries that has been described as both symbiotic and codependent (Engelmeier 1990: 8; Butchart 2016: 8). While mutually beneficial, this partnership has not been free of tension. When collaborating on a film, couturiers somehow have to adapt their métier to the demands of the industry, since their one-of-a-kind garments become costumes within the film. Couture houses have endured these production constraints because of the publicity generated by dressing major stars in significant films. As historian Marylène Delbourg-Delphis argues, cinema has been the main arbiter of fashion styles since the 1930s (1981: 161–70). This is why many couture houses have taken on film commissions, even though some of them have notoriously failed.[1]

The alliance with the film industry opened up the elitist world of couture to a wider audience. This partial democratization of couture meant that while the majority of film viewers could not afford to purchase the costumes on display, they could at least enjoy them as a visual spectacle, and even produce imitations with more modest fabrics. Of course, the gains have been reciprocal. The film industry, especially in the mid-twentieth century, also profited from selling stardom with the allure of a couture brand. In some cases, fashion proved fundamental to molding the image of a star. This was the case with Audrey Hepburn, who perhaps would not have risen to such heights if not for her long-lasting professional relationship and friendship with French couturier Hubert de Givenchy. Today, this synergetic union continues, although it is perhaps more apparent on the red carpet of major award ceremonies such as the Academy Awards and high-profile international film festivals like Cannes, San Sebastián, and Venice.

In the context of critical discussions on the couture-cinema relationship, the case of Cristóbal Balenciaga (1895–1972) demands attention, on historical as well as aesthetic grounds. He was considered the greatest couturier of his time and had a steady number of commissions for film costumes (spanning three decades). Balenciaga designed clothes for an extensive list of renowned film stars. Within Spanish cinema, he dressed Blanca de Silos, Conchita Montenegro, Isabel Garcés, María Martín, Sara Montiel, and Rocío Dúrcal. Abroad, he made his debut in French cinema when he dressed Marie Déa in *Pièges* (Robert Siodmak 1939). After that, he dressed global stars such as Ingrid Bergman in *Anastasia* (Anatole Litvak 1956), María Félix in *La estrella vacía* (Emilio Gómez Muriel 1958), Ava Gardner in *The Angel Wore Red* (Nunnally Johnson 1960), and Marlene Dietrich in *Paris When It Sizzles* (Richard Quine 1964).[2] Despite his considerable achievements, the growing scholarship on the relationship between couture and cinema has thus far overlooked Balenciaga's contributions. Notably, Christopher Laverty conducted a wide-ranging study of forty-eight designers' work for motion pictures, from the early 1920s to 2016. The extensive list of designers selected for brief commentary includes Balenciaga's contemporaries such as Chanel, Dior, and Givenchy—yet there is no mention of the Basque couturier.

Cinema was the ideal platform for flaunting the couturier's range as a dressmaker—his ability to dress women of different generations—as well as the evolution of his *métier* across time. Above all, it provided an opportunity for showcasing his relentless inquiry into the possibilities of the female silhouette, always propelled by a modernist impulse to innovate. As fashion historian Miren Arzalluz points out, "Balenciaga's formative years and early development coincided with the explosion of Modernism," which is a cultural movement "driven by an energetic desire to make a deliberate break with the past" (2016: 55). This modernist mantra became especially noticeable from the 1950s onward. In the 1950s, Balenciaga presented a number of original silhouettes that revamped the couture world, such as the "balloon dress" (1950), the unfitted middy blouse (winter 1951), the semi-fitted suit (summer 1952), the tunic dress (summer 1955), the sack dress (1957), and the A-line baby-doll dress (summer 1958).

Although they did not reach the level of abstraction of his late 1960s designs—with architectural qualities that created an exceptional degree of autonomy from the body—Balenciaga's collections in the 1950s do offer an experimentation with structure and form. Some of these innovations appeared in a 1954 film, *Alta costura* (Luis Marquina), which offers a noir plot with a police investigation during a couture show in a fashion house. Balenciaga designed the entire collection shown in the film, which becomes a crucial instrument for plot development and characterization. One of the models (played by Laura Valenzuela) dons a balloon-style dress, and later a kimono jacket that exhibits his version of Orientalizing cultural influences. Continuing with the path opened by the *tonneau* (barrel) line of coats that he first presented in 1947, this jacket incorporates a barrel-like curve at the back that forms an arc so that the jacket is detached from the waist. The unattached style of the jacket—a risky creative decision in the times of the wasp waist popularized by Dior's New Look—conceals the model's waist and breast (the two conventional pivotal points in Western women's fashion), thus illustrating Balenciaga's enduring investigation of the female silhouette. This kimono-style jacket blazes the trail in terms of the aesthetic independence of the garment with regard to the body it covers.[3]

For practical reasons, I limit my scope in this chapter to the use of Balenciaga garments as costumes with a key role in shaping Conchita Montenegro's star persona in the early 1940s. While predating his most innovative designs from the 1950s on, these costumes already contain some of Balenciaga's career-long trademarks. For instance, they show the imprint of the Spanish regional dress and the great masters of Spanish painting, two of the major artistic influences throughout his trajectory. In particular, the costumes that Montenegro wears in the films that I analyze here contain two specific inspirations. The first one is the recurring presence of black in his work, which Marie-Andrée Jouve attributes to his admiration for Velázquez's paintings of the Spanish court under Philip IV (1988: 303–6).[4] The costumes in the film *Lola Montes* (Antonio Román, 1944) also show resemblances to the *Infanta* dresses that Balenciaga launched in his 1939 collection, both in their silhouettes and the use of stitch work (ribbons and bows). These costumes prove that his immediate success in the Paris couture scene was not accidental.

Balenciaga relocated from San Sebastián to Paris in 1936 because of the Spanish Civil War (1936–9), but he already had a trajectory of twenty years as a fashion designer and entrepreneur in which he developed a unique design vision influenced by his profound knowledge of cultural and artistic traditions, as well as by a constant search for innovations in the female silhouette (Arzalluz 2011: 12–13). Before analyzing these film costumes, let me provide a bit of context of how Conchita Montenegro rose to global stardom.

The Rise and Disappearance of a Global Star

In the early 1940s, Conchita Montenegro was the biggest—and most unusual—star of the national industry. She became an international celebrity before Spanish audiences even recognized her name. After brief roles in two Spanish films (*Sortilegio* [Agustín de Figueroa 1927] and *Rosa de Madrid* [Eusebio Fernández Ardavín 1927]), Montenegro moved to Paris to study dance. Her career took a dramatic turn when she was chosen for the role of an exotic Andalusian dancer in *Le femme et le pantin* (Jacques de Baroncelli 1929), where she performed naked in front of a tavern audience in a key scene of the film. Her full-frontal nude—reflected on a bottle of champagne—caught the attention of some Metro-Goldwyn-Mayer executives, who immediately offered her a contract. Initially, she was hired for the Spanish versions of Hollywood blockbusters, but her prompt adaptation to the ways of the American industry and her quick mastery of English helped her secure star roles in English-language films such as *Never the Twain Shall Meet* (W. S. Van Dyke 1931). From 1930 to 1935, she made a total of seventeen films in Hollywood (under contract with MGM and Fox), working with high-caliber male stars like Ramón Novarro, Buster Keaton, and Leslie Howard, with whom she had a well-publicized affair (Bou and Pérez 2018: 43). When Fox Studios did not renew her contract, she continued to pursue an international career, appearing in films in France, Brazil, and Argentina.

In 1940, CIFESA[5]—the foremost production company in Spain until the mid-1950s—hired Conchita Montenegro as part of an ambitious attempt to create a star system similar to the Hollywood studio model. Montenegro was sent to Italy, where she starred in several coproductions directed by Luis Marquina. The idea was to use her as the star vehicle to sell the CIFESA brand abroad, but these coproductions failed because of their low quality (Fanés 1982: 104). Therefore, producer Vicente Casanova brought Montenegro back to Spain, where she acted in five films between 1942 and 1944: *Rojo y negro* (Carlos Arévalo 1942), *Boda en el infierno* (Antonio Román 1942), *Ídolos* (Florián Rey 1943), *Aventura* (Jerónimo Mihura 1944), and her very last film, *Lola Montes* (Antonio Román 1944). However, Montenegro did not even partake in the postproduction promotion of *Lola Montes*, because she decided to retire after marrying Ricardo Giménez Arnau, a diplomat and prominent member of the Falangist Party. In fact, she never attended an industry-related event again and refused to give any interviews except for the brief chat she had before her death with José Rey-Ximena (2008). She did not even attend an homage dedicated to her at the San Sebastián Film Festival, and declined to accept the *Medalla de Oro al Mérito Artístico* that Spain's Minister of Culture awarded to her in the 1990s (Moro 2018: 366; Ro 2017: 513–14). For all intents and purposes, Conchita Montenegro tried to disappear from the history of Spanish cinema, and she was quite successful for a long time. She only appeared in descriptive accounts of the contingent of Spanish actors who landed in Hollywood to make the foreign-language versions of American films in the late 1920s and early 1930s.[6]

Fortunately, the recent mounting interest in the reconfiguration of the star system in the 1940s has brought her back into academic discussions of Spanish cinema.[7] In addition, Montenegro has received attention even beyond the academic sphere in two recent novels that fictionalize her life story.[8] My contribution to these discussions about Montenegro's place in Spain's star system of the 1940s will center on assessing the importance of fashion in reshaping her star image. In particular, I will highlight how becoming the muse of Balenciaga in Spanish cinema—as the cover jacket of Carmen Ro's novel describes her—played a significant part in the adaptation of her image, associated with the glamorous yet dangerous vamp type, to the rigid moral codes of Francoist cinema in the early 1940s. I will employ three types of material. First, I will analyze the importance of the Balenciaga garments that Montenegro wears in *Ídolos* and *Lola Montes* as narrative devices that contribute to her performance and star image. Also, I will call attention to the functions that promotion (magazine ads and articles about her starring role in these films) and publicity (what she disclosed about herself in interviews) had in the reshaping of Montenegro as a fashionable star who had an international pedigree yet did not show signs of moral excess in her private life. A third important source will be the impact that commentaries and criticism in film magazines had on this adaptation of her image through fashion.[9]

Ídolos: Countering the *Españolada* through Fashion

Ídolos is particularly apt for reflecting upon the refashioning of Montenegro's stardom, since Florián Rey was a director who specialized in films about stars' trials and tribulations, whether they were actors, singers, dancers, or football players. *Ídolos* zooms in on the harmful side of stardom, which it portrays as incompatible with a decent life. In fact, it tells a story that echoes Montenegro's own trajectory. She plays the role of Clara Bell, a famous Parisian actor who goes on a tour of southern Spain to prepare for her next film role. During her trip, she meets an attractive *matador*, Juan Luis Gallardo (Ismael Merlo), but a jealous producer who ruins Clara's career thwarts their romance. Back in Paris, she cannot find any acting roles and has to earn a living by modeling for a fashion house. Luckily, Juan Luis tracks her down and saves her from her professional demotion by proposing to her.

In one of the film's first sequences, Clara performs a song-and-dance routine during a film shoot in Paris. A long shot taken from the back of the room shows the diva making her grand entrance onto the stage, wearing an evening gown that radiates sophistication. It is a Balenciaga black dress with inventive shoulder lines: each sleeve in the form of a ruffle—one white, the other black—is stitched to the dress.[10] This symmetrical combination of black and white is a typical element of Balenciaga's style throughout his career. For Véronique Belloir, this association in his work "brings to mind the lace-trimmed ruffs illuminating the severe costumes of Spanish monarchs, synonymous with both luxury and renunciation," and, more broadly, "the tension between light and darkness that so characterized Spanish cultural expression" (2018: 17). This contrasting effect is reinforced by the beaded and embroidered ensemble of rich, multilayered arabesques that adorns the front portion, while the lower part is made of black tulle and decorated with black fringe tassels (*madroños*). Clara completes her look with a spectacular hat also made of black tulle and ornamented with tiny black tassels that match the lower half of her dress. While performing a song, Clara walks around the room seducing the audience with sensual gestures. A tracking shot follows her, but surprisingly for a performance intended to emphasize the star's sex appeal, there are no close-ups of the flirtatious looks she directs at the intra- and extra-diegetic audience. This is a noteworthy technical decision, given that close-ups play a key role in star image-making. They are the moments seen only by us and not by other characters, "thus disclosing for us the star's face, the intimate, transparent window to the soul" (Dyer 2004: 10). With so little information available about Montenegro, close-ups could have functioned for the audience as unmediated gateways into the star's inner self—the illusion of getting a glimpse of who she really was. Instead, all shots of Clara are either medium-long or long shots, so her charm has to be conveyed through other aspects of the mise-en-scène, such as the elegant Balenciaga dress and the plasticity of the composition.

The inclusion of geometrical motifs framing the foreground, often in elaborate compositions that resemble a static painting or an altarpiece, is common in Florián Rey's films (Benet 2012: 203). In this case, the geometrical pattern underscores the seductress's agency. As Clara walks around the room, she disappears and reappears behind thick columns, which adds a touch of mystery to her alluring performance. Along with the absence of close-ups, this visual element intensifies the glamorous effect of Clara's performance. Virginia Postrel has theorized glamour as "a form of nonverbal rhetoric" that generates a subjective response in the audience, typically a sense of yearning (2013: 48). In this case, it triggers a desire for Clara's wealth, beauty, and sex appeal. While her outfit is an emblem of glamour, it is not glamour itself, as glamour does not simply exist inside a dress or any other object (Postrel 2013: 44). Glamour is something more elusive, a mechanism of persuasion that requires mystery, which Postrel considers its "defining perceptual quality," because it inspires projection (2013: 110). This is why the technical decisions about the scene's camerawork and visual composition, while initially unexpected because they partially hide the star from sight, contribute to heightening the audience's desire for her, because they compel viewers to fill in the gaps with their longings.

The scene that follows Clara's performance further underscores the significance of the dress. As Clara is walking toward the dressing room, the film's producer stops her to remind her about the upcoming shoot for her next film, set in Spain. She expresses her disgust at having to participate in this film: "I don't act in *españoladas*."[11] The daughter of a Spanish woman, Clara says that her mother always voiced her indignation at the hackneyed image of "the Spain of the tambourine,"[12] a reference to how the country was depicted and misrepresented on-screen with cheap commercial folklore to attract tourists. This is why Clara announces that she is going to Spain to learn about its authentic culture, and the visual motifs of her dress highlight this vindication of genuine Spanish culture. The decorative *madroños* of the hat and the lower part of the dress show the influence of Spain's regional dresses on Balenciaga's designs; fashion historians have noted that these dresses inspired him throughout his career. Ana Balda writes that in the archives of the House of Balenciaga in Paris, there is a copy of the book *El traje regional de España* (Isabel de Palencia 1925), which the couturier might have referred to when creating his designs (2016: 59). There is also evidence that before moving to Paris, Balenciaga traveled around Spain and learned about popular dress traditions (Bowles 2011: 187). In particular, the lower part of Clara's dress evokes the *basquiñas*, the black skirts that Spanish women wore in the nineteenth century when they went to town for shopping or social events. As Helena López de Hierro has noted, the most sophisticated versions of the *basquiñas* "were made of net embroidered and embellished with black pompons," like the *madroños* that decorate Clara's dress and hat (2018: 23). Balenciaga also drew inspiration from the paintings of Goya, especially those that depicted the dresses of the Spanish *majas*, which clearly resonate in the *madroños* of Clara's dress and hat (Arzalluz 2011: 203).

We must frame Clara's fervent position on the (mis)representation of "Spanishness" in cinema within the context of a crusade initiated in the pages of *Primer Plano*, a film magazine that channeled the Falangist views of the new regime and its attempt to appropriate cinema as a vehicle for political propaganda. The early issues of *Primer Plano* included several articles calling for the elimination of the *españolada* from the Spanish film industry. The strongest one, which appeared in issue 137 in 1943 under the headline "Alerta contra la españolada," aggressively described the *españoladas* as a despicable form of cinema that delivered a mistaken representation of Spanish culture (n.p.). The producers of *Ídolos* had to take the vitriolic views of *Primer Plano* very seriously, because this influential magazine held sway over the critical and commercial fate of the film. It is thus fitting that Florián Rey had Montenegro conveniently give a speech against the *españolada*; after all, *Primer Plano* had made Montenegro the flag-bearer of cinema in the "New Spain" by putting her on the cover of its first issue in 1940. Besides, in the early fall of 1943, several issues of the magazine contained promotional information about the upcoming premiere of *Ídolos* that consistently made use of Montenegro's stylish star image. She appeared, for example, on the cover of issue 160 wearing a spectacular white mink coat, a deliberate attempt to sell the star and the film using fashion. The cover also notes that the film would be screened "with the symbolic patronage of *Primer Plano*"[13] (1943: n.p.). This refers to the film producers' clever promotional decision—

already announced in issue 154 of September 1943—to donate all the earnings from the premiere to the *Asociación de la Prensa* with an honorable mention for *Primer Plano* (1943: n.p.). This ensured plenty of promotional coverage and, just as importantly, a favorable review after the premiere. Indeed, José Luis Gómez Tello's review of the film that appeared in issue 161 lauded the filmmaker for making a modern, versatile film with a European flair (1943: n.p.). Conchita Montenegro, with her aura of chic international celebrity, embodied that sense of European modernity.

In effect, there was a lot at stake for the producers of the film as well as for Montenegro. *Ídolos* was an expensive film with a budget of around 2.5 million pesetas, which was above average for a Spanish film at the time. Moreover, it was the first film made in the new studios of the production company Sevilla Films, an additional reason to ensure it had a lucrative commercial run (Sánchez 1991: 284). For Montenegro, it was important to succeed at the box office if she wanted to preserve her privileged position in the star system of Spanish cinema.

This was especially true after *Rojo y negro* (where she arguably delivered her best performance in a Spanish film) flopped: it was banned by the regime's authorities for political reasons and disappeared from theaters after only three weeks.[14] Carmen Rodríguez Fuentes provides evidence that Conchita Montenegro was the highest-paid Spanish actress in the early 1940s thanks to her Hollywood pedigree. She made around 150,000 pesetas per film—and some sources estimate it was 200,000 for *Lola Montes*—while her female contemporaries (such as Conchita Montes, Amparo Rivelles, Maruchi Fresno, and Ana Mariscal) were making less than 100,000 per film (Rodríguez 2002: 168). Montenegro was an expensive bet and the return on the investment was far from guaranteed. She was not popular among Spanish audiences, because neither her Hollywood films nor her European production had been seen in Spain; her celebrity was based on what film magazines reported about her success abroad.

This is why it was vital that popular and influential film magazines continued to portray her in a glamorous fashion. Montenegro kept up her side of the bargain by playing the publicity game. In an interview with Juan Ares for issue 24 of *Cámara*, she was photographed in her home performing summer leisure activities such as horseback riding, reading, and petting her dog (1943: n.p.). The interview also contained information about her impeccably decorated house. It was imperative to create an image of mysterious glamour, but also to reveal something personal that would make her seem approachable to film audiences. In this vein, Virginia Postrel notes that the mystery that is essential to glamour cannot lead to "complete inscrutability" (2013: 112). This type of publicity interview with Montenegro effectively galvanized the mechanisms of glamour by conjuring a sense of translucence. As Postrel further argues, "glamour is neither transparent nor opaque. It is *translucent*. It invites just enough familiarity to engage the imagination, allowing scope for the viewer's own fantasies" (2013: 20). The interview delivered the perfect combination of accessibility to, and detachment from, the star—inviting desire in the form of distanced identification. It offered a glimpse of Conchita Montenegro performing quotidian activities without revealing too much or breaking the glamour spell.

Promotional pressures explain why providing an "authentic" depiction of Spanish cultural traditions is a central preoccupation in *Ídolos*.[15] In this sense, the elegant Balenciaga dress that Montenegro wears in this film, with its combination of couture sophistication and traditional elements of the regional Spanish dress (like the *madroños*), is perfect for conveying the film's counterimage of Spanish culture. I am inclined to speculate that Montenegro—who donned Balenciaga in almost all of her late films and had the star power to make costume decisions—probably chose to wear this dress, and that it was not a conscious selection by the costume designer of the film, Julio Laffitte. Whatever the circumstances, this Balenciaga dress is an ideal narrative vehicle and visual spectacle—dramatically colored by *Radiocinema* in its promotional display for its issue 90—for attempting to add a touch of European modernity to Spanish folk traditions (1943: n.p.). Conversely, it also functions effectively as an element of the mise-en-scène to suggest the "Hispanization" of the female star, both the intra-diegetic Clara Bell and Conchita Montenegro. Hispanizing Montenegro entailed taming her sensual image, which in the resolution of the film is clinched through marriage. Juan Luis proposes while Clara is modeling the bridal dress in the fashion house where she works. Far from the confident and flirtatious diva she was at the onset of the film, Clara appears docile in this white bridal dress. She is barely able to look her soon-to-be husband in the eyes to accept his marriage proposal and her future as a submissive Spanish wife. The diva is transformed into a virtuous spouse.

Lola Montes: Hispanizing the Vamp

After *Ídolos*, fashion continued to be key to adapting Montenegro's star image to the sui generis Spanish film industry. In *Aventura* (Jerónimo Mihura 1944) she plays Ana Luna, a libertine actor who, while shooting a film set in a rural village, begins to seduce Andrés (José Nieto), a local married man. When she realizes how much Andrés means to his wife, she changes her mind and leaves the village without breaking up the marriage. The film pivots both thematically and ideologically between rural vs. urban and tradition vs. modernity. Radical costume differences—between Ana's lavish gowns and the local women's regional dresses—visually convey these oppositions. Montenegro's over-the-top outfits became a topic of critical discussion when *Aventura* was released in the summer of 1944, as some reviewers deemed her costumes incongruous with the story's rural setting.

On the other hand, Manuel Tovar Rodríguez defended Montenegro in the pages of *Radiocinema* by contending that negative reactions to her costume choices came from a misunderstanding of her star image, which "is closer to Culver City [California] than to Chamartín [Madrid]" (1944: n.p.).[16] Although Montenegro's outfits in *Aventura* do border on ridiculous (especially a white chiffon gown she wears for a hike and picnic in the woods), Tovar had a point in the sense that Montenegro occupied a unique niche in the Spanish star system.[17] She embodied like no other the international archetype of the glamorous vamp, which was "the antitype of the folklórica, who wore her heart on her sleeve" (Woods Peiró 2012: 78–9).

Modeling herself after her idols Marlene Dietrich and Greta Garbo, Montenegro convincingly played heartless, manipulative, and extremely intelligent women. However, to comply with the rigid moral codes of early-Francoist cinema and to get approved by the censors, those vamps had to be somewhat redeemed, or else they were punished with a tragic ending.

The extravagant costumes of a dangerous yet ultimately well-intentioned vamp were also the main attraction of *Lola Montes* (Antonio Román 1944). Montenegro plays the role of Lola Montes, an Irish-born dancer who adopted a fake Spanish identity and became an international celebrity through her performances and affairs with distinguished noblemen and kings in the mid-nineteenth century.[18] While Lola gallivants across Europe, she is being used without her knowledge by a mysterious agent of an international revolutionary movement to destabilize political regimes. Lola seduces King Ludwig I of Bavaria and provokes a serious political crisis and a popular revolt against the monarchic institution. But Carlos Benjumea (Luis Prendes), a Spanish military officer who is in love with her, rescues Lola when she is about to be put to death, and the film ends with her on a church altar, atoning for her extravagant life.

When *Lola Montes* was in the pipeline, the promotional weight shifted from director Antonio Román, one of the sacrosanct pro-regime directors of the early 1940s, to the costume designers commissioned for the film (Coira 2004: xiv).

In issue 186 of *Primer Plano* (May 1944), the critic Alfonso Sánchez drummed up excitement for the film's premiere by writing about how costume designers Pepe Caballero and Juan Antonio Morales created "fashion sketches that are a marvelous spectacle in themselves" (n.p.).[19] What the article does not reveal is that Balenciaga created many of these garments. In fact, Balenciaga received screen credit at the beginning of the film and critical praise for this collaboration in other venues. For example, a few decades later, Jesús García de Dueñas cited this film to make the case that impressive acting and costumes can make up for a bad script: "the presence of Conchita [Montenegro], splendidly dressed by Balenciaga, can save us from literary pretension" (1993: 191).[20]

Remarkably, recent accounts offer a different interpretation of the function of costume in *Lola Montes*. Núria Bou and Xavier Pérez assert that the clothes serve to neutralize the erotic potential upon which she had built her star image. They claim that the film focuses on the dresses themselves and not "on the body that wears them" (2018: 50).[21] The body is covered "with sumptuous dresses that make it hard to see the body's shape,"[22] which leads to the obliteration of Montenegro's sex appeal altogether (2018: 52). For Bou and Pérez, *Lola Montes* was the pinnacle of the moral rectification of Montenegro's trajectory since her return to Spain, and it signposted her subsequent disappearance from cinema (2018: 53). It is true that, as I have been arguing, the specific circumstances of the early 1940s in Spain and, especially, the censorship to which cinema was subjected, compelled Montenegro to tweak her star image. The challenge was to "Hispanize" her persona, which involved partially mitigating her erotic appeal, while retaining the glamour that made her suitable for roles in films set abroad. However, it is one thing to say that her erotic potential was softened, and another to claim that it was destroyed, as the title of their essay suggests.

In my view, Bou and Pérez's assessment of the function of costume in *Lola Montes* is somewhat problematic because it oversimplifies its importance with a blanket statement, neglects fashion history and, thereby, exposes an anachronistic bias. Their analysis overlooks the fact that costume plays a central role in historical dramas, since it lends crucial historical authenticity to the overall look of the film. Lola wears a number of outfits with a wide and full-length skirt supported by a *miriñaque* (crinoline), that is, a frame composed of metal hoops that functions as a petticoat to hold a woman's skirt in place. These bell-shaped dresses were bulky and covered Lola's body from head to toe, but they were not mere pretexts for concealing her body. Rather, they were common in the period in which the film takes place. The film is set sometime in the mid-nineteenth century (the real Lola Montes was born in 1821 and died in 1861), an epoch in which the crinoline was in fashion. Therefore, it seems only fitting that Lola Montes, a courtesan who had influence over noblemen and kings across Europe, would sport such styles.

Besides, the dresses resonated with film audiences because of the historicist fad in the fashion scene of the late 1930s and early 1940s. Balenciaga led the pack with his 1939 collection of *Infanta* dresses, inspired by Velázquez's seventeenth-century portraits of the Spanish royal family, which catered to "the Parisian public's fascination with the masters of Spanish painting" (Arzalluz 2011: 201). According to fashion historian Hamish Bowles, the timing of Balenciaga's *Infanta* dresses collection was perfect. That same year, Franco's regime approved an exhibition of masterworks retrieved from Spanish art institutions, including iconic paintings by El Greco, Murillo, Velázquez, and Goya. The exhibition was held in Geneva with great success: it "had a potent effect on the Parisian haute couture, and the press was quick to note the resonances in Balenciaga's work" (Bowles 2011: 35). In his first years in Paris, Balenciaga stood out for his technical perfection and the flawless cut of his suits, but it was because of his clever allusions to Spanish art and culture, imaginatively incorporated into his gowns, that he earned recognition. Some of Lola Montes's spectacular gowns bear resemblance to those *Infanta* dresses. When she pays a visit to the King of Bavaria to defend herself against her enemies, the top part of her gown is heavily ornamented, including a white lace frill that falls from the neckline to the waistline, and decorative bows and ribbons stitched to the sleeves and shoulders. It is in the decorative bows that one can detect the influence, for instance, of the *Infanta* dress designed by Balenciaga in red velvet for Madame Bemberg in 1939 (Arzalluz 2011: 201).[23]

Audiences responded well to seeing Montenegro in those particular costumes because nineteenth-century silhouettes were trendy in the 1940s. In fact, Amber Butchart claims that costumes in period films "often reveal more about the fashions of the present day than they do about those of the past" (2016: 68). In the aforementioned satin gown, Lola Montes is clearly dressed to impress, and, seduced by her stunning looks, the King asks her to dance for him at the opera house. One could even draw a direct connection between Lola's most elaborate clothing and her tempting maneuvers with men. Her obsession with chocolate, paired with her flashy gowns, underscores the image of her as a calculating vamp: she is both playful and seductive.

Costumes here play a disruptive, intrusive role in the narrative to the extent that they turn into what Jonathan Faiers calls "a negative cinematic wardrobe" in the sense that clothes adopt a function that is contrary to their expected positive image and become associated with subversive, unregulated behavior—including sexuality—that causes conflict and political turmoil (2013: 9). Throughout most of the film, she is a femme fatale with a *miriñaque*, using sartorial seduction to make things happen.

When Bou and Pérez state that Montenegro's attire erases her star image as a sex symbol, the assumption is that sex appeal is only expressed through the body. They also take for granted that her costumes are signifiers with the only function of helping the audience understand the body that wears them—in this case, to obliterate its erotic potential by concealing it. Bou and Pérez's point of departure for grasping the function of costume is therefore the body, and not clothing. This is a limited view of film costume that neglects the diverse ways costume can generate desire independent of the body it dresses. One cannot avoid, for instance, considering the potential of clothing fetishism. The textures, colors, and designs of film costumes can prompt a tactile and visual desire in the viewers that may lead to a compulsion to possess those clothes and/or erotic arousal. For Bou and Pérez, Montenegro's body disappears underneath the costumes, which leads to the eradication of the star's erotic appeal and ultimately of her own star image—since they one-dimensionally conflate it with her capacity to sexually arouse viewers with her body. I disagree with that categorical assessment. My analysis has shown that Montenegro's costumes in *Lola Montes* call attention to themselves and produce a surplus of meaning that takes the story in new directions. They are intra- and extra-diegetic instruments of the vamp's sartorial agency and sex appeal. Within the film's narrative, they become weapons to provoke seismic changes to power structures, and even a political revolution; in terms of the promotional tactics to sell the film, they serve as a strategic way to generate viewing expectations through stardom. It is true that at the end of the film her seductive energy is mitigated: Lola has an epiphany, rejects her previous life choices, and ends up on a church altar praying for forgiveness. But this is depicted as the felicitous outcome of Carlos's positive influence, the Spanish officer who shows her the path to redemption. Ultimately, the key to Lola's moral conversion lies, much like in the case of Clara Bell in *Ídolos*, in her "Hispanization," and not so much in how much flesh she shows or conceals.

Although Montenegro's sex appeal had to be tamed, it was not destroyed altogether. As Richard Dyer argued, star images "have a temporal dimension," which means that they can change or develop over time (1998: 64). Thus, certain features of a star's image can prevail in certain periods of her or his career, and wane in others (Dyer 2004: 3). In the early 1940s, it was important to de-emphasize Montenegro's sex appeal, or better yet to sublimate it through fashion and glamour, in order to make her look more "Spanish." Balenciaga was an ideal sartorial fit to promote this renationalization of her star image, because his creations always exuded an air of "Spanishness." Although he perfected his craft and ascended to the top of the couture world in Paris, the culture and traditions of his native Spain never ceased to inspire his work. Audrey Hepburn, one of the most fashion-conscious film stars, once stated—borrowing from a popular phrase attributed to Mark Twain—that "if clothes maketh man, then costumes certainly make actors and actresses" (Hepburn 1990: 11). Montenegro was already "made" when she returned to Spain, but Balenciaga's designs definitely contributed to reshaping her image for the cultural context of Francoist Spain in the early 1940s.

Notes

1 Curiously, the most infamous case was also one of the first instances of a collaboration between film and fashion. In 1931, Metro-Goldwyn-Mayer brought Coco Chanel to Hollywood with an exclusive contract (sources say it was worth $1 million). However, this partnership barely lasted a year because of Chanel's disagreements with the star, Gloria Swanson. See Leese (1976: 14); Edmonde (2009: 404–7). The designer did not want to compromise her point of view for the sake of the films.

2 See Usabiaga (2013) for a well-documented, descriptive account of Balenciaga's costumes for different films and stars.

3 For a detailed analysis of the use of Balenciaga designs in this film, see my article "The Noir Side of Couture: Balenciaga and Luis Marquina's *Alta costura* (1954)," 115–27.

4 See also *Balenciaga in Black*, edited by Véronique Belloir et al (Paris: Rizzoli Electa, 2018) for a detailed look into the Spanish cultural traditions influencing Balenciaga's recurrent use of black.

5 La Compañía Industrial de Film Español, S.A. (1932–1956).

6 See Armero (1995) and Dueñas (1993).

7 *El cuerpo erótico de la actriz bajo los fascismos*, edited by Núria Bou and Xavier Pérez (Madrid: Cátedra, 2018); Comas (2004); Fuentes (2002); Vernon and Peiró (2013: 293–318).

8 Ro (2017) and Moro (2018), which was Premio Primavera de Novela.

9 I must clarify that because of Montenegro's unique trajectory and relative dearth of archival documentation about her career (Carmen Ro and Javier Moro

mention in their novels the legend that Montenegro had all personal documents of her acting years burned by her assistants), we can only speculate about the nature of her relationship with the House of Balenciaga or believe third-party testimonies about her alleged friendship with the couturier. It is possible that the connection between Montenegro and Balenciaga was tied to their Basque origins. Montenegro grew up in San Sebastián, where Balenciaga had his own dressmaking business by the time she entered her teens. Perhaps she was already a client at that time. I tried to gather more information about her connection with the fashion house at the Museo Balenciaga that could help me explain why Montenegro was so often dressed by the Basque couturier in her later films, but the curators told me there is no record of Balenciaga's specific involvement with the films I have analyzed.

10 We know it is a Balenciaga dress because of the information provided by Pedro Usabiaga, *Un sueño de Balenciaga*. The film credits, though, do not mention any involvement of Balenciaga in the film, only the work of the costume designer, Julio Laffitte. As I explain later, this leads me to believe that this was a costume choice by Montenegro herself (or perhaps even a piece from her own wardrobe) instead of a commissioned job.

11 "Pues yo no hago españoladas" (this and further translations into English are mine).

12 "Una España de pandereta."

13 "Bajo el patrocinio simbólico de *Primer Plano*."

14 According to the information provided by Hueso (1998: 214), *Ídolos* was shown for eleven days at the Cine Alcázar in Barcelona, and an unknown number of days at the Cine Capitol in Madrid. While there is not enough data to draw a definitive conclusion, judging by its poor showing in Barcelona, it does not seem like the film came anywhere near the status of a box office hit.

15 In fact, the critics all praised this aspect of the film. For example, the reviewer for *Cámara* raved about the meticulously crafted setting and cinematography, even as he lamented the absence of an actual bullfight sequence, which he assumes is "por el temor a caer en la españolada" (to avoid falling into the españolada trope) (issue 27, December 1943). Along those lines, the reviewer of *Radiocinema* (issue 94, November 1943) speculates that the film's flaws in psychological characterization are the result of the excessive focus on providing a counterimage of national folklore, which he deems successful.

16 "Está más cerca de Culver City que de Chamartín."

17 For more on this, see Comas (2004: 85); Ximena (2008: 141); Fuentes (2002: 386).

18 That same year, a biography by Enrique Moreno, *Lola Montes, Reina de Reyes* (1944), had spurred interest in the figure of Lola Montes in Spain. Actually, as part of the promotional campaign for the film, *Primer Plano* included an interview with Moreno in its issue 212 (November 5, 1944), in which the biographer attested

to the historical rigor of the film adaptation. This is a rather interesting promotional trick, given that the film contains plenty of historical inaccuracies. For example, in *Radiocinema* (issue 98, March 1944), director Antonio Román admitted that the initial sequence of the film, which takes place in Seville is not historically accurate—the real-life Lola Montes never went to Spain.

19 "Figurines que por sí solos constituyen ya un maravilloso espectáculo."

20 "La presencia de Conchita, maravillosamente vestida por Balenciaga, nos redime de esa infección literaria."

21 "En el cuerpo que los sostiene."

22 "Vestidos suntuosos que dificultan la identificación de sus líneas."

23 It is important to point out that this was not a fashionable dress but rather a costume for a dress party around the theme of Louis XIV. The fashionable dresses dubbed *Infanta* were not nearly as close to the Velázquez paintings. I am indebted to one of the anonymous reviewers of this chapter for this observation.

References

Armero, Álvaro (1995), *Una aventura americana: Españoles en Hollywood*, Madrid: Compañía Literaria.

Arzalluz, Miren (2011), *Cristóbal Balenciaga: The Making of a Master (1895–1936)*, London: V&A Publishing.

Arzalluz, Miren (2016), "Iconoclastic Visions of the Silhouette: Cristóbal Balenciaga," in Karen Van Godtsenhoven, Miren Arzalluz, and Kaat Debo (eds.), *Fashion Game Changers: Reinventing the 20th-Century Silhouette*, 33–81, London: Bloomsbury.

Aventura (1942), [Film] Dir. Jerónimo Mihura, Spain: CEPICSA.

Balda, Ana (2016), "Two Views on the Popular Costume," in Ana Balda Arana (ed.), *Coal and Velvet: Views on the Popular Costume*, 53–72, Getaria: Fundación Cristóbal Balenciaga.

Belloir, Véronique (2018), "The Choice of Black," in Véronique Belloir et al. (eds.), *Balenciaga in Black*, 12–17, Paris: Rizzoli Electa.

Benet, Vicente (2012), *El cine español: Una historia cultural*, Barcelona: Paidós.

Bou, Núria, and Xavier Pérez (2018), "La destrucción de una sex symbol: Conchita Montenegro," in Núria Bou and Xavier Pérez (eds.), *El cuerpo erótico de la actriz bajo los fascismos: España, Italia, Alemania (1939–1945)*, 41–53, Madrid: Cátedra.

Bowles, Hamish (2011), *Balenciaga and Spain*, New York: Skira Rizzoli.

Butchart, Amber (2016), *The Fashion of Film: How Cinema Has Inspired Fashion*, London: Mitchell Beazley.

Cámara (1943), "El veraneo de Conchita Montenegro," no. 24, n.p.

Cámara (1943), no. 27, n.p.

Charles-Roux, Edmonde (2009), *Descubriendo a Coco Chanel*, Barcelona: Lumen.

Coira, Pepe (2004), *Antonio Román: Un cineasta de la posguerra*, Madrid: Editorial Complutense.

Comas, Ángel (2004), *El star system del cine español de posguerra (1939–1945)*, Madrid: T&B Editores.

Delbourg-Delphis, Marylène (1981), *Le chic et le look: Histoire de la mode fémenine et des mœurs de 1850 à nos jours*, Paris: Hachette.

Dyer, Richard (1998), *Stars*, London: BFI.

Dyer, Richard (2004), *Heavenly Bodies: Film Stars and Society*, London: Routledge.

Engelmeier, Regine, and Peter W. Engelmeier (1990), *Fashion in Film*, New York: Prestel.

Faiers, Jonathan (2013), *Dressing Dangerously: Dysfunctional Fashion in Film*, New Haven: Yale University Press.

Fanés, Félix (1982), *CIFESA, la antorcha de los éxitos*, Valencia: Institución Alfonso El Magnánimo.

García de Dueñas, Jesús (1993), *¡Nos vamos a Hollywood!*, Madrid: Nickel Odeón.

Hepburn, Audrey (1990), "The Costumes Make the Actors: A Personal View," in Regine and Peter W. Engelmeier (eds.), *Fashion in Film*, 9–11. New York: Prestel.

Hueso, Ángel Luis (1998), *Catálogo del cine español: Películas de ficción 1941–1950*, Madrid: Cátedra/Filmoteca Española.

Ídolos (1943), [Film] Dir. Florián Rey, Spain: Sevilla Films.

Jouve, Marie-Andrée and Jacqueline Demornex (1988), *Balenciaga*, Paris: Éditions du Regard.

Laverty, Christopher (2016), *Fashion in Film*, London: Lawrence King.

Leese, Elizabeth (1976), *Costume Design in the Movies*, Brembridge: BCW Publishing.

Lola Montes (1944), [Film] Dir. Antonio Román, Spain: Alhambra Films.

López de Hierro, Helena (2018), "Spanish Black," in Véronique Belloir et al. (eds.), *Balenciaga in Black*, 19–23, New York: Rizzoli Electa.

Miller, Lesley Ellis (2007), *Balenciaga: Shaping Fashion*, London: V&A Publishing.

Moro, Javier (2018), *Mi pecado*, Madrid: Espasa.

Pérez, Jorge (2019), "The Noir Side of Couture: Balenciaga and Luis Marquina's *Alta costura* (1954)," *Film, Fashion, and Consumption* 8 (2): 115–127.

Postrel, Virginia (2013), *The Power of Glamour: Longing and the Art of Visual Persuasion*, New York: Simon & Schuster.

Primer Plano (1943), "Alerta contra la españolada," 137: n.p.

Primer Plano (1943), "El estreno de la película *Idolos* a beneficio de la Asociación de la Prensa," 154: n.p.

Primer Plano (1943), 160: n.p.

Primer Plano (1943), "Ídolos," 161: n. p.

Primer Plano (1944), "El biógrafo y el guionista de Lola Montes frente a frente," 212: n.p.

Primer Plano (1944), "Lola Montes: ¡Sí, en España podemos hacer buen cine!," 186: n.p.

Radiocinema (1943), 90: n.p.

Radiocinema (1943), "Ídolos," 94: n.p.

Radiocinema (1944), 98: n.p.

Radiocinema (1944), "Rápidos," 103: n.p.

Rey-Ximena, José (2008), *El vuelo del Ibis: Leslie Howard al servicio de Su Majestad Británica*, Madrid: Ediciones Facta.

Ro, Carmen (2017), *Mientras tú no estabas*, Madrid: La Esfera de los Libros.

Rodríguez Fuentes, Carmen (2002), *Las actrices en el cine español de los cuarenta*, Benalmádena: Caligrama.

Sánchez Vidal, Agustín (1991), *El cine de Florián Rey*, Zaragoza: Caja de Ahorros de la Inmaculada.

Usabiaga, Pedro (2013), *Un sueño de Balenciaga, el cine*, Getaria: Museo Cristóbal Balenciaga.

Vernon, Kathleen and Eva Woods Peiró (2013), "The Construction of the Star System," in Jo Labanyi and Tatjana Pavlovic (eds.), *A Companion to Spanish Cinema*, 293–318. Oxford: Wiley-Blackwell.

Woods Peiró, Eva (2013), *White Gypsies: Race and Stardom in Spanish Musicals*, Minneapolis: University of Minnesota Press.

6

Rosalía and the Rise of *Poligonera* Chic

Mary Kate Donovan

The singer and songwriter Rosalía Villa Tabella, better known simply as Rosalía, exploded onto the music scene with her 2018 album, *El mal querer* (*The Bad Desire*). Her particular brand of flamenco pop has propelled her to international stardom. Rosalía trained at the Taller de Músics and later at the Escola Superior de Catalunya, where she studied under professor of flamenco singing, José Miguel Vizcaya, also known as Chiqui de la Línea. Her first album, *Los Ángeles* (2017), takes a traditional approach to flamenco music, highlighting the vocal abilities that initially brought Rosalía success in the domestic Spanish market. Her sophomore release, *El mal querer*, fuses Rosalía's vocals and flamenco rhythms with other musical styles, particularly trap and reggaetón, to produce an album that has won the singer enormous crossover success. *El mal querer* won three awards at the 19th Annual Latin Grammy Awards, Grammy for Best Latin Rock, Urban or Alternative Album at the 62nd Annual Grammy Awards, and took Rosalía on her first international tour in 2019—including appearances at Coachella and the Glastonbury Festival—further bolstering her star status and winning new audiences worldwide. Rosalía's musical style has evolved from *Los Ángeles*, an album that consists almost exclusively of Spanish-style guitar and flamenco vocals, to *El mal querer*, which incorporates digitally produced sounds and a wider range of rhythms. The result is an album with a more "urban" sound that moves away from traditional flamenco and aligns the artist with the emergence of Spanish trap and the evolution of reggaetón from its Afro-Caribbean roots to a genre with global cachet.

As Rosalía's musical style and influences have changed, so has her fashion, garnering nearly as much attention as her musical success. In December 2019, journalist Lola Gambau proposed that the key to Rosalía's success lies in the way she has combined "her love of flamenco with other styles and rhythms, like trap and reggaetón, and a large dose of experimentation while shaping an image that oscillates between a *polígono* aesthetic and a more sophisticated *mise-en-scène*" (Gambau n.p.).[1] The *polígono* aesthetic to which Gambau refers is one way of describing a style of dress that, at least since the 1990s, has been associated with the working-class outskirts of major Spanish cities like Madrid, Barcelona, and Valencia—also commonly referred to as the *extrarradio*.[2] It was with the release of *El mal querer* that Rosalía began to define what is now considered her quintessential look, which favors tracksuits, elaborate acrylic nails, and large, gold, jewelry. Along with the growing popularity of trap and reggaetón in the Spanish music scene, Rosalía's rise to fame has brought aspects of this so-called *polígono* aesthetic into the mainstream.

Like Rosalía's primary musical genre, flamenco, this *polígono* aesthetic overlaps and intersects with the culture of Spain's *gitano* or Roma community, who have often built shantytowns in abandoned lots near industrial parks in *extrarradio* areas. It is important to note that Rosalía herself is a *paya*—a term used to describe those who are not members of the Roma community—and, for that reason, her use of iconography affiliated with Roma and Andalusian cultures in her music videos has incited accusations of cultural appropriation.[3] As she experiments with musical genres and collaborates with international artists, Rosalía continues to gain traction in the US market, as evidenced by her recent Grammy and Latino Grammy wins. This chapter explores the role fashion has played in producing Rosalía's enormous success in Spain and in expanding her crossover success abroad. In particular, it reads her fashion in select music videos and performances and considers her reception in the Spanish press. Since her rapid rise to fame began in 2016, Rosalía's public image has evolved from flamenco prodigy to *poligonera* fashion icon and, more recently, *reguetonera* whose modern take on flamenco fusion appeals to a much broader audience. By framing these readings with Dick Hebdige's theorization of fashion and youth subcultures, I argue that the various positionalities Rosalía occupies through her fashion are calculated moves; they reflect not only the performer's expanding engagement with musical genres beyond flamenco but also her strategic use of fashion to market a carefully constructed star persona. While Rosalía's musical talent is undeniable, I argue that her mobilization of street fashion has played a crucial role in the performer's breakthrough into mainstream commercial success not only in Spain, but also abroad in markets throughout the United States and Latin America. Rosalía's use of fashion mirrors the way that her music plays with genres, reimagining familiar styles in new ways. However, it also reveals the complicated ways in which fashion, like music, can exacerbate racial and class inequalities by profiting from the commodification of cultural innovations produced by marginalized communities.

Fashion and Youth Subcultures

The release of "Malamente" ("Badly"), the lead single from *El mal querer*, in May 2018 marked a decisive turn in Rosalía's celebrity, both in terms of her musical trajectory and her position as a fashion icon.[4] The track constituted a turn away from the more traditional flamenco sound of her first album and signaled Rosalía's move into the more experimental flamenco fusion that has defined her rise to international stardom. Although the song's rhythm still relies heavily on the sound of *palmas*, or handclaps, the syncopated beats, and layering of synthetically produced melodies give the track a trap sound.[5] The song was received positively by critics, but it was the release of the accompanying music video, produced by the Barcelona-based team CANADA, that made "Malamente" a viral phenomenon. The music video was a key component in accelerating Rosalía's success, and also in establishing the relationship between Rosalía and the so-called *polígono* aesthetic.

The "Malamente" music video self-consciously plays with iconography associated with Spanish, and more specifically, Andalusian culture. Sequences of Rosalía performing are edited together with scenes of bullfighters-in-training (*novilleros*) in what looks like a school gymnasium, young men posing with souped-up cars, and skateboarders wearing traditional Holy Week robes skating in a bowl park under an enormous cross decorated with graffiti stickers. Just as Rosalía's music reframes flamenco vocals with trap and reggaetón rhythms, the music video reimagines traditional symbols of Spanish cultural and religious iconography within the context of contemporary youth culture, placing Rosalía at its center. Rosalía first appears wearing a red velour tracksuit, flanked by dancers wearing variations of a similar look in black and yellow—Adidas-branded tops, track pants, and white sneakers (Figure 6.1). A video brimming with national cultural references, the yellow and red wardrobe brings to mind the Spanish flag. Before cutting to a medium shot that shows the entire group, the camera opens onto a close-up of Rosalía's face and chest, her hand held up near her mouth, giving the viewer a clear view of her large, gold jewelry, red lipstick, and long, acrylic nails.

Over the course of the video, Rosalía appears in a number of other outfits, all of which feature crop tops, white sneakers, synthetic fabrics, and bright colors

Figure 6.1 Rosalía and her backup dancers wear tracksuits in the music video for "Malamente." Credit: "Malamente" music video directed and produced by CANADA.

offset by pops of white, creating a cohesive look in sync with the music video's *poligonero* setting. In addition to the gymnasium where the *novilleros* train, the video's scenes take place in parking lots, a mechanic's shop, the interior of a freight truck, alongside a highway overpass, and in empty streets lined with heavily graffitied barrier walls. Like Rosalía's wardrobe throughout the video, all of these settings refer to peripheral spaces on the edges of metropolitan centers and the people who occupy them. In a particularly noteworthy scene, Rosalía rides a motorcycle as a male companion performs bullfighting *pases* around her. In this sequence, the *novillero's* traditional dress is replaced with an Adidas tracksuit and Rosalía herself takes the place of the bull. The way in which the music video reimagines the iconography of traditional Andalusian culture such as bullfighting and Holy Week processions—one *novillero* even dons a tattoo of the Esperanza Macarena de Sevilla[6]—within a mise-en-scène that is clearly identifiable as Spanish working-class *extrarradio* suggests that the *polígono* aesthetic represents a new, twenty-first-century version of Spanish "authenticity."

Portrayals of the *extrarradio* are not a development new to contemporary Spanish cinema.[7] A marginal, working-class space similar to the one conjured in the "Malamente" video was portrayed on the big screen in Bigas Luna's 2006 feature film, *Yo soy la Juani*. The film's eponymous protagonist is a young woman living in the outskirts of Valencia where she and her boyfriend, Jonah, work in labor and service positions in order to subsidize their lifestyle, which is centered on clubbing and *tuning*, the practice of customizing and racing cars.[8]

As Abigail Loxham describes in her reading of the film, Juani is intentionally identified as a *poligonera*, and "Juani's identity is based on a particular form of self-presentation which identifies her as part of this peripheral configuration" (2016: 80). For Loxham, "*Yo soy la Juani* is Bigas [Luna]'s twenty-first-century reflection on the changing nature of Spanish youth," in which the director's "sensitivity to cultural context and his mode of representation in this film set the scene for an examination of the new feminist subjectivities encapsulated by Juani" while also constructing a meta-commentary on the nature of female stardom in the globalized era of late capitalism (2016: 81). Within the diegetic world of the film, Juani strives for self-empowerment by traveling to Madrid with dreams of "making it" in show business. As a cultural text, the film's celebration of a working-class aesthetic as a productive mode for female stardom anticipates Rosalía's contemporary deployment of a similar look more than a decade later.

In an article published in *El País* upon the film's release, journalist and film critic Ángel S. Harguindey heralds *Yo soy la Juani* as the kind of film that "consciously or unconsciously, becomes a testimony to a particular time and people" (2006: n.p.).[9] The article describes how Bigas Luna has created a film that portrays particular and interrelated youth subcultures, including *tuneros*, which refers to the practice of customizing cars for display and, in some cases, racing (2006: n.p.). For Harguindey, *Yo soy la Juani* is a markedly postmodern film, bringing to the big screen a sociocultural reality that represents an important sector of contemporary popular youth culture in Spain, one that previously had remained on the periphery of the mainstream. Harguindey quotes Bigas Lunas as claiming that modernity can be found in the periphery, and that the character of Juani, with her miniskirts, large gold hoops, and passion for souped-up cars "represents today's Spanish woman, one who is no longer the victim of Iberian brutalism and who is able to give the average *machito* a run for his money. She is free, sensitive and liberated. [...] She represents a new Iberian icon, a new national symbol" (2006: n.p.).[10] If we consider Bigas Luna's claim, nearly fifteen years ago, that Juani represents a new national symbol, then Rosalía's use of a similar *poligonera* style to define her celebrity persona reflects a distinctly millennial mode of commercializing this form of Spanish youth culture and identity.

In his groundbreaking study of youth subcultures in postwar Britain, Dick Hebdige makes an argument about the central role of popular media in the establishment and evolution of subcultural styles, particularly those of the working class (1988: 84). He suggests that the media relays "back to working-class people a 'picture' of their own lives which is 'contained' or 'framed' by the ideological discourses which surround it and situate it" (1988: 85). He goes on to theorize the incorporation of subcultural forms of style into the mainstream, claiming that "as the subculture begins to strike its own eminently marketable pose, as its vocabulary (both visual and verbal) becomes more and more familiar, so the referential context to which it can be most conveniently assigned is made increasingly apparent" (1988: 93). It is through this process, closely linked to mass media representation, that the emergence of subcultural styles, particularly those associated with youth cultures, transition from a marginal position to occupy more mainstream cultural spaces. In the case of Spain's *poligonero* culture, mass-media representations such as the "Malamente" music video can be read as one method of reclaiming this particular subcultural style and making it meaningful—and marketable—within the frame of Spanish national identity.

Breaking into the Mainstream

Following the release of *El mal querer* in 2018, Rosalía began a collaboration with the Spanish clothing company Pull&Bear. Pull&Bear is a subsidiary of the Spanish multinational Inditex, based in Galicia, whose flagship brand is Zara. Inditex appears on the *Fortune 500* list and is consistently ranked among the top ten most profitable Spanish companies.[11] An innovator in the concept of "fast fashion," Inditex is known for its unique business model in which stock for its brands is manufactured in limited quantities.[12] In accordance with customer demand, stock is replenished, and new styles are added on a weekly basis. This strategy has allowed Inditex brands to stay abreast of current style trends, something scholars have argued gives the parent company its competitive edge (Mihm 2010: 57). The release of a Rosalía-branded line in 2018 and a second collection in 2019 is in keeping with Hebdige's argument that subcultural styles that challenge dominant cultural norms are often incorporated into the mainstream through commodification and mass-production. Both the 2018 and 2019 lines feature tracksuits and urban-inspired leisurewear. However, while the 2018 line focused on apparel with graphics referencing lyrics from the early singles of *El mal querer*, Pull&Bear's second collaboration with Rosalía in 2019 most closely resembled her looks from the "Malamente" video. The 2019 line includes 1990s-inspired pieces like crop tops in neon colors, bike shorts, track pants, and platform footwear, offering consumers access to ready-to-wear versions of Rosalía's signature style. A more extensive collection, the 2019 collaboration closely followed the conclusion of the singer's first international tour and the release of multiple music videos from *El mal querer*, through which she established herself as a model of contemporary urban youth style, particularly for those who wanted to mobilize an affect associated with working-class toughness.

As Hebdige argues, subcultural innovation is often closely linked to the processes of commodification and commercialization of mass culture. Writing about youth subcultures in postwar Britain, he suggests that it can be difficult "to maintain any absolute distinction between commercial exploitation on the one hand and creativity/originality on the other, even though these categories are emphatically opposed in the value systems of most subcultures" (1988: 95). On the contrary, "the creation and diffusion of new styles is inextricably bound up with the process of production, publicity and packaging which must inevitably lead to the defusion of the subculture's subversive power" (1988: 95). In the case of Rosalía and Pull&Bear, the performer's fame and the popularity of her celebrity image as represented through music videos and stage performances provided an opportunity for one of Spain's largest fashion conglomerates to capitalize on styles that have been associated with peripheral urban communities since at least the 1990s. Media coverage of the Pull&Bear by Rosalía line placed great emphasis on its subcultural character, noting its "urban air" (*El Periódico*), "urban style" (*La Voz de Galicia*), "street inspiration," and how it combines an urban style with "a hint of trash and a sporty touch" (*La Vanguardia*).[13]

The Pull&Bear collaboration was advertised as a reflection of Rosalía's personal style. Media coverage of its release described the line as inspired by her lifestyle and her unique "urban" style that "has impacted the world not only through her songs, but also her flashy outfits" (*La Voz de Galicia*).[14] Celebrity and fashion have a long history of symbiosis. In his foundational writing on celebrity and fan theory, Richard Dyer makes the argument that the phenomenon of celebrity necessarily extends beyond the scope of a performer's talent to include aspects of her or his personal life, paying particular attention to the role of women stars as fashion icons. Dyer poses the question, "what meanings are packed into the recurrent image of women stars as leaders of fashion?" (1979: 38). Writing about Hollywood's star system, Dyer presents his theory through a series of case studies in which he demonstrates how celebrity is constructed through the circulation of transmediatic representations of a film star. These images rely just as much on facets of her persona off-screen—such as her fashion choices—as they do on her on-screen performances. Dyer reads fashion as a potential tool of audience manipulation, and suggests that "fashion in this sense is a much less superficial or trivial phenomenon than it appears. . . . [A] change in physical style is also always a change in social meaning" (1979: 14). Rosalía's expansion into the fashion industry, and particularly the media's focus on her style, reveal a similar phenomenon to Dyer's theorization of film stars and their audiences. As Rosalía's musical scope has expanded to include genres—like trap and reggaetón—that are historically affiliated with working-class and racialized communities, her fashion sense has followed suit, constructing a cohesive and marketable celebrity persona.

Nicole M. Fleetwood writes about the commercialization of hip-hop culture through popular fashion and the role of popular media representations such as music videos, magazines, and advertisements in this process (2005: 334). She notes the double-bind produced by the relationship between fashion and hip-hop, one that makes hip-hop palatable for a largely white, suburban audience while also serving to provide economic advancement for the community—or at least certain figures—that produces the culture through fashion (2005: 335). In her study of fashion and American hip-hop, Fleetwood follows Dorinne Kondo's theorization of male Japanese business fashion as potentially political in that it signifies subcultural style and ethnic/racial pride in order to critique "notions of subcultural authenticity by focusing on the strategic production and performance of racial authenticity through hip-hop fashion wear" (2005: 327). Fleetwood's examination of hip-hop fashion as a lens through which to critique the intersection of masculinity, racial or ethnic alterity, and national identity provides a productive model according to which we might consider the implications of Rosalía's mobilization of subcultural fashion trends. Considering Bigas Luna's claim that the *poligonera* represents a new "Iberian icon," Rosalía's commercialization of this aesthetic can be read as a strategy to align her celebrity persona with particular affective qualities of working-class subcultures—like grit, an anti-establishment attitude, and perhaps even a certain anti-intellectualism—in a way that appeals to contemporary Spanish youth. The Pull&Bear line achieves this by recycling symbols that have been associated with the Spanish *extrarradio* for decades, such as the tracksuit, and combining them with fashion trends that signal Rosalía's membership in a contemporary, globalized youth culture, such as her elaborate acrylic nails.

Crossover Success and Cultural Appropriation

It is also important to recognize that the flamenco music in which Rosalía's success is grounded and the *poligonera* style she has popularized both have strong connections to the culture of Spain's Roma community. At the thirty-third

Goya Awards in February 2019, Rosalía performed an acoustic rendition of the *rumba calera* hit "Me quedo contigo" ("I'll Stay with You"). She was accompanied by the Cor Jove de l'Orfeó Català, perhaps a nod to the singer's Catalan heritage, and the lack of additional musical accompaniment during the stunning performance highlighted Rosalía's vocal prowess. "Me quedo contigo" was originally performed by Los Chunguitos on their 1980 album, *Pa ti, pa tu primo*, and became a hit as the soundtrack for the final scene of Carlos Saura's *Deprisa, deprisa* (1981) the following year.[15] Indeed, the entire soundtrack for the film consists of tracks by Los Chunguitos, a *rumba* group formed by three brothers from a Roma family originally from Extremadura and based in the working-class district of Madrid, Puente de Vallecas. The 1981 film by Carlos Saura is one of the most well-known examples of the *cine quinqui* subgenre that emerged in the years following the dictatorship of Francisco Franco, who came to power during the Spanish Civil War (1936–9) and remained in power until his death in 1975. While *quinqui* films were initially designed to attract and scandalize audiences by displaying the horrors of delinquent youth during Spain's Transition to democracy, the subgenre ultimately became a mirror that reflected the lived experience of marginalized, working-class Spanish youth at the time.[16] The films generally represent young Spaniards living on the margins of society, often played by nonprofessional actors whose lives echoed those of the characters they portrayed on screen. For example, José Antonio Valdelomar, who played the male lead in *Deprisa, deprisa* was convicted of armed robbery shortly after the film wrapped, and a decade later, after a series of subsequent incarcerations, died of a heroin overdose in the Carabanchel prison. Like the *quinqui* films in which their music appeared, Los Chunguitos' lyrics often focused on drug use, delinquency, and poverty, themes also commonly associated with working-class Roma communities in Spain.

Rosalía's performance of "Me quedo contigo" at the 2019 Goyas engages with the history of flamenco-inspired music and its relationship to marginality and youth culture in Spain on a number of levels. For the performance, Rosalía appeared on stage wearing a red, floor-length gown, a clear departure from the *poligonera*-styled wardrobe that has become synonymous with her stardom. The reserved elegance of her costume choice for the performance seems to reflect the seriousness of the event, in essence an homage to the musical history of the genre that has inspired her. Los Chunguitos, however, represent a particular facet of flamenco's history. As evidenced by the group's relationship to *cine quinqui*, their legacy highlights an association with marginality, poverty, and drugs. The group's original composer and lead singer, Enrique Salazar, died tragically at the young age of twenty-five after contracting hepatitis, perhaps through intravenous drug use. At the height of their fame, Los Chunguitos were an early example of a crossover musical success, pushing generic boundaries and capitalizing on their mainstream exposure via *Deprisa, deprisa.* Although they achieved popular success with "Me quedo contigo," their music was nevertheless affiliated with marginality. By performing their most well-known track, Rosalía not only pays tribute to the legacy of Los Chunguitos but does so in a way that reinforces how her own music celebrates marginal subcultural style and challenges the generic boundaries of traditional flamenco.

As a Catalan *paya*, Rosalía's engagement with musical genres that share a long history with Spain's Roma community has been viewed as problematic. In *White Gypsies: Race and Stardom in Spanish Musicals*, Eva Woods Peiró outlines how the performance of *gitana* characters by white stars played an important role in the construction of modernity under Franco. Through her study of Franco-era *españoladas*, or folklore-infused musicals, Woods Peiró argues that "White Gypsy heroines penetrated the heart of the conversation on Spain's nationalism and its place in global modernity: to be modern meant manipulating hybridity by assimilating racial difference or by excluding it from the definition of Spanishness" (2012: 24). The double-bind that Woods Peiró theorizes is one way of framing Rosalía's performance of Spanishness through flamenco and flamenco-inspired music for an increasingly international audience. The way in which Rosalía interprets a particular vision of Spanishness, constructed via the appropriation of the *polígono*'s mise-en-scène, signals the celebration of Spanish difference while eliding the racial or ethnic alterity inherent in that difference, embodied by Spain's Roma.

Although Rosalía has faced criticism for performing flamenco as a *paya*, her vocal talent has given her a "pass" among some flamenco traditionalists. The release of the "Malamente" music video, however, ignited a fiery debate about cultural appropriation in her music and, more specifically, in the recorded performance. The Roma community accused Rosalía of cultural appropriation, not only for her performance of flamenco but also for the music video's aesthetic. Noelia Cortés, a student and *gitana* from Almería, articulated her frustrations via Twitter comments that were subsequently picked up by news media outlets in Spain and abroad: "Being *gitana* is not an aesthetic. If it were a *gitana* singing what [Rosalía] sings, the same people wouldn't be listening to it on their phones. You use your expensive clothes, your fake nails, and your stuff to achieve a fake look that is associated with *lo gitano* but that erases the racial factor and its consequences" (@thelazaruslady).[17]

She adds that Rosalía's pronunciation of certain lyrics with an Andalusian accent—one that, she notes, Rosalía doesn't have while speaking—constitutes another example of cultural appropriation. Cortés makes the point that Rosalía's music and fashion draw on a long history of Roma and Andalusian cultures that have thrived on the margins of Spanish society while being coopted as representative and "authentically" Spanish for centuries.[18] She also highlights the way in which Rosalía markets herself with the use of working-class and *gitana* fashion while also signaling her celebrity status by wearing designer brands. For example, at Coachella in 2019, Rosalía was pictured wearing a velour tracksuit with an oversized Louis Vuitton print. She wore a similar pair of pants by Louis Vuitton in the music video for the track "Con Altura," her collaboration with the Colombian reggaetón artist J. Balvin. In the video, Rosalía sports the Louis Vuitton pants with a beaded corset and yellow slides by Versace as she and her dancers perform a choreographed routine in the cabin of a private jet decorated with roses in shades of pink (Figure 6.2). Rosalía's look, as well as those of her dancers, blend fashion trends associated with marginalized and working-class communities— such as tracksuits, crop tops, gaudy patterns, and high ponytails—with designer brand recognition. The success of Rosalía's star persona hinges on the allure of the *poligonera* aesthetic, but presents a version of it in which its appeal is distilled and thereby distanced from the lived reality of the communities it ostensibly represents.

Since the release of *El mal querer* in 2018, Rosalía has collaborated increasingly with reggaetón and trap artists such as J. Balvin. The Spotify streaming rates for

Figure 6.2 Rosalía wears Louis Vuitton pants and slides by Versace in the music video for "Con Altura." Credit: "Con Altura" music video directed by Director X.

"Con altura" and "Yo x ti, tú x mi," a 2019 single with the Puerto Rican trap and reggaetón singer Ozuna, have surpassed those of "Malamente," the most popular track from *El mal querer*. Her work with Ozuna and J. Balvin signals that Rosalía's forthcoming third album is likely to push the genre boundaries of her music even further and target an ever-wider set of audiences. Her fashion has also evolved in a way that continues to associate her with the Spanish *poligonero* culture, while also making her style readable to international audiences of "urban" music, particularly Latinx audiences in the United States. The music video for the second single off her third album, "Aute Cuture," which was released in May 2019, offers productive insights into the way her fashion has evolved in tandem with her celebrity persona.

Just like the "Malamente" and "Con altura" videos, the "Aute Cuture" video features Rosalía flanked by a team of female dancers. It is also set in a working-class neighborhood, in this case clearly identifiable by the architecture and the neighbors who emerge to check out Rosalía and her "girl gang" when they arrive. The "Aute Cuture" video displays a level of theatricality and production value that far supersedes the "Malamente" music video, in large part because of how it is organized around a cinematic narrative. In the opening credits, Rosalía is introduced with a close-up shot of her hand clad in acrylic nails, which double as a weapon, and her dancers are presented as the "Sisters of the Beauty Gang" (Figure 6.3).

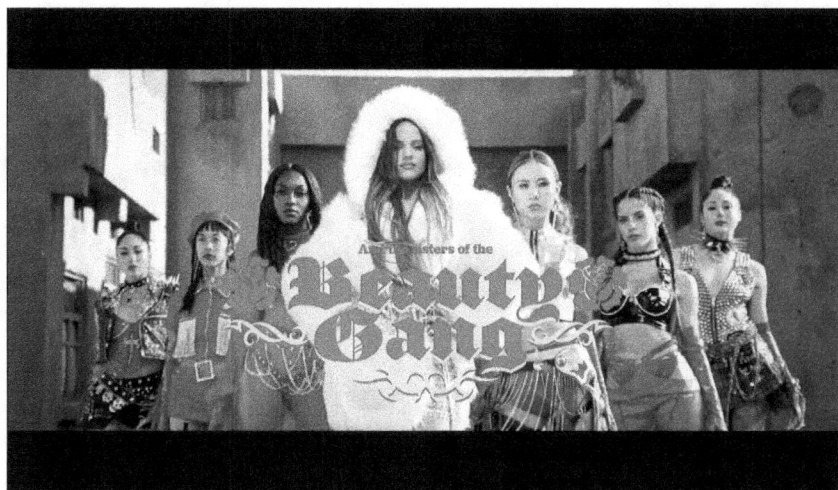

Figure 6.3 In the "Aute Cuture" music video, Rosalía appears wearing a white fur reminiscent of Blaxploitation-style cinema from the 1970s. Credit: "Aute Cuture" music video directed and produced by Bradley and Pablo.

The sequence's editing, including extreme close-ups and zooms in and out, is reminiscent of 1970s exploitation cinema, a reference that is further reinforced by the large white fur that Rosalía wears in the opening scene. The use of English titles suggests that the video is targeting a much broader (i.e., non-Spanish) audience than the more culturally specific "Malamente" video, as does the greater racial and ethnic diversity of the dancers cast for "Aute Cuture." Throughout the video, Rosalía and her "Sisters of the Beauty Gang" open a nail salon, bringing the pleasures of baroque and architectural nail art to the residents of this small, working-class community. It is implied that the neighborhood consists mostly of Roma residents, first identified as such in the opening scenes by stereotypical wardrobe choices such as large, gold jewelry, and later by the way they perform flamenco *palmas* with their newly adorned nails. (Figure 6.4)

An evolution of Rosalía's nail art has accompanied the performer's rise to fame with *El mal querer*. Absent from the video for her breakout track "Antes de morirme," with Spanish rapper C. Tangana, long acrylic nails and increasingly elaborate nail art have become part of Rosalía's signature style since the release of *El mal querer*. This reflects a broader trend of nail art in Spain, particularly among Spanish rap and trap performers. In February 2019, the fashion section of *El País* published an article titled "Uñas de trapera" that describes nail art as central to the celebrity image of performers like Rosalía.[19] A trend recently arrived in Spain, nail art has a much longer history in the US and Latin

Figure 6.4 A close-up of three sets of hands performing *palmas* in the "Aute Cuture" draws the eye to their elaborate nail art. Credit: "Aute Cuture" music video directed and produced by Bradley and Pablo.

American contexts, one that is steeped in racial, ethnic, and class implications. Although nail art can be traced back centuries to practices in China, Egypt, and Greece, the modern acrylic nail was developed in the United States during the 1950s. The trend became popular among Black and Latina women, gaining more mainstream recognition during the 1990s. More recently, the Kardashian sisters made the fashion of wearing long, and sometimes elaborately decorated acrylic nails more common among white women in the United States, further popularizing a trend that was pioneered by Black and Latina women decades ago. Furthermore, because of its association with working-class women of color, the trend had often been criticized as tacky, low class, or "too much" prior to its massification via the Kardashian phenomenon. In 2012, a salon called Ghetto Nailz opened in Madrid, one of the only salons to offer acrylic nails in the city. The salon's English-language name reveals an awareness of the fashion as affiliated with racialized and classed communities in the United States, and presents a problematic celebration of the term "ghetto" in ways that elide the history of the term's racial and class connotations.

The *El País* article on nail art and Spanish trap goes on to describe the fashion as "una tendencia ratcheta" ("a ratchet trend") (Armas 2019: n.p.). Like the use of the term "ghetto" in the Madrid-based nail salon's English-language name, the choice to describe the nail art trend as "ratchet," a US term heavily steeped in racial and class implications, is a troublesome one. The article suggests that this "ratchet" fashion transcends the derogatory categorizations of *choni* or *hortera*, Spanish terms that could be considered the closest equivalents to "ratchet."[20] The article cites another Spanish performer, La Zowi, as defining "ratchet" as "someone like me, who combines clothes from Bershka with designer knock-offs and who, because I feel excluded from the system, is more concerned with having their nails done than with voting in the elections."[21] (Armas 2019: n.p.). L. H. Stallings explains that the term "ratchet" can be defined as "foolish, ignorant, ho'ishness, ghetto, and a dance. It is the performance of the failure to be respectable, uplifting, and a credit to the race" (2013: 136). In opposition to these definitions, she offers a theorization of what she terms "The Black Ratchet Imagination" as a strategy of resistance that offers values "especially with regard to gender and sexuality" (2013: 136). Similarly, Therí A. Pickens recovers the derogatory term "ratchet" as a performative strategy employed by Black women within the context of reality television (2015: 43). La Zowi's definition seems to be gesturing in a similar direction, using the term to describe a method of apolitical resistance against traditional social hierarchies, but her use of the racially marked term "ratchet" as opposed to—and also in opposition to—autochthonous terms like *choni* and *hortera* treads into the complicated territory of cultural appropriation. Rosalía may have made nail art mainstream in Spanish fashion, but the style has long been affiliated with hip-hop and reggaetón music. For example, Ivy Queen—also known as The Queen of Reggaetón—has been known for her elaborate acrylic nail art since the 1990s.

With its focus on nail art, the music video for Rosalía's "Aute Cuture" is one of her most fashion-focused pieces. The track's title also makes a fashion reference; its misspelling of the French term "haute couture"—referring to custom garments produced in Paris—mocks the distinction between high and low-brow fashion and reads more like *cutre*, a colloquial term used to describe something of poor taste or bad quality. Like La Zowi's endorsement of the Bershka brand—another affordable ready-to-wear Inditex line, like Pull&Bear—and designer knock-offs, both the "Aute Cuture" music video and lyrics celebrate styles that might otherwise be considered tacky. In the chorus, Rosalía sings about polka-dots, fringe, dark eyeliner, and animal prints, all fashion trends often associated with Spain's Roma community. Like the "Malamente" music video, the "Aute Cuture" video positions Rosalía within the context of Roma and Andalusian cultures in Spain. However, unlike "Malamente," "Aute Cuture" relies heavily on Black American and Latinx cultural references, such as nail art and the montage style it borrows from Blaxploitation cinema. Like her recent collaboration with reggaetón and trap artists from the United States and the Caribbean, this shift in Rosalía's fashion seems to be an intentional one, aligning her more closely with trends associated with Black and Latinx communities and promoting her appeal for a more international and culturally diverse audience.

Rosalía's four wins at the Latin Grammy Awards in 2019 and her more recent win at the 2020 Grammy Awards in the Latin category have ignited a renewed debate surrounding Rosalía and the politics of cultural appropriation, this time in regard to her categorization as Latina.

There is a tradition of Spaniards winning Latin Grammys that includes Julio and Enrique Iglesias as well as Alejandro Sanz, who took home three Latin Grammys in 2019 as well as the Grammy for Best Latin Pop Album in 2020. Nevertheless, Rosalía has faced harsher criticism and more allegations of cultural appropriation than any of the aforementioned male artists. This is perhaps due to Rosalía's performance of reggaetón, a musical genre with a distinctly Afro-Latino heritage. Petra R. Rivera-Rideau argues that reggaetón serves as a site for the negotiation of racial politics in the Caribbean, and Puerto Rico specifically. She notes the ways in which the notion of *Latinidad* has historically distanced itself from Blackness and how, "within the Latin music industry, reggaetón has been labeled *música urbana*," a term that "carries with it racial and class connotations that speak to the music's affiliations with blackness" (2015: 12). Rosalía's success as a crossover artist has come largely from her foray into reggaetón as well as trap.

Rosalía's ability to blend musical genres has brought the artist international fame and crossover success. Her unique sound has been credited with heralding in a new kind of "Latin" music. Similarly, her fashion has brought marginal styles into the mainstream and won her recognition as a style icon. What remain largely unrecognized amidst her breakout success, however, are the much longer traditions of music and fashion on which her contemporary stardom is built, traditions that belong to marginalized and racialized communities. The evolution of Rosalía's fashion from the release of the "Malamente" video to the debut of the "Aute Cuture" video a year later shows an evolution in her fashion, one that has expanded from the *poligonero* style of the Spanish *extrarradio* to an "urban" look that draws heavily on fashions pioneered by Latina and Afro-Latina performers. It also suggests that Rosalía markets herself as a product that can yield profit through the process of remixing fashion and music references.

This shift has made Rosalía more marketable as a crossover performer, fashioning not only her music but also her style to suit a more culturally diverse international audience. In the globalized era of digital culture, we have unprecedented access to fashion trends from around the globe. As is the case with musical genres, fashion in the era of late-stage capitalism is increasingly susceptible to cross-pollination. Greater access to information has also made historically marginalized communities more aware of the power of their own voices to push back against the forces that strive to commodify and mass-produce their cultural expressions. Rosalía's musical innovation has revolutionized transatlantic Latin music and is driving fashion trends across Europe and the Americas. However, it is important to recognize the ways in which Rosalía's success builds on the shoulders of Black and Afro-Latina women whose groundbreaking performances and fashion is rarely recognized as such, but who have set the stage for the contemporary culture of the remix.

Notes

1 "Su inicial querencia por el flamenco con otros estilos y ritmos, como el trap y el reggaetón, y con una gran dosis de experimentación al tiempo que conformaba una imagen propia que oscila entre la estética de polígono y la más sofisticada puesta en escena."

2 In the Spanish context, a *polígono* is an industrial park, almost always located on
   the outskirts of a city or town. Stricter noise regulations in downtown areas have
   pushed some clubs into these areas that are semi-abandoned at night. The term
   poligonero/a, then, is a derogatory way to refer to the patrons of this nightlife
   culture (often working-class youth that live in the neighborhoods adjacent to these
   industrial parks) and is considered synonymous with low-brow taste.

3 *Payo/a* is a term used primarily within Spain's Roma communities to refer to those
   who are not members of the ethnic group and culture.

4 Rosalía wrote the song and it was produced by Pablo Díaz-Reixa, better known as
   El Guincho, who has collaborated with artists such as C. Tangana and J. Balvin.

5 Trap refers to a subgenre of rap that originated in the southern United States in the
   1990s and has been growing in popularity in Spain since the early 2010s.

6 The María Santísima de la Esperanza Macarena Coronada is a wooden statue of the
   Virgin Mary, which dates to the seventeenth century and is housed in the Basílica
   de la Macarena in Sevilla. The statue is a central figure of Sevilla's Holy Week,
   during which time it is processed through neighborhood streets. Commonly known
   as la Esperanza Macarena, the figure is a symbol of Sevilla and inspires a large
   number of devotees in its home city and elsewhere.

7 The *extrarradio* is a centerpiece of the *quinqui* subgenre of the 1980s. Pedro
   Almodóvar's early films also portray the *extrarradio*, *¿Qué he hecho yo para merecer
   esto?* (1984) being one particularly noteworthy example. Fernando León de Aranoa's
   films *Barrio* (1998) and *Princesas* (2006) are two more examples that are set, at least
   in part, in Madrid's *extrarradio*. *7 vírgenes* (2005), directed by Alberto Rodríguez is
   another example of a film that highlights the *extrarradio*, reimagining the *quinqui*
   subgenre in the twenty-first century.

8 Jonah is played by Dani Martín, the front man of the Spanish pop rock group El
   Canto del Loco.

9 "Consciente o inconscientemente, se [convierte] en testimonio de un tiempo y unas
   gentes."

10 "Representa a la mujer española de hoy, esa que ya no es víctima del brutalismo
   ibérico, capaz de poner a caldo al machito de turno. Una mujer libre, sensible y
   liberada. [. . .] Representa un nuevo ícono ibérico, un nuevo símbolo nacional."

11 Founded by Galician entrepreneur Amancio Ortega in 1985, Inditex is the biggest
   fashion group globally and consists of eight brands including Zara, Zara Home,
   Massimo Dutti, Bershka, Oysho, Pull&Bear, Stradivarius, and Uterqüe. Operating
   75,000 stores worldwide, the success of the Inditex brands has made Ortega one of
   the richest people in the world.

12 Zara's garments are generally manufactured either in Spain or in countries that are
   geographically close to Spain, such as Portugal, Morocco, and Turkey. This gives the
   brand the ability to have shorter production runs and produce new items quickly,

since its supply chain is much closer to Spain than other popular manufacturing sites in Asia.

13 "algo de *trash* y un punto deportivo."

14 "Ha impactado al mundo no solo con sus canciones, sino también con sus estilismos llamativos."

15 The group's name plays on the slang *chungo*, used to describe something of bad quality or an unfortunate situation. When it is used as a noun to describe a person, *chungo* or *chunga* implies that the he or she is deviant or dangerous.

16 For more on the history and influence of *quinqui* cinema, see also: Amanda Cuesta (2009); Joaquín Florido Berrocal et al. (2015); Tom Whittaker (2020).

17 "Ser gitana no es una estética. Si lo que cantas lo cantase una gitana no lo llevaría la misma gente en el móvil. Tú con tu ropa cara y tus uñas y tus cosas consigues una estética falsa que se relaciona con lo gitano pero quita el factor racial y sus consecuencias."

18 For a more thorough and historical perspective on the collapsing of Roma and Spanish identities see Lou Charnon-Deutsch's *The Spanish Gypsy: The History of a European Obsession.*

19 The term *trapera* refers to a woman who performs trap music. Incidentally, in the nineteenth century the term *trapero/a* was used in Spain to describe an individual who collected used clothing, rags (*trapos*) and other objects in order to re-sell them.

20 *Choni* is a derogatory slang term used to describe a woman who dresses and acts in a way that might be considered to be cheap, vulgar, or of bad taste. It is often used as a synonym to *poligonera* and strongly implies that the person is of a low social standing or class. *Hortera* is a term originating in the nineteenth century to describe a male shop attendant, but it evolved in contemporary slang to describe something or someone considered to demonstrate bad taste.

21 "Alguien como yo, que combina ropa del Bershka con imitaciones de marcas caras y que, como se siente excluida del sistema, se preocupa más por tener las uñas bien hechas que por votar en las elecciones."

References

Armas, Eva (2019), "«Uñas de trapera», la tendencia 'nail art' que llevan desde Rosalía a Blanca Suárez," *El País*, February 15: n.p.

Charnon-Deutsch, Lou (2004), *The Spanish Gypsy: The History of a European Obsession*, University Park: Penn State Press.

Chunguitos, Los (1980), [Vinyl] "Me quedo contigo," *Pa ti, pa tu primo*: Odeon.

Cortés, Noelia (@thelazuruslady), [Tweet] "Ser gitana no es una estética," December 27, 2017.

Cuesta, Amanda (2009), "Els Quinquis del barri," in Amanda and Mary Cuesta (eds.), *Quinquis dels 80. Cinema, Premsa I Carrer*, 14–47, Barcelona: Centre de Cultura Contemporània de Barcelona.

Deprisa, Deprisa (1981), [Film] Dir. Carlos Saura, Spain: Cinematog.

Dyer, Richard (1979), *Stars*, London: The British Film Institute.

Fleetwood, Nicole R. (2005), "Hip-Hop Fashion, Masculine Anxiety, and the Discourse of Americana," in Harry J. Elam, Jr. and Kennell Jackson (eds.), *Black Cultural Traffic: Crossroads in Global Performance and Popular Culture*, 326–45, Ann Arbor: University of Michigan Press.

Flamenco, flamenco (2010), [Film] Dir. Carlos Saura, Spain: Acciona.

Florido Berrocal, Joaquín, Luis Martín-Cabrera, Eduardo Matos-Martín, and Roberto Robles Valencia (eds.) (2015), *Fuera de la ley: asedios al fenómeno quinqui en la Transición Española*, Granada: Editorial Comares.

Harguindey, Ángel S. (2006), "El 'glamour' de la periferia," *El País*, October 8, n.p.

Hebdige, Dick ([1979] 1988), *Subculture: The Meaning of Style*, New York: Routledge.

Loxham, Abigail (2016), "'Sí valgo, yo valgo seguro' Spain's New Peripheral Female Subjects in *Yo soy la Juani*," *Studies in Spanish and Latin American Cinemas* 13 (1): 79–92.

Mihm, Barbara (2010), "Fast Fashion in a Flat World: Global Sourcing Strategies," *International Business & Economics Research Journal*, 9 (6): 55–64.

"Nueva colección de Rosalía para Pull&Bear" (2019), *La Voz de Galicia*, May 7: n.p.

Pickens, Therí A. (2015), "Shoving Aside the Politics of Respectability: Black Women, Reality TV, and the Ratchet Performance," *Women & Performance: A Journal of Feminist Theory* 25 (1): 41–58.

Rivera-Rideau, Petra A. (2015), *Remixing Reggaetón: The Cultural Politics of Race in Puerto Rico*, Durham: Duke University Press.

Rosalía (2019), "Aute cuture" [Video] Dir. Bradley & Pablo, Spain: Sony. Released May 30.

Rosalía (2019), "Con altura" [Video] Dir. Director X, Spain: Sony. Released March 27.

Rosalía (2018) "Malamente," [Video] Dir. CANADA, Spain: Sony. Released May 30.

Stallings, L. H. (2013), "Hip Hop and the Black Ratchet Imagination," *Palimpsest: A Journal on Women, Gender, and the Black International* 2 (2): 135–9.

Tarragó, Alba (2018), "Chándales y mucho 'Tra tra' en la nueva colección de Rosalía para Pull and Bear," *La Vanguardia*, November 12: n.p.

Whittaker, Tom (2019), "Accelerated Rhythms and Sonic Routes: Mapping the Sound Cultures of Bakalao," *Journal of Spanish Cultural Studies* 2 (3): 287–99.

Whittaker, Tom (2020), *The Spanish Quinqui Film: Delinquency, Sound, Sensation*, Manchester: Manchester University Press.

Woods Peiró, Eva (2012), *White Gypsies: Race and Stardom in Spanish Musicals*, Minneapolis: University of Minnesota Press.

Yo soy la Juani (2006), [Film] Dir. Bigas Luna, Spain: Media Films, 2006.

Part IV

Museums

From Closets to the Cloud

7

The Museo del Traje's Research on Spanish Prêt-à-Porter

Juan Gutiérrez

Introduction

From the moment it opened in 2004, Madrid's Museo del Traje has worked to recover and preserve ready-to-wear creations made by designers in Spain since the 1960s, when the industry first adopted this production model.[1] This initiative is complex and challenging because fashion consumers have only recently become aware of the heritage value of textile products, and most designers have not kept archives or preserved their unsold garments. Collecting clothes that exemplify the history of Spanish fashion design is, therefore, an urgent priority for the museum. Exploring private wardrobes and reviewing archival documentation such as brochures or photos enables the museum's curatorial staff to reconstruct the recent history of Spanish fashion.

Toni Miró, Juanjo Rocafort, Francis Montesinos, Ágatha Ruiz de la Prada, Manuel Piña, and Sybilla are well-known names in Spain's prêt-à-porter industry. However, we have limited knowledge of their careers and of pioneering runways such as *Moda del Mediterráneo* (Mediterranean Fashion), which supported a new concept of fashion and aided the commercial launch of creative designers. This chapter examines the museum's continued research efforts on the history of modern Spanish fashion, an endeavor that has led to several temporary exhibitions. I consider a number of exhibitions from the last two decades to highlight the types of questions our research has raised. My goal is to highlight how the museum has redefined its approach from its beginnings as an ethnographic institution to its current emphasis on ready-to-wear. I devote the most space to Antonio Alvarado, the fashion designer perhaps most closely affiliated with *la Movida*, an underground cultural phenomenon that transformed art and lifestyles as it went mainstream. *La Movida* has become a significant research topic in contemporary Spanish cultural studies, which has intensely debated its definition, boundaries, and outcomes (Marí 2009; Nichols and Song 2014). As the enfant terrible of Spanish fashion in the mid-1980s, Alvarado was behind some of the most memorable images in Pedro Almodóvar's films (Gutiérrez 2016). Nowadays, his work is being collected and researched by the Museo del Traje to better understand not only his approach to fashion design but also his role as one of the leading agents in renewing aesthetic narratives in the 1980s and 1990s.

To this end, this chapter highlights one of the museum's main objectives: to preserve Spanish fashion and textile heritage and to disseminate knowledge about the latter. Compared to the tremendous attention paid to other creative fields, fashion—which produces highly perishable materials—remains secondary in collecting efforts. While the unique one-off pieces of couture are reasonably well represented in museum collections because of their prestige and value, ready-to-wear has not enjoyed the same recognition. With the changes in the fashion industry that took place in the 1970s and 1980s, the legacy of great brands and designers disappears as quickly as people renew their wardrobes. Hence the sense of urgency and mission that drives the work of the museum in collecting and preserving Spanish prêt-à-porter items.

The Museo del Traje is a young institution. Its origin dates back to 1925, when Madrid hosted the *Exposición del Traje Regional e Histórico* (Exhibition of Regional and Historical Dress) in which Spanish regional and historical dress received renewed cultural and scholarly attention (García-Hoz 2016: 14–23). The ethnologist Luis de Hoyos, director of the exhibition, worked alongside a group of scholars and art patrons to collect traditional garments, most from the eighteenth and nineteenth centuries.[2] Hoyos and others had been researching and teaching about Spanish traditional culture since 1914 at the *Seminario de Etnografía, Folklore y Artes Populares* (Seminar of Ethnography, Folklore, and Popular Arts) (Hoyos 1922).[3] In 1922, Hoyos published *Etnografía Española, cuestionario y bases para el estudio de los trajes regionales* (Spanish Ethnography, Questionnaire and Foundations for the Study of Regional Dress) in which he described his positivist methodology, which he later applied to his study of the regional dress displayed at the exhibition. The 1925 exhibition, like much of Hoyos's work, reflected a sense of urgency: the vernacular practices he studied were on the verge of extinction. His efforts to collect pieces resulted in the preservation of many traditional garments, but his ultimate objective was to define the local ethnic features of each region in Spain, and in turn, illuminate a presupposed *volksgeist*.[4] The critical framework he employed was not as scientific and empirical as Hoyos made it sound, as its founding premise was the existence of a "true" Spanish cultural identity, the keys to which were to be found in traditional dress.[5]

The exhibition was a resounding success. Hoyos went on to create the Museo del Traje Regional e Histórico (Museum of Regional and Historical Dress) to permanently display the rich and varied cultural heritage that had been collected. In 1934, however, the collections were transferred to the newly created Museo del Pueblo Español (Museum of the Spanish People), an institution that would attempt to bring together the country's diverse ethnographic heritage, including many objects beyond dress (Berges 1996; Carretero 2002). The Spanish Civil War (1936–9) prevented this museum from opening its doors, and except for a brief period between 1971 and 1973, it remained closed to the public for most of the Franco era.[6]

Spanish Ready-to-Wear on Display: The Exhibition as Research

The museum was reopened to the public in 2004 as the Museo del Traje, Centro de Investigación del Patrimonio Etnológico (CIPE, Ethnological Heritage Research Center). The regional dress brought together for the 1925 project once again took center stage, becoming the basis for the new museum (Carretero 2004). While the museum adhered to some traditional ethnographic methods, it also began to embrace new areas of study. A team of fashion and textile historians, led by museum director and anthropologist Dr. Andrés Carretero Pérez, adopted methodologies from fashion history to organize exhibitions and establish policies that expanded the museum's collection. Additional pieces from the nineteenth and twentieth centuries, mostly donated, joined the collection.[7] Collecting efforts focused primarily on historical periods and couture creations. During 2003, the ill-fated *Geometría y Trazas* (Geometry and Traces) exhibition gave much-needed attention to ready-to-wear designs, greatly modernizing the collection.[8]

This new approach meant that ready-to-wear fashion would be treated as the cultural heritage of the State (Carretero 2007: 22). The museum's first task was to catalog and preserve the most significant part of the collection it had already acquired, attempting a comprehensive assemblage of the many fashion designers that emerged mainly during the 1970s and 1980s. The second task was to incorporate ready-to-wear into the museum galleries. The collection efforts driven by the *Geometría y Trazas* exhibition project also marked the start of a word-of-mouth initiative to inform people of the museum's existence, awakening strong public awareness that in turn facilitated more donations. Many designers donated the pieces on loan for *Geometría y Trazas* to the Museo del Traje, whose collection was already underway (García Serrano 2010: 44).

Designers welcomed the Museo del Traje's approach because it was the first State institution to treat fashion as cultural heritage (Carretero 2007: 13). This marked the start of a "legitimation" process regarding the artistic and cultural purposes of fashion. The Museo del Traje's strong reputation and its commitment to fashion as cultural heritage ended the debate on whether fashion should be included in museums and whether it had its own discourse. This followed a trend on the international stage after the 1971 Victoria and Albert exhibition "Fashion: An anthology by Cecil Beaton" in London, which included a number of Balenciaga garments, followed in 1973 by a Balenciaga exhibit at the Metropolitan Museum of Art, (Mata Torrado 2003: 229). The 1980s saw the consolidation of the idea that fashion deserved space in museums. This trend, however, did not flourish in Spain until 2001, when an exhibition of Giorgio Armani at the Guggenheim Museum in Bilbao met with unprecedented success. The exhibition traveled from its original venue in New York and opened on March 22 (the same day Hubert de Givenchy laid the first stone of the future Balenciaga Museum in Getaria, the designer's birthplace). It became the most outstanding cultural event of the season, opening a heated debate in Spain on the mission of museums because of the hypothetical conflict between the mercantile interests of fashion firms and the educational missions of publicly funded museums, a discussion that this exhibition sparked elsewhere, too (Steele 2018: 201).

Prior to this debate, the fashion industry was already contemplating the need to promote fashion culture in Spain. This objective was driven by the Asociación de Creadores de Moda de España (ACME), the country's leading association of designers that had been created in 1998. In response to the changes in fashion design that forced ateliers to close—caused in part by the success of Spanish fast-fashion firms such as Zara and Mango—the Spanish government in 2001 launched a Global Fashion Plan, with the participation of the Ministries of Economy, Science, and Technology and Education, Culture, and Sports. The plan intended to raise awareness of the importance of couture as national cultural heritage. Specific initiatives were proposed, such as a large exhibition at the Reina Sofía Contemporary Art Center Museum dedicated to the figure of Spanish fashion designer Manuel Pertegaz (2003), and the creation of a museum for the preservation of textile and fashion heritage, which took shape in the Museo del Traje itself (2004).

The strategies launched by the Museo del Traje were so successful that donations started to flow in, reaching 122,335 items by September 2020.[9] The vigor and urgency that had guided the collection's creation during Luis de Hoyos's term thus reappeared in the early 2000s. Hoyos's main objective had been to collect the traditional forms of dress that were at risk of being obliterated by industrial standardization. For the museum's curators in the early twenty-first century, however, the priority became to collect Spanish fashion pieces—both in spite of and because of the previous minimal interest in preserving examples of this sartorial legacy. Hoyos had had several advantages when he founded the collection: the compilation of ethnographic materials, a positivist methodology and even a nationalistic bias to guide him. By contrast, the challenge that the museum faced in 2004 was the general lack of academic interest in the evolution of Spain's fashion industry.

This explains why researching and writing the recent history of Spanish fashion is so important. Although an authoritative bibliography on regional and historical fashion in Spain had been compiled by the time the Museo del Traje was founded in 2004, the historiography of contemporary fashion was still at that point in its early stages. In the case of the prêt-à-porter industry, the lack of critical work was even more flagrant. Even today, few critical works have been written about this field.[10] Until the beginning of the twenty-first century, the only historiographical attempt to address Spanish fashion as a whole was the catalog for the temporary exhibition *España, 50 años de Moda* ("Spain: 50 Years of Fashion"), which took place in Barcelona in 1987 (Ajuntament de Barcelona 1987).[11]

As a result, the collection process necessitated research efforts to establish a historical context that would make interpreting fashion possible, using the analysis of the objects as material culture as the primary method to study each individual item. Elsewhere, Valerie Steele has proposed reassessing the museum's potential as a fashion research center, based on the proximity of the object (1998). This idea was further developed in successive works (Woodward 2002 and 2015; Küchler and Miller 2005; Scaturro 2018), leading to specific terms such as "renewed materialism," that gathers anthropological, ethnographic and sociological approaches focused on recovering the materiality of the fashion object (Rocamora and Smelik 2016: 14). Following this material turn, the museum became a research center with a key role in writing the history of fashion in Spain, while simultaneously introducing recent museum studies theory and praxis applied to fashion.

Throughout the years, the Museo del Traje has developed a specific methodology regarding the synergistic processes of collecting, researching, and exhibiting. Three distinct steps (acquisition, analysis, and exhibition) mark the process by which pieces are collected, documented, and displayed to the public. The collecting of pieces happens either through private offers (donations or sales, which are accepted or rejected based on their relevance to the museum's mission) or through the initiative of the collections department, which may request that the Spanish government purchase objects of relevant cultural interest.[12] A technical committee, formed by curators and conservators of the museum, evaluates offers and regularly deals with pieces devoid of any information other than the oral histories that the owners recount. The interview before the acquisition thus constitutes an important part of the Museo del Traje's method, often providing the only information available in the absence of other sources to help contextualize the piece. The information gathered is compared and contrasted with an initial formal material analysis, and ultimately informs acceptance (or rejection) of each piece.

Once an object is accepted, the in-depth analysis begins. Curators, textile specialists, and conservators all participate in the process. This multidisciplinary approach seeks both to outline the historical context of the piece, and to establish preventive conservation measures. The study of the items as material culture is complemented with the interpretative tools of disciplines such as history and art history, political economy, industrial techniques and materials, cultural studies, fashion studies, and gender studies, to name a few relevant fields. The resulting analysis from this work seeks to validate the significance of the piece and insert it into the broader cultural history of its time. This phase is not limited to the museum alone. As a public institution, the museum welcomes external researchers who support its work, and facilitates their access to collections. The final step in this phase comes when the museum's multidisciplinary team of specialists discusses possible future temporary or permanent displays in which the new acquisition could be featured.

The commitment to today's fashion, as stated in the museum's mission statement, was initially carried out through exhibitions and round table discussions with designers that were open to the general public.[13] The first significant exhibition that included prêt-à-porter creations as a part of Spanish culture was *Genio y Figura. La influencia de la cultura española en la moda* (Genius and Figure. The Influence of Spanish Culture on Fashion) which opened in 2006 and was curated by Manuel Outumuro.[14] This renowned fashion photographer established a dialogue between works of art and fashion pieces of different time periods using some of the most recognizable images of Spanish culture. Thanks to his extensive experience working with Spain's best designers, Outumuro included pieces by Manuel Piña, Sybilla, Jesús del Pozo, and Francis Montesinos in the exhibition, highlighting the dialogue between contemporary designers and local traditions.

In 2008, the museum held its first retrospective exhibition of Spanish fashion devoted to a living designer: Elio Berhanyer (1929–2019). Sociologist and journalist Pedro Mansilla, who has chronicled Madrid's fashion scene since the 1980s, curated this exhibition. Berhanyer was renowned for his *alta costura* designs as well as his signature designs for mass production, a niche in which he was a pioneer in Spain. Berhanyer revamped the fashion language and communication strategies of his time and experienced his most significant professional success at the New York World's Fair in 1964–5. He was one of the few Spanish designers whose atelier produced popular trends.

Berhanyer is one of the first Spanish designers in the modern sense. In contrast to Balenciaga, who could masterfully carry out the entire process of making a garment from idea to pattern and from pattern to cutting and sewing, Berhanyer confessed, "I do not know how to sew a button." He exemplifies the modern designer focused exclusively on the concept, leaving the process and production to other professionals.[15] Berhanyer's architectural but organic language, composed of basic shapes and vast stretches of color, as well as his early adoption of recognizable branding, fit perfectly with the mass-production model. By 1970, he had diversified his manufacturing initiatives by creating prêt-à-porter clothing lines for the Spanish market. Despite the research carried out for the exhibition project and catalog (*Elio Berhanyer* 2008), significant gaps in scholarship regarding the transition from *alta costura* to a ready-to-wear mass market remain, offering an exciting field to analyze the transformation of Spanish fashion.

Thanks to the success of the Berhanyer exhibition and the growing awareness of the relevance of Spanish fashion, donations to the museum have greatly increased. Noticeable among these are donations from national prêt-à-porter firms. The creation of the National Fashion Design Award in 2009 by the Spanish Ministry of Culture further expanded the fashion industry's visibility in the collective consciousness.[16]

The Museo del Traje has continued to evolve under the leadership of fashion curator Helena López de Hierro, who was appointed director in 2011. She launched a new strategic plan, marking a new era in the institution's history. From that point on, the museum has prioritized research efforts aimed at clarifying and displaying the history of Spanish prêt-à-porter fashion, and has organized public activities to promote it. López de Hierro and her team's strategic plan aims to raise public awareness of the museum's identity as an institution focused on dress and fashion. This means that the museum's original focus on ethnography has shifted to fashion, and as a result, on hiring the necessary staff to carry out the reinvigorated mission. A reassessment was made in all sections of the collections department to reflect upon, analyze, and identify their respective strengths. Due to the rapid growth of the collection since 2004, a new policy was established to prioritize contemporary fashion. This updated policy will also be reflected in the program of exhibitions and activities. If until 2011, the curatorship of exhibitions dedicated to Spanish fashion had been based on external initiatives, from this moment on, the projects would be the result of internal research.

The plan also formalized relationships with the fashion industry and scholars focusing on dress and fashion, and sought to promote joint initiatives with local, national, and international universities. This recent period has seen the museum integrate into a network of relationships including business initiatives such as the abovementioned ACME, the Mercedes-Benz Fashion Week in Madrid (the museum leadership forms part of the selection committee), and organizations dedicated to sustainability such as Ecoembes and Slow Fashion Next. Outreach and collaborations also include higher education centers such as fashion design schools, university departments, foundations and museums, and fashion journals, to name a few. Joining these networks has allowed the Museo del Traje to become a point of confluence and a space for reflection for fashion cultural communities in Spain and abroad.[17]

The first major initiative aimed at recovering the history of Spanish prêt-à-porter fashion was launched in 2012. It began with a research project on Manuel Piña, one of the key designers from the 1980s. The resulting exhibition *Manuel Piña, diseñador de moda (1944–1994)* (Manuel Piña, Fashion Designer) opened in 2013, curated by Concha Herranz and me. We secured the collaboration of the Museo Manuel Piña (Manzanares, Ciudad Real), which holds many pieces donated by the designer in addition to an extensive archive. Using materials on loan, the fifty items by this designer kept at the Museo del Traje, along with information and objects collected through several months of fieldwork, it was possible to reconstruct his career. Without formal apprenticeships in design, Piña progressed from salesperson to manufacturer and only later to designer.[18] His professional development exemplifies the informal circumstances in which the Spanish prêt-à-porter industry evolved.

After the Manuel Piña exhibition, the museum continued to work on fashion analysis of the post-1975 democratic period, and developed another exhibition with a more ambitious idea. The intention was to update the historiography from the 1987 *España, 50 años de Moda* exhibition to include and appraise design that emerged in the 1970s and 1980s with a wider lens. The temporary exhibition *España de Moda* (2014) re-contextualized the museum's collections, and used documentation from the museum's library and archives, particularly fashion journals. Although there was no catalog, the exhibition attained worldwide digital dissemination when it was included in *Google Arts & Culture*, where some of the content is available to the public.[19] This platform has made it possible to share some of the research conclusions, which detailed the origins of the Spanish fashion industry. The exhibition offered an integrative view of *alta costura*, prêt-à-porter, and fast fashion, along with a display of the pop aesthetics and consumer material culture that permeated Spain from the 1960s.

The Museo del Traje's research on Berhanyer, Piña, and other designers has led to an extensive historiographical review of the industry's evolution, and by extension, to an innovative reading of the museum's permanent collection (2015–18). Spanish fashion produced after 1970 did not appear in the permanent collection until 2015. In that year, the Museo del Traje extended its treatment of Spanish fashion to include recent history, which now covers up to the present day. The galleries now explain not only the rise of Spanish *alta costura* during the Franco era but also the emergence and evolution of mass-produced prêt-à-porter, a particularly strong industry in Spain. By broadening the perspective, and including apparel from department stores, decades of Spanish fashion and its history were added to the narrative.

As a result, the museum's permanent displays now present two key eras corresponding respectively to the final decades of Franco's regime and the restoration of the constitutional regime in 1975. The gallery section on the twentieth century includes the period of growth that took place from 1959 with the State "Development Plans," which drove the Spanish economy until the industrial reorganization that began with the textile sector in 1981.[20] During this time, many pioneering initiatives were established, such as *Moda del Sol* (a textile and clothing association created in 1963) and *Moda del Mediterráneo* (a trade show and fashion runway between 1977 and 1983), in addition to fashion journals such as *Vestirama* (1971) and *Centro Moda* (1972). Concurrent with these initiatives, the language of fashion photography was renewed by Leopoldo Pomés, Oriol Maspons, Antoni Bernad, Gianni Ruggiero and others (see chapter four). Above all, the museum presents fashion design as a professional field, and includes in its exhibits such pioneering designers as Esteban Pila, José María Fillol, Andrés Andreu, and Juanjo Rocafort. [21]

The second period represented in the museum collection started in the 1980s when prêt-à-porter designers stepped into the national spotlight and the industry began to assume its current form. Fashion became a critical instrument in what Guillem Martínez referred to as the "culture of the Transition" (2012), as well as in what Giulia Quaggio termed "socialist culture" (2014)—the years when the PSOE, the Spanish Socialist Worker's Party, attempted to update the national image by promoting cultural expression.

At this point in time, the museum's goal is to offer a comprehensive yet concise view of the evolution of Spanish ready-to-wear, and to explore the implications of fashion within its historical context by connecting the multiple events and actors involved in developing fashion labels and design. One pivotal year in that history is 1985. In that year, the government implemented the *Plan for Promoting Design and Fashion: Intangibles-Textiles*, which forged a new relationship between the fashion industry and the government (Ministerio de Industria y Energía).[22] Among other initiatives, this plan helped to establish and support Spain's two major fashion shows: Gaudí (established February 1984, currently called "080 Barcelona Fashion") and Cibeles (called "Pasarela Cibeles" from 1985 to 2008; "Cibeles Madrid Fashion Week" 2008–12; and now known as "Mercedes-Benz Fashion Week"). Both shows established themselves by highlighting leading Spanish designers and international brands. Although economic and structural issues ultimately prevented many 1980s Spanish designers and labels from being successful, the Gaudí and Cibeles fashion shows have managed to survive to this day.[23] Despite its tribulations, the period between the Transition and the early years of democracy was a crucial moment for introducing new dress codes and modern approaches to fashion creation in the artistic, industrial, and commercial arenas.

During the Transition, fashion design grew in popularity while multiple creative fields—literature, film, music, visual arts, and photography—explored personal and collective modes of self-expression that had been limited during the dictatorship. Germán Labrador describes this process of personal and collective autonomy, democratization, and creativity in his study of underground literary movements during the Transition (2017: 201). The political and cultural processes moving Spanish society away from the uniformity imposed by Franco's dictatorship, as well as the "emergence of new subjects," such as the queer community (Smith 2000: 2), created the perfect breeding ground for fashion to evolve. In addition to the development of the ready-to-wear industry, unconventional social behaviors and the liberation from the strict dress codes of the former regime paved the way for the success of Spanish fashion. Identity-oriented fashions, such as subcultural styles and subjective interpretations of their codes, appeared on the streets as a sign of restored liberties in public spaces. People using the codes of subcultures to express their own identity through personal image and style began to spread even before the birth of the collective cultural phenomenon known as *la Movida*, whose reverberations in mass media helped to popularize those styles. One of *la Movida*'s "stars" was the multidisciplinary creator Tino Casal, to whom the Museo del Traje dedicated a retrospective exhibition in 2017.

The singer, composer, producer, artist, sculptor, designer, and stylist Tino Casal (1950–91) was known for his ability, much like David Bowie or Madonna, to transform his public persona. The Tino Casal exhibition project (2017) studied the transformations of Spanish fashion from a contemporary perspective. The biography of this polymath musician shows that, since his earliest days, Casal understood and employed advanced concepts to develop a public persona that served both his identity and his commercial ventures. From the mid-1960s on, Casal started to shape his identity in a paradigmatic case of "authentic inauthenticity" (Grossberg 1988: 136), an approach that considers personal image as a flexible language to express personal subjectivity. He showed a notable tendency toward accumulation and excess (Gutiérrez 2017: 39–44).

Gathering references from a range of alternative aesthetics, Casal created a visual universe that amplified his public and private image. For instance, his direct contact with the latest trends emerging from London allowed him to adopt features of Edwardian, glam, punk, and neo-Romantic styles. These he mixed with local Spanish garments and fetishes related to the esoteric and religious.[24] His successful career, despite his somewhat marginal status given the difficulty that the record industry encountered in labeling and marketing such an eclectic persona, must be attributed in large part to the visual and conceptual impact he caused. His commitment to radical differentiation, fidelity to imposture, and sexual ambiguity led the Spanish mainstream media to push him to the margins. So that the wider public could experience Casal's unique story, the museum gathered more than 300 pieces, including garments, visual art, mass media, and decorative objects. The research behind the exhibition, as well as its conclusions (which are published in the exhibition catalog) reveal Casal to be a key, albeit underestimated, figure for understanding Spanish culture in the 1980s (Gutiérrez 2017).

Exhibiting Antonio Alvarado

Antonio Alvarado was a close friend of Casal and produced some of the exotic designs he wore (Gutiérrez 2017: 107, 121, 153). Born in 1954, Alvarado is one of the most significant and unique designers in Spain. He entered the fashion world in the 1970s, and toward the end of that decade, he participated with his *Polo de Limón* label at the *Moda del Mediterráneo* runway, forerunner of the aforementioned major fashion shows that took off in the mid-1980s. Alongside Antonio Miró, Daniel Carbocci, Pedro Morago, and Francis Montesinos, Alvarado belonged to the generation that developed signature design firms.[25] Early on, he employed a unique lexicon that would transform him into the enfant terrible of Madrid's fashion scene. Alvarado's work followed principles of camp, an aesthetic that would be adopted by many in *la Movida*. In the Spanish case, reappropriating religious symbols and popular folklore—the dominant archetypes of Francoist culture—underscored the break with dictatorship (García-Torvisco 2010). The newfound freedom in fashion practices during the early stages of democracy allowed designers like Alvarado to radicalize their collections by playing with signifiers that until then had been outside the fashion vernacular.

Fashion as a conscious communicational practice was a concept introduced in Spain during the 1970s by individuals like Casal, whose DIY practices played a key role in Alvarado's work. Traditional tailoring—Alvarado's technical mastery can be seen in many of his pieces—was combined with punk influences through deconstruction, assemblage, and collage, all mixed together with the intention of scandalizing the establishment. The titles of Alvarado's early collections and of his shows held in Madrid's Rock-Ola concert venue (the epicenter of *la Movida*) reflect this irreverent attitude toward fashion. For example, the "Baja Costura" ("Low Couture" 1981) collection plays with double meanings. On the one hand "Baja Costura" plays implicitly off both the Spanish term *alta costura* and the French term "haute couture"; yet it also alludes to the fact that Spain is a country located bajo ("below," or "south of") France. The title was intended neither to endorse traditional hierarchies of prestige nor to dismiss Spanish fashion as of lower quality. Rather, Alvarado was making a strong and playful statement about a completely different fashion made in the South and capable of competing at the highest level.

One of Alvarado's very first shows in Madrid, titled "Pitita presenta..." (1980), alluded ironically to the wealthy customers still loyal to traditional couture, for by the 1980s, bespoke couture was less in demand.[26] From the early 1980s on,

Alvarado's iconoclastic approach was aligned with the international avant garde of that era. He reinterpreted the classically tailored suits of Chanel with a punk sensibility, and later did the same with one of Franco Moschino's. He also made Pop-Art versions of popular Spanish kitsch iconography taken from flamenco, bullfighting, or Catholic rituals. Finally, everyday objects became fashion accessories, such as his popular *baguette* bags made of discarded vehicle license plates. Alvarado's reputation for redefining Spanish fashion was magnified thanks to his interactions with those involved in *la Movida*. He dressed the pop group Mecano, Tino Casal, and Alaska—three popular music icons covered extensively by the media, thanks in part to their striking personas.[27] Among many other projects, Alvarado designed the wardrobe for the film *Women on the Verge of a Nervous Breakdown* (Pedro Almodóvar 1988).

After retiring from the catwalks in 2011, in 2014 Alvarado turned to documenting and preserving his legacy. His awareness of his work's ephemeral nature, coupled with the limited number of designs he had preserved, gave rise to this latest endeavor.[28] Between 2014 and 2018, Alvarado gathered information from almost 100 clients, documenting the location of his pieces in private wardrobes. Following this period of research, Alvarado contacted the Museo del Traje to apply professional standards to the documentation, study, and conservation of his work.

Thanks to Alvarado's motivation, the museum has launched a research project that may culminate in another retrospective exhibition. To carry out this initiative, we adopted the interdisciplinary methodology developed in previous projects, including interviews with his many customers and collaborators. The original number of fifteen Alvarado pieces owned by the museum has increased to 233 garments loaned, as of 2020, by different lenders for analysis. As an example of the challenges of this project, there are some pieces attributed to Alvarado of which he has no recollection. Other documented pieces, furthermore, have been found to be missing.[29] The discovery of these forgotten pieces has only been possible thanks to a detailed charting of Alvarado's career and personal interviews with the collaborators, friends, or clients who were at his side at the time of creation and manufacture. As the designer's biography is researched, the collected items are individually described and catalogued by the museum's curators and assistant curators, whose efforts also include studying privately owned collections outside of the museum.[30]

Alvarado's project exemplifies the type of work that the Museo del Traje carries out. With any donation or acquisition, the curators in charge write a brief description of the designer's career and contextualize it within the history of

Spanish fashion. In the same document, the curator makes a formal analysis that highlights (a) the intrinsic value of the piece and its qualities as a fashion item, (b) the connection with the formal trends of the moment, and (c) the first hypotheses about the symbolic value of the design within its historical context. The report may include data culled from interviews, which will later be verified and cross-referenced. Regardless of the information obtained during these first steps of the evaluation, the curators follow Prown's method (1982), which includes three stages: description, deduction, and speculation, after which the contextualization phase can begin through external evidence and with the support of archival material. In this way, the first descriptive analysis carried out is "substantial" (Prown 1982: 7–8), a physical analysis which is absolutely required for conservation and quite useful for fashion historians because it provides them with essential context for their work.

Alvarado's ensembles reveal interesting qualities in this first stage: the use of silk with a synthetic mixture in patterned fabric for men; high-quality cotton and wool textiles, dyed in different tones due to exhaustive production controls; and the presence of nontextile materials without any functional purpose. His work displays Spanish iconography, as observed in a women's ensemble from the museum collection (MT104140-MT104143): the jacket presents a map of the Iberian Peninsula with a red star, and the text "TACÓN AMARGO" ("bitter heel") referring to the tragic pathos of flamenco crosses the tie vertically from the same ensemble. The textile label itself, sewed to the collar, presents the silhouette of a flamenco dancer standing over the map of Spain. The asymmetrical ruffles of her skirt cannot move because of the stitches and heavy textile that were used. Alvarado's "fight of opposites" develops a dialectic of tradition versus modernity that equally emerges in his material selection, contrasting rough/soft, precious/cheap, or heavy/light, compelling the wearer to extract meanings from materiality (Woodward 2015). Alvarado's designs thus offer different levels of reading and understanding that must be considered in order to integrate the symbolic and material aspects of his designs into a coherent narrative.

Later phases of analysis comprise sensory engagement, along with intellectual and emotional responses. The "ghost labor" of fashion conservation takes place (Scaturro 2018: 23–7) in the museum workshops, where close contact with the pieces gives valuable information to the curator, in dialogue with conservators and restorers. To understand Alvarado's effort to combine style and comfort, his designs must be studied in terms of their functionality: the sensuality of shapes and textures as against the protection the garment provides. At the same time, an intellectual approach must consider the provocative nature of some of Alvarado's garments. As the ensemble described above illustrates, his work often appropriates symbols formerly associated with Franco's regime, offering a social and political message about the cultural overhaul of the Transition. In turn, the curator needs to evaluate the complicity of those clients willing to transfer this semantic load to the general public by wearing Alvarado's creations. It is at this point that the emotional response sought by the designer comes into play. For instance, the ensemble illustrated here is harmonious in its lines and faithful to certain conventions of elegance, but harsh in detail to the point of breaking the traditional aesthetic balance.

One suggestive conclusion that arises from analyzing these pieces is their apparent ambivalence: they reflect the juxtaposition of classic tailoring with the street aesthetic that characterized some *la Movida* productions, or hybrids that mix Spanish iconography with American "preppy style." Vacillating between these distant poles maintains the tension between the neatness of tailoring with (often disheveled) DIY aesthetics. Alvarado's work represents prêt-à-porter of the highest quality, carefully produced, and directed to an exclusive and elitist niche market. Further research needs to be conducted to explain how exactly these two extremes find their balance in the context of *la Movida* and the mainstreaming of underground culture in 1980s Spain. The ultimate goal of the future exhibition will be to accurately position the designer's work within Spanish cultural, social, and political circumstances during the Transition. While the Museo del Traje explores the transformations that took place at this pivotal time of Spanish history as expressed in fashion, it continues to develop analysis and exhibition methods in search of a more embodied approach to fashion (Pecorari 2018: 194).

Conclusion

Over time, the Museo del Traje has refined its methodology for documenting and studying Spanish fashion. Though it started out with an ethnographic framework guiding its initial collections, the museum has introduced methodologies specific to fashion studies in recent years. One challenge faced by the museum was the lack of established fashion studies as a comprehensive discipline at the university level in Spain. The museum solved this problem by conducting research through temporary exhibitions, which allowed a methodology to emerge, one inspired by tools borrowed from Anthropology, Art History, and Sociology.

Since its foundation in 2004, the Museo del Traje has sought to establish a narrative of the history of Spanish fashion, in parallel to starting and developing a collection of items that represents this history. Because of the museum's role as a public institution, research and the dissemination of contemporary fashion collections through exhibitions have been carried out simultaneously. This work has served to define the evolution of fashion in Spain, from *alta costura* to mass production, while strengthening public awareness of the value of fashion as cultural heritage.

Recent Spanish historiography owes a debt to fashion, whose impact on the arts and culture at large is often underestimated. The museum highlights the role of ready-to-wear and of the new identities that emerged during the Transition, when a new democratic sensibility was materializing. Concurrent changes in film, music, photography, and the visual arts are crucial to understanding the context of ready-to-wear in this period. Furthermore, in the midst of social transformations in Spain in recent decades, fashion design has gained a relevance that the Museo del Traje continues to explore, in hopes that the academic world will pay due attention to a subject that has too often been relegated to oblivion.

Notes

1 The museum was founded as Museo del Traje, CIPE (Centro de Investigación del Patrimonio Etnológico), by the Spanish Ministry of Culture and Sports. It is housed in a prize-winning building designed in 1969 by architects Jaime López de Asiaín and Ángel Díaz Domínguez. Purposely built as a museum, the building was originally home to the Spanish Contemporary Art Museum until 1986, when the Museo Nacional Centro de Arte Reina Sofía was founded.

2 Luis de Hoyos joined the project to fill the role of the deceased Juan Comba García, who had held the first research chair created in Spain at the Real Conservatorio de Música y Declamación. A painter and illustrator, Juan Comba García was a pioneer of fashion studies in Spain. He wrote two unpublished works on the history of fashion: *Historia del traje en España y de las artes suntuarias españolas* and *La indumentaria del reinado de Felipe IV en los cuadros de Velázquez del Museo del Prado*. For more see Soria (2012).

3 For additional information about Luis de Hoyos's career, see Ortiz García (1988).

4 The exhibition guide contained information about the methods used, which were described as "comparisons of human geography," and highlighted the value of dress as a "geo-ethnographic" element. *Guía. Exposición del Traje Regional*, Madrid, 1925.

5   The collection was guided by the *Instrucciones para la recogida de datos y objetos en aras de salvaguardar el traje nacional,* in which Luis de Hoyos defined a method that gave priority to gathering empirical data. Regarding the ideological bias of interpretations during the years when folklore was at its peak, Joan Prat has pointed out that the "objectives were, to put it mildly, manipulated to such a degree by other non-scientific objectives that it is difficult to situate them in a relatively neutral 'scientific' perspective" (1991: 27).

6   Even though the museum was closed, the collection kept growing and research efforts continued, but the marginal position of the institution resulted in a lack of definition of its methods and purposes. For more than ten years (1942–53), the museum was led by Julio Caro Baroja. In an article published by the newspaper *El País* (Caro Baroja 1977), this famous anthropologist documented the state of neglect experienced by the institution over several decades.

7   This team included scholars and specialists such as Amelia Leira, Dr. Amalia Descalzo, Dr. Mercedes Pasalodos, Lucina Llorente, Juan Antonio Rodríguez Menéndez and Concha Herranz. For information on the museum's original setup, see the first number of *Indumenta,* the museum journal (2007).

8   The exhibition never opened. The participating designers, however, donated the collected pieces so they could form part of the future Spanish fashion museum. For more see García Serrano (2010: 43–46).

9   According to numbers from the museum database, between 1934 and 2003, a total of 92,553 pieces were received, of which 13,294 were classified as "clothing." From 2004 to the present day, the museum has acquired 29,782 pieces, of which more than half belonged to the clothing category. The numbers represent a new focus giving priority to prêt-à-porter over regional and historical garments.

10 Luis Casablanca's doctoral dissertation on Jesús del Pozo's career (Casablanca 2007) and Francis Montesinos's catalog (IVAM 2004) are the only in-depth approaches to Spanish designers' work, along with overviews by journalists such as Lola Gavarrón (1982), Rosa María Pereda (1986) and Josefina Figueras (2011), and the vast handbook by Francisco de Sousa (2007) who broadly but superficially covered the topic at hand.

11 The exhibition, curated by Pilar Garrigosa, was originally the idea of fashion designer Margarita Nuez. Rosa María Martín i Ros was the exhibition adviser. It established the first timeline of its kind for Spanish fashion, recovering forgotten names and paying special attention to prêt-à-porter designers.

12 The museum does not have a budget line to purchase new items. The decision and funds to acquire new objects comes from the Ministry of Culture and Education. There, the *Junta de Calificación, Valoración y Exportación de Bienes del Patrimonio Histórico Español* (Board for the Qualification, Valuation, and Export of Spanish Historical Patrimony) approves each purchase after reviewing the application

and technical brief produced by the museum. The museum competes for these funds with all other museums under the administrative purview of the Ministry of Culture.

13 "Showcasing the historical evolution of fashion; analyzing its technical, social, ideological and creative implications through diversity and ever-changing fashion trends; and combining the necessary informative elements with actual exhibits, from the oldest eras that can be documented through the present day which should be permanent; and chronicling the evolution and achievements of contemporary fashion design"(Museo del Traje website: www.culturaydeporte.gob.es/mtraje/m useo/mision.html [accessed September 30, 2018] [Translation by the author]).

14 For more information, see Ana Cabrera and Lesley Miller (2009).

15 Stated by the designer in the documentary *Elio Berhanyer, maestro del diseño* (2013, directed by Diego Galán, España: Altube Filmeak, and Dos de Catorce Producciones).

16 The three first awards went to Manuel Pertegaz, Paco Rabanne, and Berhanyer. That Rabanne, a Basque-born designer like Balenciaga, received this award shows the interest in establishing a wider historical perspective on Spanish fashion in which a leading figure such as Rabanne, despite his French career, is recognized as a national figure.

17 Full information is available on the website: www.culturaydeporte.gob.es/mtraje/i nicio.html

18 Unfortunately, it was not possible to print the catalog due to a lack of funding, although the curators wrote the corresponding *Modelo del Mes* (Gutiérrez 2013; Herranz 2014). Since 2004, the *Modelo del Mes* is a short lecture held in the museum galleries critically highlighting the important pieces displayed. Attendees receive a free printed copy summarizing the conference (the lecture notes can be found at: www.culturaydeporte.gob.es/mtraje/biblioteca/publicaciones/publicacion es-periodicas/modelo-mes/ediciones-anteriores.html)

19 To see this online: *España de moda: los diseñadores contemporáneos crean marca*, Google Arts & Culture, available online: https://artsandculture.google.com/exhibit/ uQJCmYCGMyawKA?hl=es (accessed October 20, 2018).

20 This plan marked the first time that a clear understanding of fashion's intangible value was put into words, and since then it has received strong institutional support: "The plan promotes improving the production, financial and commercial infrastructures. It facilitates adapting supply to demand variations; fosters other competitive factors, such as textile technology and the use of design, fashion, brand and quality as competitive tools to create markets; and provides incentives for improving corporate structures and management techniques" (published in BOE [*Spanish Official State Gazette*] no. 217, September 10, 1981, 20843–20846).

21 During his short career, Esteban Pila (Sant Cugat, 1937–Torredembarra, 1968) led the renovation of male fashion; José María Fillol (1928–2019) was the creative

director of the collective brand *Moda del Sol* for more than thirty years; Andrés Andreu (Tarragona, 1940); designed *alta costura* and started with prêt-à-porter from 1966; Juanjo Rocafort (Madrid, 1943) was renowned as the only youth fashion designer in Madrid during the 1960s.

22 See Feito (1986) for an explanation of the reasons that led to the plan's creation.

23 The institutional support strategy for Spanish fashion undergoes an accurate comparative critique in Gimeno-Martínez (2011).

24 For example, Casal used to dress in Vivienne Westwood's "Pirates" collection pieces, which he combined with a traditional *zamorana* blanket adapted by designer Pepe Rubio, and exotic furs (Gutiérrez 2017: 82–99).

25 Miró (Barcelona, 1947), Carbocci (Burdeos, 1947), Morago (Valladolid, 1943) and Montesinos (Valencia, 1950) spearheaded a new approach to fashion design and industrial production in the 1970s. They were commercially successful under their own brands (Antonio Miró, Francis Montesinos) or designing for labels such as Falstaff, 11 3 42 or Maíz.

26 In colloquial terms, the word "pitita" continues to be used when referring to an older woman with a conservative yet sophisticated look. The word originally referred to Esperanza "Pitita" Ridruejo (Madrid, 1930–2019), a renowned member of Spain's high society.

27 Mecano, made up of brothers Cano and Ana Torroja, was the most popular pop band in Spain. Their initial style, commissioned by producer Miguel Ángel Arenas "Capi" to Alvarado, reflected the new romantic style. Casal and Alaska, both main figures in Spanish pop music during the 1980s and local media icons, frequently requested Alvarado's services.

28 It could be said that despite its key role during *la Movida* era, fashion has been late to join what is known as the "accelerated fossilization process," a characteristic phenomenon on the redefinition of recent Spanish culture (Bermúdez 2009).

29 This is not surprising given the zeitgeist of the moment. Alvarado was one of the most active people in Madrid's nightlife scene during *la Movida* era, and as he has stated on numerous occasions: "When I presented 'La Santa Faz' at Cibeles, I didn't sleep for ten days" (Gallero 1991: 190).

30 This task had already been started by the museum before the collaboration with Alvarado. The first notes used to reconstruct Alvarado's career are available online in Gutiérrez (2016).

References

Bermúdez, Silvia (2009), "Memoria y archivo: La Movida, Alaska y procesos de arqueología cultural," *Arizona Journal of Hispanic Cultural Studies* 13: 107–81.

Berges Soriano, Pedro (1996), "El Museo del Pueblo Español," *Anales del Museo Nacional de Antropología* III: 65–88, Madrid: Dirección General de Bellas Artes.

Cabrera, Ana and Miller, Lesley (2009), "Exhibition Review: *Genio y Figura. La influencia de la cultura española en la moda*," *Fashion Theory* 13:1, 103–10, DOI: 10.2752/175174109X381391

Caro Baroja, Julio (1977), "Instituciones 'corpore insepulto'," *El País*, December 13. Available online: https://elpais.com/diario/1977/12/13/opinion/250815602_850215 .html (accessed on October 16, 2018).

Carretero Pérez, Andrés (2002), "Colecciones a raudales," *Anales del Museo Nacional de Antropología* IX: 13–37, Madrid: Dirección General de Bellas Artes.

Carretero Pérez, Andrés (2004), "El Museo del Traje. Centro de Investigación del Patrimonio Etnológico," *Revista de Museología* 29: 88–95.

Carretero Pérez, Andrés (2007), "El Museo del Traje: breve Presentación," *Indumenta. Revista del Museo del Traje* 00: 13–22, Madrid: Secretaría General Técnica, Ministerio de Cultura.

Casablanca Migueles, Luis (2007), *La moda como disciplina artística en España: Jesús del Pozo y la generación de los nuevos creadores*, PhD diss., Universidad de Granada.

Comín, María Pilar et al. (1987), *España, 50 años de moda* (1987), Barcelona: Regidoria d'Edicions I Publicacions, Ajuntament de Barcelona.

Feito, Miguel Ángel (1986), "Las razones de la política de promoción de diseño y moda," *Análisis e Investigaciones Culturales. Moda española*, 11–18, Madrid: Secretaría General Técnica, Ministerio de Cultura.

Figueras, Josefina (2011), *Moda española: una historia de sueños y realidades*, Madrid: Ediciones Internacionales Universitarias.

Gallero, José Luis (1991), *Solo se vive una vez. Esplendor y ruina de la movida madrileña*, Madrid: Árdora.

García-Hoz, Concha (2016), "El traje popular como objeto cultural: la exposición de 1925," in *Carbón y terciopelo: miradas sobre el traje popular*, 14–23, Getaria: Fundación Cristóbal Balenciaga.

García Serrano, Rafael (2010), "The Museo del Traje in Madrid," *Her & Mus* 5, II (3): 43–6.

García Torvisco, Luis (2010), "La narrativización del excesivo yo de la 'Movida' en Patty Diphusa (1983–1984) de Pedro Almodóvar," *Actas del XVI Congreso de la Asociación Internacional de Hispanistas. Nuevos caminos del hispanismo* Vol. 2: [CD-ROM], España: Iberoamericana.

Gavarrón, Lola (1982), *Mil caras tiene la moda*, Madrid: Pentathlon Ediciones.

Gimeno-Martínez, Javier (2011), "Restructuring Plans for the Textile and Clothing Sector in Post-industrial Belgium and Spain," *Fashion Practice* 3 (2): 197–223, London: Routledge.

Grossberg, Lawrence (1988), "Rockin' with Reagan, or the Mainstreaming of Postmodernity," *Cultural Critique* 10: 123–49, University of Minnesota Press.

Gutiérrez, Juan (2013), "Conjunto de Manuel Piña, 1982," Museo del Traje. Available online: www.culturaydeporte.gob.es/mtraje/dam/jcr:00eacdb4-953f-4f9c-a272-718a 2c2425dd/12-2013.pdf (accessed on July 30, 2019).

Gutiérrez, Juan (2016), "Conjunto para hombre, de Antonio Alvarado, 1987," Museo del Traje. Available online: www.mecd.gob.es/mtraje/dms/museos/mtraje/biblioteca/pub licaciones/publicaciones-periodicas/modelo-mes/ediciones-anteriores/2016/05-2016 .pdf (accessed on 30 June 2018).

Gutiérrez, Juan (2017), *Tino Casal. El arte por exceso*, Madrid: Ministry of Education, Culture and Sports. Documents and Publications Office.

Herranz, Concha (2014), "Jersey de Manuel Piña, 1986," Museo del Traje. Available online: www.culturaydeporte.gob.es/mtraje/dam/jcr:8f71e07f-db52-408f-ab07-782a eeac400b/01-2014.pdf (accessed July 30, 2019).

Hoyos Sainz, Luis de (1922), "Etnografía española: cuestionario y bases para el estudio de los trajes regionales," *Actas y Memorias. Sociedad Española de Antropología, Etnografía y Prehistoria*, Vol. I: 91–128, Madrid: National Anthropology Museum.

IVAM (Institut Valenciá d'Art Modern) (2004), *Francis Montesinos. Catálogo razonado 1972–2003*, Valencia: Institut Valenciá d'Art Modern.

Labrador, German (2017), *Culpables por la literatura. Imaginación política y contracultura en la transición española (1968–1986)*, Madrid: Akal.

Mansilla, Pedro et al. (2008), *Elio Berhanyer, 50 años de moda* (2008), Madrid: Subdirección General de Promoción de las Bellas Artes.

Marí, Jorge (2009), "La Movida como Debate," *Arizona Journal of Hispanic Cultural Studies* 13: 127–41.

Martínez, Guillem (ed.) (2012), *CT o la cultura de Transición. Crítica a 35 años de cultura española*, Barcelona: Debolsillo.

Mata Torrado, Francisco Manuel (2003), "Las exposiciones temporales de moda," *Museo. Revista de la Asociación Profesional de Museólogos de España* 8: 227–34.

Miller, Daniel (2005), "Introduction," in Susanne Küchler and Daniel Miller (eds), *Clothing as Material Culture*, 1–19, Oxford: Berg.

Ministerio de Cultura (2007), *Indumenta, Revista del Museo del Traje*, No. 00, Madrid: Secretaría General Técnica. Ministerio de Cultura.

Ministerio de Industria y Energía (1985), *Plan de Promoción de Diseño y Moda. Intangibles-Textiles*, Madrid: Ministerio de Industria y Energía.

Nichols, William J. and H. Rosi Song (2014), "Back to the Future: Towards a Cultural Archive of La Movida," in William J. Nichols and H. Rosi Song (eds.), *Toward a Cultural Archive of la Movida: Back to the Future*, 1–15, New Jersey: Farleigh Dickinson University Press.

Ortiz García, Carmen (1988), "Luis de Hoyos Sainz. Founder of the National Museum of Spanish People," *Anales del Museo del Pueblo Español*, Vol. IV: 147–68, Madrid: Subdirección General de Promoción de las Bellas Artes.

Pecorari, Marco (2018), "Beyond Garments: Reorienting the Practice and Discourse of Fashion Curating," in Hazel Clark and Annamari Vänskä (eds.), *Fashion Curating. Critical Practice in the Museum and Beyond*, 183–97, London: Bloomsbury.

Pereda, Rosa María (1986), *Vestir en España*, Madrid: Ediciones del Dragón.

Prat, Joan, Martínez, Ubaldo, Contreras, Jesús and Moreno, Isidoro, eds. (1991), *Antropología de los Pueblos de España*, Madrid: Taurus Universitaria.

Prown, Jules D. (1982), "Mind in Matter: An Introduction to Material Culture Theory and Method," *Winterthur Portfolio* 17 (1): 1–19, Chicago: University of Chicago Press.

Quaggio, Giulia (2014), *La cultura en transición. Reconciliación y política cultural en España (1976–1986)*, Madrid: Alianza.

Rocamora, Agnès and Anneke Smelik (2016), "Introduction," in A. Rocamora and A. Smelik (eds), *Thinking through Fashion. A Guide to Key Theorists*, 1–27, London: I. B. Tauris.

Scaturro, Sarah (2018), "Confronting Fashion's Death Drive: Conservation, Ghost Labor, and the Material Turn within Fashion Curation," in H. Clark and A. Vänskä (eds.), *Fashion Curating. Critical Practice in the Museum and Beyond*, 21–38, London: Bloomsbury.

Smith, Paul Julian (2000), *The Moderns. Time, Space and Subjectivity in Contemporary Spanish Culture*, New York: Oxford University Press.

Sociedad Estatal para Exposiciones Internacionales (2005), *Genio y Figura. La influencia de la cultura española en la moda*, Madrid: SEEI.

Soria Tomás, Guadalupe (2012), "Las enseñanzas teatrales en el cambio de siglo: la apertura de la Cátedra de Indumentaria en el conservatorio de música y declamación (1903–1922)," *Don Galán. Revista de Investigación Teatral*, 2. Available online: http://teatro.es/contenidos/donGalan/donGalanNum2/pagina.php?vol=2 &doc=2_5&pag=1 (accessed on October 20, 2018).

Sousa Congosto, Francisco (2007), *Introducción a la historia de la indumentaria en España*, Madrid: Istmo.

Steele, Valerie (1998), "A Museum of Fashion Is More Than a Clothes-Bag," *Fashion Theory* 2 (4): 327–35, Oxford: Berg.

Steele, Valerie (2018), "La calidad del Museo y el auge de la exposición de moda," in A. Palmer and V. Steele (eds.), *Fashion Theory. Hacia una teoría cultural de la moda*, 189–213, Buenos Aires: Ampersand.

Woodward, Sophie (2002), "Making Fashion Material," *Journal of Material Culture* 7 (3): 345–53. Doi: 10.1177/135918350200700305.

Woodward, Sophie (2015), "Object Interviews, Material Imaginings and 'Unsettling' Methods: Interdisciplinary Approaches to Understanding Materials and Material Culture," in *Qualitative Research* 16 (4): 359–74. Doi: 10.1177/1468794115589647.

Curating Catalan Cultural Identity through Dress in the Virtual Fashion Museum of Catalonia

Nicholas Wolters

Introduction

As early as 1883, at the height of the *Renaixença* or "rebirth" of Catalan language, art, culture, and literature, the Town Council of Barcelona began to collect historical textiles and items of clothing with the intention of displaying them publicly. For collectors and exhibitors, dress displays gave visibility to Catalonia's long history as an important center for sartorial production, while also memorializing its commercial and industrial identity and prowess within Spain and transnationally. Collectors and museum directors curated and hosted a number of expositions during the turn of the century and showcased a wide array of items, ranging from the exotic (e.g., swatches of ancient Coptic textiles from Egypt) to the familiar (e.g., Manila shawls, fans, civil and ceremonial dress, and liturgical vestments), all of which suggested Catalonia's historical relevance to domestic and foreign networks of sartorial manufacture and trade (Carreras and Tafunell 2016: 170). The collection and display of historically significant textiles were both made possible by the heterogeneous interests of artists, private collectors, merchants, industrialists, and museum personnel, who tacitly recognized the symbolic weight of clothing in a place where garments and textiles were so much a part of the cultural, social, and economic fabric (Carbonell Basté 2016: 153).

Historical personages like Joaquim Folch i Torres (1886–1955)—director-general of Catalan art museums between 1918 and 1926—and Eusebi Güell i López (1877–1955), for example, played decisive roles in contributing to narratives of Catalan identity through the curation and donation, respectively, of sartorial heritage (Vidal i Jansà 1991: 87; Bassegoda 2016: 68). The interests of prominent specialists, collectors, and donors in extending the life of patrimonial objects through museological activity recall Xavier Roigé Ventura and Iñaki Arrieta Urtizberea's observation that, "all museums, in one way or another, play a decisive role in the definition and reshaping of local, national, and regional identities through the appropriation and valorization of heritage" (2010: 540).[1] In the twenty-first century, new technologies and social media platforms have begun to usher in a variety of innovations related to the preservation and sharing of cultural heritage that go beyond traditional strategies of maintenance of objects in store and on display.

For example, since clothing and textiles are notoriously fragile and difficult to maintain, innovative online solutions to traditional problems associated with the exhibition of sartorial heritage have become attractive and ethical alternatives that also afford wider access to museum objects and the many stories they have to tell.

A particularly illustrative example of such novel approaches is the Virtual Fashion Museum of Catalonia (*Museu Virtual de la Moda de Catalunya*).[2] Inaugurated on March 15, 2018, the sleekly designed Museu Virtual has built up digitized profiles of over 600 clothing items held in physical storage in small, municipal museums scattered throughout Catalonia: from large urban centers like Barcelona and Tarragona to more remote locales such as Esterri d'Anéu (Lleida). With objects whose timelines span the seventeenth to the twenty-first centuries, the meticulously digitized collection of men and women's civil apparel catalogs elegant *robes à la française* from the Ancien Régime, bourgeois capes and vests/jackets dating to the Industrial Revolution, and everyday clothing created by contemporary Catalan fashion designers: all reminders of Catalonia's involvement in the garment industry and, by extension, its place within transnational webs of production and consumption. Not unlike the user-friendly, commercial websites maintained by popular fast-fashion brands like Zara and couture labels like Palomo Spain, each clothing item is reproduced with the help of a number of angle and zoom options and boasts an impressively well-documented datasheet with relevant details about fabric, textures, and cut (to name only a few relevant technical specifications). Accompanied by generous bibliographies and links to other digital archives, entries for individual garments provide the virtual museumgoer with detailed descriptions of historical context that cater to the curiosity and interest of specialists and nonspecialists alike. The brainchild of Walden Group researcher Laura Casal-Valls, and constructed in cooperation with DigitalBakers thanks to a 100,000-euro award from the Fundació Carulla, the Museu Virtual threads together Catalonia's rich contributions to Spain's sartorial and industrial history at the same time that it presents a space for users to imagine and visualize the aspirations of a regional-national space that exists "in a constant process of articulation and construction" (Vialette 2018: 135).

The Museu Virtual represents an effective (if still nascent) solution to questions related to the innovative preservation and display of or access to cultural heritage. The cultural narratives that emerge in the form of an official blog and occasional posts to social media accounts range from the spotlighting of women's "ghost labor" in the creation of clothing and women's sometimes overlooked contributions to the development of the region's history and economy, to Catalan department stores' role as catalysts for the distribution and consumption of fashion in Catalonia and Spain more broadly. Facilitated by the website's intuitive design and layout and integration with platforms like Facebook, Twitter, and Instagram, virtual museumgoers are also encouraged to discover, share, or develop, if they so choose, their own relationship to newly displayed objects once destined to occupy storage in small municipal museums. The Museu Virtual's capacity as both a forum for and container of plural narratives foregrounds the democratic potential of this type of museum, a potentiality that is particularly compelling in a sociopolitical climate in which Catalan cultural identity—along with its erstwhile and current place in Spain and Europe—is in a constant process of legitimization and rearticulation. As we shall see, the Museu Virtual's innovative approaches to and strategies for displaying Catalan heritage (e.g., dynamic visual presentation of archival materials, robust historicization, and active, if still limited presence on social media platforms) speak to the museum's stated mission to restore visibility to previously invisible objects with the intention of encouraging engagement with diverse sets of visitors.

This chapter describes and analyzes the Museu Virtual's museological innovations and strategies in order to shed light on the ways the virtual space functions as an excavation site for cultural narratives that restore the latent historical memory of clothing items previously housed exclusively in underground or offsite storage (where roughly 95 percent of Catalan sartorial heritage remains) (Casal-Valls 2017: 78). Despite the virtual museum's many limitations related to its small social media presence and questionable reach, problems that I will later address and explain, its display of once inaccessible and apparently marginalized archival pieces works toward restoring a "voice to those forgotten objects"—to echo the suggestive language used by Museu Virtual director Laura Casal-Valls upon her receipt of the Fundació Carulla's award that funded the project. The award-winning website's deployment of an attractive and user-friendly interface, its carefully researched and targeted historicizing strategies, along with its dedication to engagement with the public via relevant social media platforms like Instagram invite museumgoers to consider and appreciate the role to be played by once-forgotten objects in the construction of cultural narratives in the Catalan context. Thus, this chapter focuses on the project's museological precedents, aesthetic and historicizing strategies, and social media presence. What it finds is that the Museu Virtual's heterogeneous display of Catalan dress contributes to cultural narratives of regional-national identity that are, at the same time, constitutively interconnected and transnational in character. To be sure, the website and its admittedly limited social media presence fall short of matching the efforts of its public, "brick-and-mortar" analogs—the project is, after all, an aggregator of small municipal museum collections that lacks the resources of larger institutions. However, the Museu Virtual makes up for any shortcomings in its dedication to the ethical and sustainable preservation and display of garments, its capacity for democratic or nonhierarchical access to cultural knowledge, and the visibility it grants to the work carried on behind the scenes in the museum.

Museums as Sites for Identity Narratives

Individual museums may vary according to content, mission, and scope, but their interest in telling the stories of people and their art, belief systems, cities, culture, and inventions make them all generative sites for personal and collective identity formation. While the most famous institutions—such as the Louvre or the Prado—began as ways for monarchies and nations to broadcast imperial might or to shield themselves behind the aegis of a hegemonic or unified image, twenty-first-century museum exhibitions have become, to borrow Tiina Roppola's phrasing, "enticingly complex spaces":

> as facilitators of experience; as free-choice learning contexts; as theatres of drama; as encyclopedic warehouses of cultural and natural heritage; as two-, three- and four-dimensional storytellers and as sites for an engaging day out. A key task for exhibition designers is to sensitively orchestrate interpretive content and interpretive media, in relationship with the overall vessel of the institution's building, so that visitors are supported in meaningful and accessible ways. (Roppola 2012: 6)

In their attempts to meet the interests and needs of individuals and communities in interactive ways—a result of changes in how museums are funded and maintained, to be sure—institutions have begun to supply museumgoers with the information and, in some cases, interpretive tools they might need to make their own experience-based meaning from sporadic or regular visits. Such features range from multiple angles and zoom options, abundant bibliographical suggestions, as well as methods for sharing, commenting upon, or, more generally, interacting with objects. Though the particular features for engaging visitors may vary from space to space, John Falk points out that "whether a [museum] visitor is maintaining or building identity," with these interactive tools, "he or she is actively engaged in using the social and physical context of the museum to make personal meaning" (2006: 162).

In spite of the historical tendency for larger museums to prioritize "grand narratives" of empire or nation, today, the turn toward more personal or polyvalent interactions and narratives—as evidenced by the social media presence and efforts of museums like the Prado or the Museo del Traje— reflects museums' increasing awareness of the need to broaden access while embracing diversity and the pedagogical potential in democratic engagement with culture and the materials through which it is constructed. In Andreas Huyssen's *Twilight Memories*, the author alludes to the need for institutions to insist on the heterogeneity or plurality of historical accounts (as opposed to the grand narratives he sees enshrined in the traditional panoramic museum) in order to reflect the cultural diversity, values, and interests of the modern-day museumgoer, whose identity is, as ever, heterogeneous and intersectional:

> What needs to be captured and theorized today is precisely the ways in which museum and exhibition culture in the broadest sense provides a terrain that can offer multiple narratives of meaning at a time when the metanarratives of modernity, including those inscribed into the universal survey museum itself, have lost their persuasiveness, when more people are eager to hear and see other stories, to hear and see the stories of others, when identities are shaped in multiply layered and never-ceasing negotiations between self and other, rather than being fixed and taken for granted in the framework of family and faith, race and nation. (1994: 34)

Even if they are valuable pursuits for their own sake, Huyssen's considerations are worthwhile in the efforts of institutions to cultivate what Peter Dahlgren and Joke Hermes have coined "cultural citizenship" (2020: 18). For Dahlgren and Hermes, cultural citizenship "elucidates how culture offers the possibility to build and reflect on social cohesion. Popular culture, especially, can make clear to us, its users, what binds us. Key factors are its accessibility, its inclusiveness, its low-threshold offer of 'community' and connection" (2020: 118). Just as turn-of-the-century Catalan collectors and patrons were eager to invest in and display items of dress as signs of cultural or ethnic particularity (or as part of their longing for recognition of Catalonia as a national or imperial space), the Museu Virtual, in a more ideologically ambiguous way, seeks to contextualize and educate Spanish and Catalan speakers about the region's rich cultural heritage. In making it available to those interested in consuming or learning about their past, and the place of that past in the present, as we shall see, the virtual museum promotes a kind of democratic, nonhierarchical engagement with the sartorial heritage to which it gives visibility across its various interfaces: from the website (museudelamoda.cat) itself to its small but growing social media presence.

As mentioned in the introduction of this chapter, costume and fashion museums have often played an important role in the way that Spaniards engage with regional and national identity. As Jesusa Vega articulates in her chapter on the history of physical exhibitions of Spanish dress and fashion, displays of sartorial heritage have historically been a part of "modern Spain's visual construction" (2005: 207). Contributing to this trend, the Museu Virtual identifies dress and fashion as necessary loci for the construction of modern narratives of Catalan identity. While generally applicable across geopolitical contexts, this is especially relevant for Catalonia, given the region's long and significant history as an industrial center for the production, distribution, and consumption of clothing and textiles. For example, as Marta Vicente points out, the transnational networks of manufacture and trade—especially in the case of *indianas* or printed cottons whose networks stretched from the Iberian Peninsula across the Atlantic Ocean—had a profound and dialogic relationship with the values and virtues associated with the private and political lives of Catalans during the eighteenth century, including pride in local commerce and métiers, craftsmanship, and family legacies (2006: 3). In the nineteenth century, between 88 percent and 95 percent of raw cotton that entered Spain was made into cloth in Catalan factories, and by 1900 the vast majority of industrial machinery related to textile manufacturing was located in the prosperous northeastern region: "Thanks to the industrialization process based on the cotton sector, the Catalan economy—unlike that of the rest of Spain—transformed over the course of the nineteenth century into an industrialized economy" (132006: 170).[3] As we will see, even as the Museu Virtual's monographic emphasis on the production, display, and collection of fashion within Catalonia is front and center, it indirectly points to the ways that Catalan cultural identity—at least insofar as it relates to cultural and economic circuits traversed by items of dress and fashion—is constitutively a transnational enterprise.

In the late nineteenth and early twentieth centuries, an increased appreciation for the collection of art and historical fabrics and costume swept Catalonia as it did in the rest of Europe, not least of all because it was during this time that "representation through dress [had] crystallized as the modern way of seeing the nation" (Vega 2005: 208). Sílvia Carbonell Basté observes that during the turn of the century in particular, the collecting craze for historical dress and textiles was not just an esoteric hobby for antiquarians, but it was also considered relevant to attempts at diversifying and promoting the regional economy (2016: 125). While collectors were able to satisfy their appetite for beautiful, valuable pieces of historical interest, cultural producers (e.g., artists, clothiers, and designers) drew inspiration from and capitalized on both domestic and exotic patterns to promote local métiers and industries, thus solidifying the region's identity as a center for sartorial culture. During the turn of the century, wealthy businessmen and industrialists—together with their wives—stored and later donated historical garments for public display in diocesan or municipal museums, some of which constitute the collections whose garments now appear on the Museu Virtual's pages. Donations from prominent bourgeois collectors such as Güell i López and Manuel Rocamora Vidal (1892–1976), to name only two significant examples, became the foundations of displays that now constitute the permanent collections of Madrid's Museo del Traje and Barcelona's Museu del Disseny, respectively.[4]

With the rise of practical applications for digital technologies, wireless networks, and social media platforms during the final decades of the twentieth century, patrimonial sites like the Museo del Traje have begun to make their collections more accessible to and interactive with visitors, since greater access means, potentially, a larger audience and a more obvious raison d'être (García Navarro and Gómez Gómez 2007: 39). Museums can now extend beyond their brick-and-mortar dimensions, and so there is a greater imperative for such institutions to provide meaningful opportunities for users to interact with collections online. The internet obviates barriers of space and time, and simultaneously augments the ways in which a greater number of potential visitors can continuously interact and identify with collections and didactic materials (González Rodao 2007: 49).

In Spain the digitization of dress and fashion collections at the end of the twentieth century and the beginning of the twenty-first has generally followed a pattern according to which museums provide more or less information about collection highlights on their homepages, and the digital museum networks (e.g., Red de Bibliotecas de Museos [BIMUS] or the Red Digital de Colecciones de Museos [DOMUS]) provide a virtual, searchable inventory that conveniently catalogs most objects on display and in storage. However, such practices are not uniform across the Spanish museum network: smaller museums, such as those whose items provide the main content of the Museu Virtual's online collection, are sometimes forced to rely on webspace provided by their municipality, and not all objects are digitized. In Paül i Agustí's estimation, many of the websites hosted by patrimonial museums and collections in Catalunya in 2015 suffered various states of construction, or failed in their presentation of up-to-date information about the physical collections held in archives and buildings (this could have been a result of a lack of funds or intellectual capital to support such maintenance) (2015: 85, 94). As Joan-Isidre Badell points out, well under half of the museums that participated in the collective *Museos en línea de Cataluña* (Catalan Museums online) in 2013 had no social media presence, and many of those that did continue to face a number of issues: "they don't always have updated information; some links produce error messages; there are problems related to access; the regional government directory does not contain updated URLs; there is little presence on Twitter, on blogs, etc." ("*Museos en línea de Cataluña* en la web 2.0 y en las redes sociales": 87).[5] The Museu Virtual de la Moda de Catalunya provides an alternative for many of the issues facing Spanish museum websites, while simultaneously doubling as a tool for users to learn those details about Catalonia's sartorial heritage most relevant to their interests and needs.

In order for museumgoers to engage meaningfully with stories related to Catalan and Spanish material culture and its histories, institutional websites must provide an attractive and intuitive interface for access to objects on display. Through its collaboration with art historians, commercial web developers, and far-reaching cultural institutions, the Museu Virtual seamlessly overcomes the aforementioned challenges facing smaller, municipal museums, particularly in an environment in which even the most iconic public museums are obliged to rely on increasingly scarce public funds (Prats 2007: 69).

Whether cognizant or not of these issues broadly faced by Catalan patrimonial collections, the Fundació Carulla's decision to award the Museu Virtual's project—headed by art historian Laura Casal-Valls—is a sign of the "growing sense of respectability" (Breward 2003: 9) attributed by institutions to the study of dress and fashion in a range of cultural and social contexts. At the same time, it is illustrative of the fact that the Fundació was well aware of the potential for displays of historical dress and fashion, in particular, to broadcast and reinforce Catalan cultural identity. [6] The Fundació's prestigious award confers a considerable degree of distinction and visibility. Additionally, in its recognition of the Museu Virtual's preventative conservation efforts, it also reaffirms fashion's unique ability to bespeak narratives of Catalonia as a historical motor for economic growth, given the region's historical preeminence in the Iberian Peninsula's garment industry from the late eighteenth century through the early twentieth. In light of this historical context, it is clear that the Museu Virtual represents a logical next "technology-driven" step in a long history of sartorial curation in Catalonia and Spain while indirectly providing actionable solutions to some of the methodological and financial challenges facing art and fashion museums, including interrelated issues such as cost, preservation, storage, display, access, and outreach.

Virtual Window Dressing

One of the features distinguishing the Museu Virtual from less connected or "tech-savvy" museum websites in Catalonia—such as those referenced earlier by Badell and Paül i Agustí—is its attention to cultivating sleek visuals, elegantly designed pages, and seamlessly animated transitions between pages. To be sure, the electronic format of a fashion museum necessarily relies on the deployment of a number of innovative "technologies of display" (Rose 2007: 184), given that "[t]ouch is a primary means by which we come to understand cloth and clothing. We handle materials, try on garments, and personally experience new shapes and fit, which we continually re-evaluate" (Palmer 2015: 32). To resolve this issue effectively, the museum had to, at the very least, bridge the spatial gap separating the viewer from the garment.

To echo Fiona Anderson (2001: 372), the dialogue between form and function that plays out in the virtual fashion museum exposes the affinities that weave through academic and commercial interests as they meet in fashionable objects: museums and other cultural institutions must actively pursue their audiences in order to stay relevant, a fact that dramatically mobilizes the kinds of blockbuster exhibits like some of those hosted in the last decade by The Costume Institute at the Metropolitan Museum of Art in New York (e.g., "Alexander McQueen: Savage Beauty" [2011]; "Heavenly Bodies" [2018]; "Camp: Notes on Fashion" [2019]), the Musée des Arts Décoratifs in Paris (e.g., "Dries Van Noten—Inspirations"

[2014]; "Christian Dior: Couturier du Rêve" [2017]), and the Victoria & Albert Museum in London (e.g., "Balenciaga: Shaping Fashion" [2017–18]; "Christian Dior: Designer of Dreams" [2019]).

Aesthetically, the Museu Virtual is less like those traditional websites hosted by brick-and-mortar museums like the Museo del Traje. Instead, its presentation more closely resembles clothing and fashion websites such as those maintained by commercial fashion labels. In its simulation of e-commerce retailers, the Museu Virtual further connects its online presence with the expectations of the twenty-first-century museumgoer or Instagram user in mind. Digital Bakers, the third-party company responsible for developing the Museu Virtual's online catalog and general layout, alludes to the design of the website as the by-product of a confluence of factors including the legibility of the website's architecture and contents to a heterogeneous audience made up of "specialists and general public," each with different backgrounds, desires, and needs. Such diversity necessitated the inclusion of a variety of filters and an intuitive interface ("Museu Virtual de la Moda de Catalunya"). The Museu Virtual's decision to model itself after the approachable format of an e-commerce website demonstrates an attempt to familiarize the experience of browsing fashion collections for viewers who are perhaps less familiar with museum websites, but who do have experience shopping for their clothes online. The bespoke design also collapses the historical time separating the twenty-first-century user and the premodern producer or consumer—given the access to sartorial filigree it provides—and in the process emphasizes the discursivity, everyday character of fashion versus its consecration as a fine art object.

Worldwide physical displays of dress and fashion have tended to dramatize their recreation of social contexts across various historical periods (Steele 2008: 10)—as is the case in permanent exhibitions on display at the Museo del Traje and the Museu del Disseny, where clothed mannequins reenact concerts, strolls in the park, runway shows, and other social gatherings. However, the Museu Virtual opts for the discreet presentation of individual garments, which viewers may organize and rearrange (or "curate") according to a number of categories.

The filters used by the museum to catalog its sartorial contents hew to some of the same criteria with which users of online fashion retailing websites have become accustomed, especially since the start of the twenty-first century: garment type (e.g., blouses, shirts, dresses, etc.); gender; novelty/chronology; colors; texture ("tacte"); ornamentation (e.g., buttons, floral, or vegetal motifs); fabric (silk, cotton, wool); authorship (i.e., signed or unsigned); label; institution (e.g., Museu d'Història de Sabadell, Museu del Disseny, etc.); and type (e.g., indumentària civil femenina [women's civil apparel], indumentària civil masculina [men's civil apparel], indumentària de ceremonia femenina [women's ceremonial dress]). The result is a series of carefully photographed, downloadable clusters of vignettes that privilege attention to detail, sartorial craftsmanship and, as a result, a recentering of the manual labor invested into the confection of the garment, with a secondary emphasis on the constructedness of fashion displays themselves.

Such attention to sartorial filigree satisfies a number of purposes. On the one hand, it fosters the development of a "scientific understanding of the details of couture garments that the visitor could not otherwise see," while providing a "more intimate understanding" of garments, and an efficacious, "substitute for the absence of touch" (Palmer 2015: 52–3). The use of polished and intuitive design elements and practical filters is yet another way in which the Museu Virtual fuses academically sound approaches with commercial realities for the purpose of appealing to (while empowering) contemporary audiences well accustomed to navigating the webpages of global e-commerce websites.

In order to compensate for the viewer's digitally mediated experience of clothing items, while democratizing the visitor's museum experience, the website also provides multiangle shots of garments, exposing the threads that are usually restricted to curators and conservators. Depending on the garment, virtual museumgoers are granted access to inside seams, clothing labels, warps and wefts, and individual imperfections, all of which open up once-concealed pockets of Catalan sartorial history; such views are not made accessible to virtual visitors of the Museo del Traje or the Museu del Disseny, and, thus, represent a particularly effective innovation by the virtual museum. Casal-Valls justifies this approach using the language of experience-based knowledge and sensoriality: "We sought to transmit sartorial heritage in a sensorial way, emulating the same form in which we relate to contemporary fashion" (2017: 76).[7] By way of an example, the various views of a blouse by fashion designer Fanny Ricot Ruet (1855–1947) are illustrative of the potentialities of such interactive features (Figure 8.1 and Figure 8.2).

Because most items of dress prior to the mid- to late twentieth centuries were seldom labeled, garments rarely included the signature of the tailor or seamstress. Access to what otherwise might be considered sartorial minutiae situates the virtual museumgoer in a more privileged position, similar to that traditionally reserved for the curator or the conservator, which is yet another way in which the Museu Virtual insists on democratic, nonhierarchical engagement with and

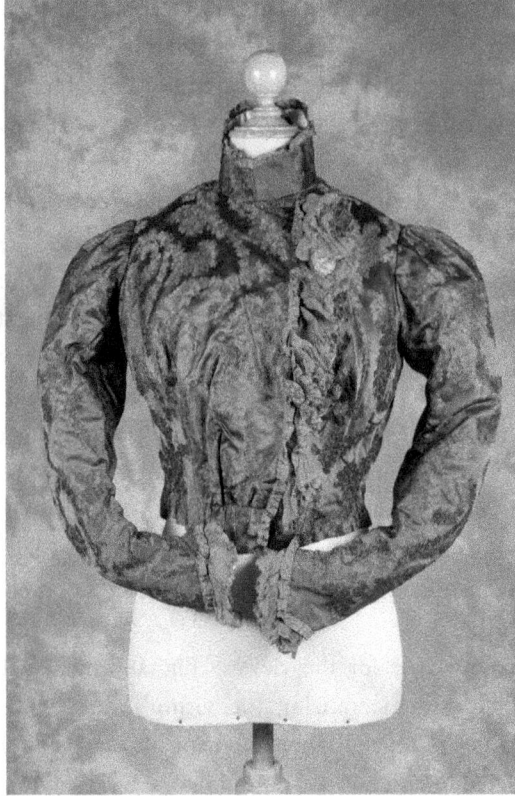

Figure 8.1 Woman's blouse by Fanny Ricot Ruet. Credits: Courtesy of the Museu Virtual de la Moda de Catalunya, 2020.

acquisition of sartorial knowledge and intellectual capital, at least for those with access to a smartphone, personal computer, internet café, or library.

Aside from labels and previously invisible interiors, highly functional zoom options encourage users to compensate with their eyes what cannot be attained by their sense of touch. In a vibrant chartreuse suit dating to the final decades of the eighteenth century "Conjunt de seda format per casaca i calçons" ("Silk suit composed of coat and knee breeches")—visitors are able to use the maximized zoom feature to reveal a figured-velvet garment with a bumpy surface texture ("llavorat" in Catalan/"aterciopelado" in Castilian) (see Figure 8.3 and Figure 8.4).

This aspect of the object only comes into focus when viewed in this way, since the spectator's immediate connection to or experience with dress is primarily tactile (Palmer 2015). The museum gives users the ability to grasp these visual feats, to imagine via tactile memory what a given fabric might feel like. Even in the enhanced displays of brick-and-mortar museums like the recently renovated

Figure 8.2 Detail of Figure 8.1. Credits: Courtesy of the Museu Virtual de la Moda de Catalunya, 2020.

Museu del Disseny, this kind of (tactile) knowledge is seldomly available as part of the museum-going experience and represents a major benefit to the virtually mediated format.

The virtual museum also responds to ethical concerns vis-à-vis the collection and display of garments: "The fundamental difficulties involved in exhibiting costume and textiles are because light irreversibly weakens fibers and fades dyes. Gravity also pulls on the artifacts and can misshape them. Conservation is best achieved by leaving the materials lying in drawers in the dark, whilst animation and public display undeniably contributes to a more rapid deterioration" (Palmer 2015: 36). Garments stored digitally will remain online for at least as long as servers are maintained, while the physical clothing made of vegetal fibers will eventually decay, even while carefully tucked away in boxes or closets in dark storage rooms. The virtual museum's project of continuing to digitize Catalan fashion collections stored in museums scattered across the region will ensure the use of cultural heritage for posterity, particularly welcome in moments when the appreciation of physical collections is difficult (due to geographical distance) or impossible (due to the exigencies of containing virus spread amidst a global pandemic).

In these ways, the Museu Virtual's "scopic regime" (Rose 2007: 2) privileges various types of knowledge that we might describe as democratic

Figure 8.3 Eighteenth-century men's suit. Credits: Courtesy of the Museu Virtual de
la Moda de Catalunya, 2020.

or nonhierarchical; zoom options and camera angles of photos, as links to
historical data—which I examine in the following pages—merely complement
each other. The Museu Virtual's dynamic and downloadable window displays are
meant to appeal to the curiosity and interest of specialists at the same time that
they accommodate twenty-first-century museumgoers well versed in surfing
increasingly sleek commercial fast fashion and haute couture websites. Their
ethically minded curation is supported by an emphasis on the technique and
skill that accompany manual labor that is often obviated in the display of art
objects and sartorial commodities. Though some of the objects it curates were

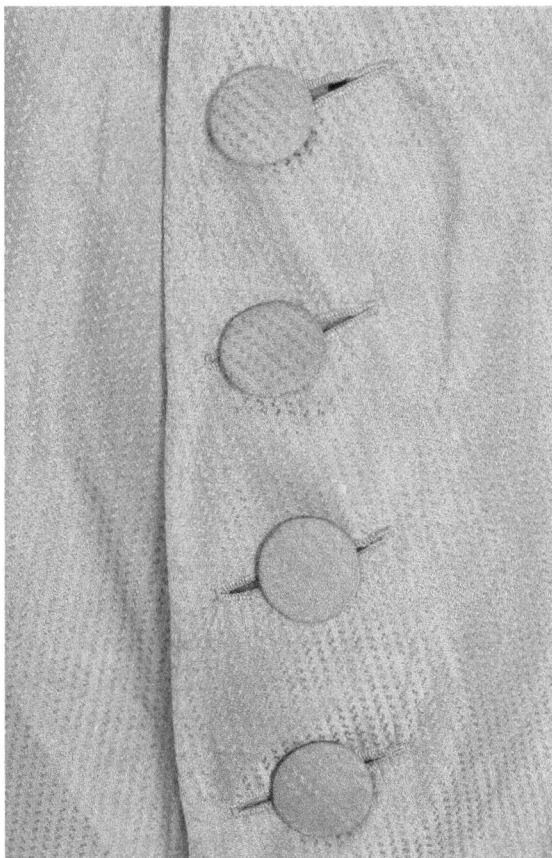

Figure 8.4 Detail of Figure 8.3. Credits: Courtesy of the Museu Virtual de la Moda de Catalunya, 2020.

produced elsewhere in Europe and only later brought into Spain by collectors, the Museu Virtual spotlights the role of individuals and social groups in Catalonia's historical clothing trade while also foregrounding the website's constructedness as an avatar for narratives of cultural identity across a plethora of contexts.

Threading Together Past and Present

The Museu Virtual's elegant aesthetic is bolstered by its historically contextualized content, which ultimately points to the interconnectedness of Catalan cultural identity and fashion history to that of its neighbors in Spain and elsewhere in Europe. In order to legitimize the value of Catalan sartorial heritage on display, the Museu Virtual's individual pages include rigorously researched datasheets with drop-down menus that encourage viewers to consult texts and images hosted by international libraries and museums. Relevant details include information about production, detailed prose descriptions of the origins and context of a particular garment (when available), and generous bibliographies. By linking virtual museumgoers primarily to Catalan, Spanish, and French-language archives and bibliographies, the site's architects and curators indirectly point to the transnational character of the clothing trade (in both the past and the present) as well as Catalonia's situatedness in pan-European fashion history more broadly. This strategy bespeaks the region's active participation in European commercial and industrial networks and its protagonism, function, and influence as a reference point for fashion and fashionable material culture in the Iberian Peninsula.

Links to archives at the National Libraries of Spain and France, and museums such as the Metropolitan Museum of Art and the Rijksmuseum—among others—vary in genre, cutting across visual cultural (e.g., portraiture, prints, advertisements) and periodicals (e.g., culture and lifestyle manuals, journals, fashion magazines, etc.). Garments from the eighteenth and nineteenth-century collections, for example, link viewers directly to Spanish and French fashion plates and prose descriptions included in coetaneous journals from the eighteenth century onward. In an example I mention above—"Conjunt de seda format per casaca i calçons" ("Silk suit composed of coat and knee breeches")—visitors are directed to both portraits by Francisco de Goya and John Singleton Copley, and textual evidence such as the eighteenth-century periodical *Le Journal de la Mode et du Goût* (Journal of Fashion and Taste). The pages scanned by the National Library of France's online database Gallica offer corresponding descriptions in French, while an ephemeral print represents a fashionable gentleman sporting a coat in a cut that is similar to the one displayed by the Museu Virtual. Instead of providing one "correct" interpretation for viewers, the museum's architects decided to leave the comparative (and narrative) leaps to museumgoers—if they choose to do so, it is the visitor who is tasked with making significant comparisons and connections with the relevant evidence provided. While fashion historians perform the initial legwork, visitors may perform the role of casual curator or researcher, dependent, of course, on their reason for visiting.

The bibliography, as is to be expected, directs sartorial sleuths to key texts in pan-European fashion history and theory, including seminal studies by an eclectic selection of scholars like Joanne Entwistle, James Laver, Gilles

Lipovetsky, Aileen Ribeiro, and a handful of others that focus on the Iberian eighteenth century specifically, including texts by historian Amelia Leira Sánchez. The reliance on French source material, in the case of the eighteenth-century *chartreuse* suit previously mentioned, as in many others, is warranted, given the Bourbon ascension to the Spanish throne as a result of the War of Spanish Succession (1701–14): "this dynastic change was reflected especially in the manner of dress of the kings, the court, and affluent, urban society in general" (Leira Sánchez 2007: 87).[8] The museum's abundant, academically sound details reflect innovations in the maintenance and display of historical garments in museological displays, as well as the transnational character of cultural and economic networks of dress and fashion since the eighteenth century.[9] The Museu Virtual's interconnectedness with and within transnational archives and museums in the present-day frames dress and fashion as relevant to both local and transnational webs of meaning that also connect virtually mediated physical collections to a variety of social media platforms like Instagram.

Instagramming the Archive (#fashionhistory #fetacatalunya)

In order to encourage the dialogue between museumgoers and a slowly expanding online collection—which represents one of the universal aims of modern museums in general—the Museu Virtual has begun to establish a presence on Instagram, a globally popular social media platform founded in 2010. Even though the account is, like the museum itself, only in a nascent phase, it extends the project of the virtual museum by commenting on highlights from the collection, while creating a space for online communities, drawing attention to events occurring in other museums, and spotlighting those activities occurring behind the scenes related to maintenance and "ghost labor" more generally.

The strategic use of hashtags (e.g., #patrimoni) and geotags (e.g., Barcelona, Spain; Terrassa, Catalunya, Spain; etc.) tethers the Museu Virtual's posts to other images that share the same labels, which amounts to a virtual "imagined community" of sorts, even if it is limited by those able to read and deploy such signifiers (Anderson 2016 [1984]: 6). While perusing the media catalogued under the hashtag "#lamoda," for example, Instagram users may stumble upon the Museu Virtual, allowing them to browse through their selection of collection highlights on display before visiting the website for the complete archive. The sporadic inclusion of videos or Instagram stories—videos that remain on the account's site only temporarily—further enriches viewers' experiences of the collection. Even as hashtags and geotags would appear to identify the Catalan character of its social media presence, its foray into virtual space hosted by an American web application transcends geopolitical boundaries and recalls the interconnected, transnational character of Catalan cultural identity as read through earlier discourses and displays of dress and fashion.

Perhaps one of the most novel and meaningful contributions of the Museu Virtual's Instagram account is the visibility it gives to the labor that is not visible in museum displays, a strategy that recuperates the various individuals who have had a hand in the confection of Catalan cultural identity. The careful, gloved hands of fashion conservators—most of whom appear to be women—sometimes foreground historical garments in photos, and restore visibility to a significant but often-invisible segment of the fashion museum that one scholar has referred to metonymically, and suggestively, as "ghost labor" (Scaturro 2017: 23). In the Museu Virtual's Instagram posts, gloved hands hold open waistcoats and bodices, while others prop up grey panels to test and strengthen the color accuracy of photographs (see Figure 8.5 and Figure 8.6).

The inclusion of the conservator's hand in the realm of the Museu Virtual draws attention to both the labor invested in the creation of the garments, or that which continues to maintain and conserve the items of dress to preserve them for posterity, as well as the seamstresses responsible for clothing manufacture in domestic and industrial settings in the eighteenth and nineteenth centuries. Especially in the context of eighteenth- and early-nineteenth-century guilds, men were generally in charge of the tailoring trade. Until the official dissolution of the guilds around the 1830s, in Barcelona as elsewhere in Spain, for example, "[male] [t]ailors were the only ones who could produce clothing for sale and this was ordained by municipal regulations" (Casal-Valls 2013: 377).[10] However, the domestic production of clothing, along with many of the tasks associated with garment manufacture during this period of industrialization and urbanization, was realized by women. On the one hand, the increased visibility of "ghost labor" by the Instagram handle demonstrates recent innovations in museological strategies deployed by other Spanish museums—including the Museo Cerralbo and the Museu del Disseny, both of which have uploaded similar posts in their regularly updated online stories. On the other, it also, if indirectly, points to the protagonism of women in the development of the Catalan garment industry, a fact reflected in the way in which clothing labels are revealed, such as that of Ricot Ruet mentioned above, and a topic to which Casal-Valls has devoted much of her own scholarly work.

Figure 8.5 Instagram post from March 14, 2018. Museu Virtual de la Moda de Catalunya.

The significance of the Museu Virtual's Instagram account in its mission should not be overstated; the account reports only 1,212 "followers" or subscribers as of the writing of this chapter. Readers may compare this number to those currently sustained by the Instagram accounts of institutions with much wider collections, audiences, and resources, like the Museu Nacional d'Art de Catalunya (Museum of National Art of Catalonia or MNAC) and the Museu del Disseny (Design Museum): each boasts over 44,000 and 42,000 followers, respectively.

Another questionable strategy, not included in the initial rollout of the website, includes a facile rating system for garments. With the help of a rectangular widget, users are encouraged to vote on what they think of garments according to four categories: tacky (*hortera*), sexy, elegant, and hipster. Despite its uncertain use-value, the widget is yet another sign of the broad net cast by the museum's designers. While such a tool may seem gauche or useless to the

Figure 8.6 Instagram post from June 4, 2018. Museu Virtual de la Moda de Catalunya.

more seasoned or academic museumgoer (who would likely be more attracted to bibliographies and hyperlinks to relevant material culture), widgets and social media integration, however small, might appeal to the more casual visitor or even children who might be encouraged to peruse the website by parents or teachers. Furthermore, such response mechanisms might be of potential use to future researchers and educators interested in understanding what our contemporaries understood from what they saw.

In spite of these limitations, the museum's expansion into social media platforms—it also has an active presence on Facebook (663 followers) and Twitter (487 followers)—reflects its desire and willingness to realize its own social ambitions as a repository and broadcaster of Catalan culture, along with those of the Fundació Carulla. In its representation of the "ghost labor" that goes into the maintenance of museological collections, the Museu Virtual's use of social media coincided with other efforts to broadcast Catalan cultural identity. Given its quota of representation in Spanish national media, as Aurélie Vialette has convincingly argued, "the dissemination of Catalan national life is done through many channels: online videos, social media in general, live streaming of political life, protests, interviews, to name a few" (2018: 134). The democratic potential of social media outlets would appear to coincide with the interests of the Museu Virtual, which hopes to give access to a variety of users interested in learning and retelling the stories of Catalonia by way of those "little histories" represented by once hidden fashion objects. Indeed, as Vänska and Clark mention with regard to popular networking applications and sites more broadly, "the rise of social media has enabled anyone to share their opinions, to select and present, or *curate*, a scenario, and thereby to function as an expert" (2017: 9).

Of course, visitors do not become experts by virtue of repeat visits to the virtual museum or to its social media pages. To be sure, the discursive space provided by social media platforms is heterogeneous and limited. Facebook, for example, is routinely under fire for the ways its various forums function as echo chambers or silos, where meaningful content and debate is often eclipsed by "fake news," ad hominem attacks, and spam. However, social media's heterogeneity or unevenness does not detract from its ability to be instrumentalized in meaningful ways. Brick-and-mortar museums and other cultural hubs, like the Museo del Traje or the Museu del Disseny, have used platforms like Instagram to bolster their educational outreach while also broadcasting the many ways museum objects relate to everyday life for tens of thousands of (real or potential) visitors. While the Museu Virtual was born online, its limited resources and size prevent it from achieving the visibility attained by larger, national cultural institutions. Still, the virtual museum's nascent engagement of users on social media vouchsafes its conservation and pedagogical mission, while it remains an adaptable tool for use by future visitors.

Conclusion

By attempting to combine the many little stories contained by once forgotten sartorial objects, the Museu Virtual privileges the incremental steps that must be taken in the articulation of any pattern of Catalan historical memory and identity. As the optics of Catalan cultural identity continue to shift, so too will the Museu Virtual's constitutively malleable form. But then this is always true of the ever-evolving shape of the "nation-space," which, as Homi Bhabha reminds readers, "is neither unified nor unitary in relation to itself, nor must it be seen simply as 'other' in relation to what is outside or beyond it" (4). In cementing its virtual (though no less real) footprint through digitized displays of dress and fashion in the present moment, it is clear that the Museu Virtual is well-positioned to play a decisive role in producing generative narratives of Catalan identity as it continues to be articulated, mapped, and reshaped. Much like the sartorial objects and stories it has begun to discover, photograph, and curate, the Museu Virtual is a small but efficacious medium through which to preserve and broadcast the historical shapes and shades of Catalan cultural identity, particularly as it continues to be imagined and refashioned.

Notes

1 "Todos los museos, de una forma u otra, juegan un papel decisivo en la definición y recomposición de las identidades locales, nacionales y regionales, mediante la apropiación y valorización del patrimonio."

2 I have shortened the name to the "Museu Virtual" throughout the chapter. All translations from Spanish and Catalan are my own.

3 "Gracias [al proceso de industrialización basado en el sector algodonero] la economía catalana—no así la española—se transformó en el curso del siglo XIX en una economía industrializada."

4 It is worth pointing out that both men and women were responsible for the collection and preservation of historical textiles and clothing. Many of the dresses in the Rocamora collection originally belonged to Rocamora's mother, Ana Vidal i Sala, who saved her dresses at the end of every season (used dresses often went into recirculation through the secondhand market or, in the case of the wealthiest members of society, were passed down to staff working on the family estate).

5 "No siempre disponen de información actualizada; algunos enlaces dan error; hay algunos problemas de acceso; el mismo directorio de la Generalitat no tiene las URL actualizadas; presentan muy escasa presencia en Twitter, en blogs, etc."

6 Only two years before the death of Francisco Franco (1892–1975), Spain's dictator between 1939 and 1975, and whose regime stifled cultural expression in languages other than Castilian—the Carulla Foundation was founded in order to act on behalf of Catalan cultural initiatives in an attempt to "promote the language, culture, and values that constitute Catalan society, with the goal of encouraging a

sense of ownership" ("Qui som?" 2018). The virtual/social character of the other two projects nominated alongside the Museu Virtual demonstrates the Fundació's dedication to spreading Catalan cultural identity through the latest technological innovations. Another finalist, Surtdecasa.cat, is a digital platform that aggregates cultural and social activities around Catalonia. The other finalist, Proscenium, seeks to promote the international reach of Catalan dramatic arts through the diffusion of video recordings of performances and relevant documentation.

7 "Buscábamos transmitir el patrimonio del vestido de una manera sensorial, emulando la misma forma en la que nos relacionamos con la moda contemporánea."

8 "Este cambio [dinástico] se reflejó de manera muy evidente en la manera de vestir de los reyes, de la Corte y de la sociedad adinerada y urbana en general."

9 Despite the museum's best efforts, it is worth mentioning that mannequins used for the garments very often do not fit properly, as they would if they had been conserved for a museum display. This is a weakness for items that were made to fit, or adjusted to fit, and is an area in which the Virtual Museum does not excel because it simply does not have the resources to mount every garment safely and soundly.

10 "Els sastres eren els únics que podien produir vestits per a la seva venda i així ho ordenaven els reglaments municipals."

References

Anderson, Benedict (2016), *Imagined Communities. Reflections on the Origin and Spread of Nationalism*, London: Verso.

Anderson, Fiona (2001), "Museums as Fashion Media," in Stella Bruzzi and Pamela Church Gibson (eds.), *Fashion Cultures: Theories, Explorations, and Analysis*, 371–89, New York: Routledge.

Badell, Joan-Isidre (2013), "Museos en línea de Cataluña en la web 2.0 y en las redes sociales," *Ibersid: revista de sistemas de información y documentación* 7: 81–90.

Badell, Joan-Isidre (2015), "Los museos de Cataluña en las redes sociales: resultados de un estudio de investigación," *Revista Interamericana de Bibliotecología* 38 (2): 159–64.

Bassegoda, Bonaventura (2016), "Eusebi Güell i López (1877–1955), segon vescomte de Güell, col·leccionista de dibuixos," in Bonaventura Bassegoda and Ignasi Domènech (eds.), *Col·leccionistes, antiquaris, falsificadors i museus: noves dades sobre el patrimoni artístic de Catalunya al segle XX*, 63–80, Barcelona: Memoria Artium.

Bhabha, Homi (1990), *Nation and Narration*, Abingdon: Routledge.

Breward, Christopher (2003), *Fashion*, Oxford: Oxford University Press.

Carbonell Basté, Sílvia (2016), "La formació dels museus tèxtils a Catalunya: Col·leccions I col·leccionistes," in Bonaventura Bassegoda and Ignasi Domènech (eds.), *Col·leccionistes, antiquaris, falsificadors i museus: noves dades sobre el patrimoni artístic de Catalunya al segle XX*, 125–55, Barcelona: Memoria Artium.

Carreras, Albert and Xavier Tafunell (2016), *Historia económica de la España contemporánea (1789–2009)*, Barcelona: Crítica.

Casal-Valls, Laura (2013), "La figura de la modista i els inicis de l'alta costura a Barcelona. Trajectòria professional i producció d'indumentària femenina (1880–1915)," PhD diss., Universitat de Barcelona, Barcelona.

Casal-Valls, Laura (2017), "Un museo virtual de la moda: de proyecto a realidad," in Sílvia Carbonell (ed.), *Libro de Actas del I Coloquio de Investigadores en Textil y Moda. 17 y 18 de noviembre de 2017*, 76–9, Terrassa: Centre de Documentació i Museu Tèxtil.

Dahlgren, Peter and Joke Hermes (2020), "The Democratic Horizons of the Museum. Citizenship and Culture," in Andrea Witcomb and Kylie Message (eds.), *Museum Theory*, 117–38, West Sussex, UK: John Wiley & Sons.

Falk, John H. (2006), "An Identity-Centered Approach to Understanding Museum Learning," *Curator* 49 (2): 151–66.

García Navarro, Jesús and Alicia Gómez Gómez (2007), "Medios interactivos y audiovisuales. Una realidad en el Museo del Traje," *Indumenta*, 00: 39–48.

González Rodao, Carmen (2007), "http://museodeltraje.mcu.es." *Indumenta*, 00: 49–55.

Huyssen, Andreas (1994), *Twilight Memories: Marking Time in a Culture of Amnesia*, Abingdon: Routledge.

Leira Sánchez, Amelia (2007), "La moda en España durante el siglo XVIII," *Indumenta*, 00: 87–94.

"El Museu" (2018), *El Museu Virtual de la Moda de Catalunya*. Available online: https://www.museudelamoda.cat/ca/el-museu (accessed on October 13, 2018).

"Museu Virtual de la Moda de Catalunya" (2018), *Digital Bakers*. Available online: www.digitalbakers.com/en/projects/museu-virtual-de-la-moda-de-catalunya (accessed on October 13, 2018).

Palmer, Alexandra (2015), "Untouchable: Creating Desire and Knowledge in Museum Costume and Textile Exhibitions," *Fashion Theory* 12 (1): 31–63.

Paül i Agustí, Daniel (2015), "Uns museus encara poc digitals: la presència dels museus catalans a internet," *Anàlisi* 52: 81–96.

Prats, Carme (2007), "Redes de museos en Cataluña: territorio e identidad," *mus-A: Revista de los museos de Andalucía* 5 (8): 66–75.

"Qui som?" (n.d.), *Fundació Carulla*. Available online: www.fundaciocarulla.cat/ca/qui -som (accessed on October 31, 2018).

Roigé Ventura, Xavier and Iñaki Arrieta Urtizberea (2010), "Construcción de identidades en los museos de Cataluña y País Vasco: entre lo local, nacional y global," *Pasos. Revista de Turismo y Patrimonio Cultural* 8 (4): 539–53.

Roppola, Tiina (2012), *Designing for the Museum Visitor Experience*, Abingdon: Routledge.

Rose, Gillian (2007), *Visual Methodologies. An Introduction to the Interpretation of Visual Materials*, Thousand Oaks, CA: Sage.

Scaturro, Sarah (2017), "Confronting Fashion's Death Drive: Conservation, Ghost Labor, and the Material Turn within Fashion Curation," in Annamari Vänska and Hazel Clark (eds.), *Fashion Curating: Critical Practice in the Museum and Beyond*, 21–38, London: Bloomsbury.

Steele, Valerie (2008), "Museum Quality: The Rise of the Fashion Exhibition," *Fashion Theory: The Journal of Dress, Body & Culture* 12: 7–30.

Vega, Jesusa (2005), "Spain's Image in Regional Dress: From Everyday Object to Museum Piece and Tourist Attraction," in Susan Larson and Eva Woods (eds.), *Visualizing Spanish Modernity*, 207–27, New York: Berg.

Vialette, Aurélie (2018), "Disobedience and the Dangers of Nationalism: A Perspective from the Pro-Independence Left in Catalonia," *Catalan Review* XXXII: 129–37.

Vicente, Marta (2006), *Clothing the Spanish Empire: Families and the Calico Trade in the Early Modern Atlantic World*, London: Palgrave Macmillan.

Vidal i Jansà, Mercé (1991), *Teoria i crítica en el Noucentisme: Joaquim Folch i Torres*, Barcelona: Institut d'Estudis Catalans.

Contributors

Inés Corujo-Martín is Assistant Professor in the Humanities Department at New York City College of Technology of The City University of New York, where she teaches courses on fashion and Hispanic studies. Her research focuses on Spanish literature and culture, feminist theory, and visual and material culture. Her most recent publications explore the relationship between gender and fashion in modern and contemporary Spain.

Mary Kate Donovan is Assistant Professor of Spanish at Skidmore College, USA, where she teaches courses on Iberian cinema and culture. Her research focuses on race, migration, and popular culture in modern and contemporary Spain and has been published in the *Revista de Estudios Hispánicos*, the *Arizona Journal of Hispanic Cultural Studies*, the *Journal of Spanish Cultural Studies*, and the *Bulletin of Hispanic Studies*. She is currently working on a book project that examines representations of Spain's Chinese community.

Francisco Fernández de Alba is the Howard Meneely Professor of Hispanic Studies at Wheaton College (MA), USA, where he teaches courses on modern and contemporary Spanish culture. He is the author of *Sex, Drugs, and Fashion in 1970s Madrid* (2020) and the coeditor of two volumes of essays on Violence and Transatlantic studies. He has published several articles and book chapters in *Bulletin of Hispanic Studies*, *Hispanófila*, *Revista de Estudios Hispánicos*, and *Symposium*. He is currently working on a book project about mountains and politics.

Marcela T. Garcés is Professor of Spanish at Siena College (Loudonville, New York, USA). She has authored articles and book chapters on *la Movida madrileña*, contemporary Spanish film, and culinary culture in journals such as *Revista de Estudios Hispánicos* and *La Nueva Literatura Hispánica*. She is scriptwriter of the documentary film The *Txoko Experience: The Secret Culinary Space of the Basques* (2017). She is the author of the forthcoming graphic novel *Me llamo Marcela: The Story of a Heritage Speaker Learning Spanish in the U.S.*

Juan Gutiérrez is Fashion Curator at the Museo del Traje in Madrid, Spain. His research interests focus on contemporary fashion, with special attention to the Museum's collections and the history of fashion in Spain. He has extensive experience in coordinating and curating fashion exhibitions, a field in which he explores the relationship of fashion with the body, space, and the public. He has published on contemporary fashion and the history of Spanish fashion and is the author of *Tino Casal. El arte por Exceso* (2017). He is currently preparing a history of the ready-to-wear industry in Spain, to be published by the Asociación de Creadores de Moda de España in late 2020.

Jorge Pérez is the Peter T. Flawn Centennial Professor of Spanish and the University of Texas at Austin, USA. He is the author of *Cultural Roundabouts: Spanish Film and Novel on the Road* (2011), *Confessional Cinema: Religion, Film, and Modernity in Spain's Development Years* (2017), and *Fashioning Spanish Cinema: Costume, Identity, and Stardom* (2021). He is also the co-editor of *The Latin American Road Movie* (2016), and has published articles on Spanish cinema, literature, and popular music in journals such as *ALEC, Film, Fashion and Consumption, Hispanic Research Journal, Journal of Spanish Cultural Studies, MLN, Revista Canadiense de Estudios Hispánicos, Revista de Estudios Hispánicos,* and *Studies in Hispanic Cinemas.*

Olga Sendra Ferrer is Associate Professor at Wesleyan University, USA, in the Department of Romance Languages and Literatures. Her research interests focus on contemporary peninsular literature, photography, and urban studies. She has published on photography, urbanism, and gender studies in Barcelona during the Franco dictatorship. Her most recent book is *Barcelona, City of Margins* (2021).

Kathleen M. Vernon is Associate Professor in the Department of Hispanic Languages and Literature at Stony Brook University, USA. She has published widely on Spanish-language cinema from the 1930s to the present and is the editor of books on the Spanish civil war and the visual arts and the films of Pedro Almodóvar. She is currently completing a cultural history of film sound, music, and voices in Spain, titled *Listening to Spanish Cinema*, to be published by Liverpool University Press. Her work in progress includes the multi-authored book, *Cinema and Everyday Life in 1940s and 1950s Spain: An Oral History.*

Alberto Villamandos is Associate Professor of Spanish in the Foreign Languages and Literatures Department, University of Missouri-Kansas City,

USA. His research focuses on Spain's graphic fiction since the 1970s, and more recently on cosmopolitanism and Europeanism in 1980s Spanish literature. He has published a book on the cultural production of Barcelona's intelligentsia during the late 1960s, *El discreto encanto de la subversión. Una crítica cultural de la gauche divine* (2011).

Nicholas Wolters is Associate Professor of Spanish at Wake Forest University, USA. His research interests focus on modern Spanish and Iberian literature and visual culture, masculinities studies, and fashion. His work on these and related topics has been published or is forthcoming in edited volumes and peer-reviewed journals, such as the *Journal of Spanish Cultural Studies* and *Revista de Estudios Hispánicos*. His first book, *Masculine Figures: Fashioning Men and the Novel in Nineteenth-Century Spain*, investigates depictions of men and the masculine norms they enact and resist in nineteenth-century realist novels, fashion advertisements, and other commercial ephemera.

Index

www.ingramcontent.com/pod-product-compliance
Lightning Source LLC
Chambersburg PA
CBHW050428280326
41932CB00013BA/2037